PUT A
WET PAPER
TOWEL ON IT

D1339814

PUT A WET PAPER TOWEL ON IT

LEE PARKINSON
AND ADAM PARKINSON

Illustrated by Tim Sadler

HarperCollins*Publishers*

HarperCollins*Publishers*
1 London Bridge Street
London SE1 9GF

www.harpercollins.co.uk

HarperCollins*Publishers*
1st Floor, Watermarque Building, Ringsend Road
Dublin 4, Ireland

First published by HarperCollins*Publishers* 2021
This edition published 2022

10 9 8 7 6 5 4

Text © Lee Parkinson, Adam Parkinson and Tim Sadler 2021
Illustrations © Tim Sadler

Lee Parkinson, Adam Parkinson and Tim Sadler assert the moral right to
be identified as the authors of this work

A catalogue record of this book is available from the British Library

ISBN 978-0-00-847421-8

Printed and bound in the UK using 100% renewable electricity at CPI
Group (UK) Ltd

MIX
Paper from
responsible sources
FSC™ C007454

FSC
www.fsc.org

This book is produced from independently certified FSC™ paper to
ensure responsible forest management.

For more information visit: www.harpercollins.co.uk/green

To Grandma

We wish you could have been here to read this book.
We hope we've done you proud.

Contents

About the Authors   ix

Who's Who?   1
Introduction   7
Mr P's Journey into Teaching   14
The Journey of 'Mr P'   28
Adam's Route into the Classroom   39
The Staff List   44
The Classroom   82
The School Day   105
The Real Superheroes of Primary Schools   124
Behaviour   144
Classroom Crazes   172
School Assemblies   183
School Performances   202
PE   214
Parents   224
School Trips   246
Dinner Times   255
The Staffroom   266
Everything Wrong with Education (in the UK)   281
Two Mr Ps' Final Thought   313

Acknowledgements   319

About the Authors

Lee and Adam Parkinson are two brothers from Manchester who work in primary education. They are the hosts of the hilarious *Two Mr Ps in a Podcast*, which takes a lighthearted look at life in the classroom. Over the past few years they have been discussing all the quirks of teaching in a modern-day primary school. The podcast has amassed over three million listens (as of April 2021) and sold out live shows all over the UK.

Lee, otherwise known as 'Mr P', has been a class teacher working in a primary school for the past 13 years. He now works part-time in class and part-time as an educational consultant, running courses on raising teaching standards using technology in the UK and overseas. His training, courses and conferences have inspired thousands of teachers to embrace technology creatively to make learning more accessible, purposeful and empowering. He campaigns to help teachers work smarter, not harder, and to challenge them to reflect on best practice to achieve a decent work–life balance. From sharing his ideas, approaches and humorous insights into life in the classroom, he has become the most-followed UK teacher online.

Adam, or 'The Other Mr P', as he is known, is Lee's much funnier (apparently) younger brother. Adam works as a higher-level teaching assistant (HLTA). He likes Turkey Twizzlers and wrestling.

Hello, and welcome to *Put a Wet Paper Towel on It* – the book, with me, Mr P ...

... and the Other Mr P.

Can you believe this? We have managed to write our own book! Could you imagine the look on some of our teachers' faces if they knew that!

Yes, I have been thinking a lot since we started writing this book. Remembering my old teachers – some of whom will get a fair share of the word count we need to reach. There have been times during this writing process when I have pictured some of them, for example one teacher, who in a fit of rage once turned to me and shrieked, 'YOU MONKEY CLOWN, GET OUT!' I wonder what he must think knowing the child who directly contributed to him balding and turning grey before 35 is now a published author!

Yes, it is certainly going to be a surprise for some. I wonder whether we should send a signed copy of the book to our old school so it can be displayed on the wall of fame. I assume most schools have this, usually next to the trophy cabinet at the front of the building. It proudly showcases the achievements of past pupils who have managed to contribute something positive to society. This is usually at the entrance to convince prospective parents that this will definitely happen to their child if they choose the school. It'd be amazing to have a wall of shame, too, so you can compare the two. We have had two pupils who have represented Great Britain at the Olympics, but also taught the Manny Massive, the gang who pulled off the jewellery heist two years ago. We take great pride in the fact our curriculum was able to equip those pupils with the skills to pull off one of the most famous robberies in recent history.

Our other brother has a framed shirt on the wall of fame at our old school, doesn't he?

I think so, he's only mentioned it the odd time ... NOT!

And there it is, people, just a little taster of the quality banter you can expect to be delivered in bucket loads through our barely understandable use of proper English.

But yes, our middle brother, Ryan, played rugby to a very respectable level, even representing England Counties on a tour of Canada, and because he got three caps that equates to a full cap for England. So he has a shirt on the wall of the school hall.

But I think it needs this literary masterpiece sitting next to it?

Absolutely!

Done, I will send a copy! Brilliant, we managed to give our other brother a mention in the first few pages, meaning he will (hopefully) not get another one for the rest of the book.

Agreed.

Now you are officially a published author, I know for a fact you'd be dropping that in as a chat-up line if you were single. You know, as opposed to telling ladies you fancied that you were a primary school teacher.

Shh, Lee! You're cramping my style!

Seriously, Adam's go-to chat-up line when he was younger and out on the pull was that he was a primary school teacher.

Worked though, didn't it?

Did it? We're talking well over a decade ago. I reckon if you tried the 'I am a primary school teacher' line now, it'd get you nowhere. In fact, you'd probably be lectured on how it is your fault that society is falling apart and you shouldn't complain as you get all those holidays! Even in my relatively short 13-year teaching career the general level of respect towards teachers has nose-dived to shockingly low levels.

Yeah, parents often just turn round and have a go at me for daring to question their child and then blame me for their child being unable to tie their shoelaces or wipe their own arse.

Right, so back to the book. If you haven't already worked out, this is a joint venture between Adam and me. I initially assumed you would have been able to work out who is speaking based on the fact that Adam's writing would be barely comprehensible, but then the publishers told us the book would go through numerous edits by people who are exceptionally qualified ... unlike the editing and marking I have done as a teacher, which usually consists of reading the first couple of lines, making a decision, and picking and writing out something from the generic bank of comments I have stored in my teacher brain:

Let me guess:

Great effort – *You finished the task, but let's be fair, the quality of what you wrote was way off.*
Fantastic – *Decent.*
Good – *Barely readable.*
Good start – *You spent 25 minutes and only managed ONE sentence. Are you taking the p**s?*

Yeah, pretty much. Now, you might be thinking, how can a teacher say this? Well, as you will find out, we are going to be extremely honest about our views on modern-day education. We are no experts, but we do have valuable experience of actually doing the job, unlike those who make most of the decisions around education ...

Oh, here he goes, ranting, and we're barely a page in to the book.

No, the point I am making is this book will share our views on life in the classroom, the ups and downs, the things we do that are a complete waste of time, like ... marking. Every teacher knows that 99 per cent of the time written marking is not done for the benefit of the child. Let's face it, whatever I did write in a child's book, said child wouldn't read it because they either couldn't ... or couldn't be arsed.

Yeah, to be fair, when my teachers used to mark my work I would just count the ticks. If I got more ticks than crosses I knew I wasn't looking at another detention.

Ok, so instead we decided that to help you differentiate between us, our words will be set in different fonts. Originally, I was hoping to go for something robust and reliable like Arial. I feel this represents my professionalism as a teacher, my well-established, reasoned approach to education and the fact I have spent the past few years sharing my wealth of knowledge with teachers all over the world. Tell everyone which font you originally wanted, Adam.

Comic Sans, baby!

Our readers will be delighted to learn that there was no chance of this happening. For starters, it's banned in too many schools and it makes some teachers' skin crawl. Also (as our publishers have reliably informed us) it turns out that Comic Sans is far too expensive as a font for a book about teaching! The irony!

Dear readers, from now on, if you see this font, expect comedy gold and genius insights because it's <u>Adam</u> writing.

Yeah, best of luck with that!

According to Benjamin Franklin, the only two certainties in life are <u>death</u> and <u>taxes</u>.

Far be it for us to disagree with the great man, but we feel that there should be a third. The only things certain in life are death, taxes and ...

PRIMARY SCHOOL CHILDREN ARE THE WEIRDEST, FUNNIEST, MOST DISGUSTING CREATURES IN THE WORLD!

Don't believe us? Ask any primary school teacher, teaching assistant or parent of a child aged between five and 11 years old. Babies are cute, toddlers are 'terrible' apparently, teenagers are ... well ... a flipping nightmare, but primary-aged children are the finest unintentional comedians you'll ever meet. Despite the bogies, the post-roast-dinner flatulence and the random faecal matter, getting to work with them is a privilege and working in education is the best job in the world ... or at least it should be.

As educators, it's our job to help give the children in our care those important life lessons and experiences that will hopefully mould them into the best versions of themselves. Saying that is easy, but doing it can be a rollercoaster for everyone involved. On either side of the school gates, we all (hopefully) want what's best for the little darlings, and we hope this book will be the perfect place to encourage an honest and positive dialogue between parents and school staff; a dialogue through which teachers can be forgiven for not casting little Chloe as the Archangel Gabriel in this year's nativity, and equally, parents will not be reported to social services for forgetting a quid for mufti day.

'These are the best years of your life!' I'll never forget hearing those words from Mrs Kerrigan, the lunchtime supervisor (or dinner lady in old money) when I was in Year 5. Primary school is a time of innocence, a time for discovery and enjoying the blissful simplicity of being a kid. Your biggest dilemma back in the day was whether to have a cheese whirl or a Turkey Twizzler (before Jamie Oliver put a spanner in the works) for lunch.

Turkey Twizzlers ... my word!

Yes, more on that later. Life really was much simpler back then; no bills to pay, no wages to chase.

No doubt we'd all love to go back, even just for a day. It's these tales of less-complicated times that inspired my brother Adam (the Other Mr P) and me to start our podcast – the No. 1 Educational Comedy Podcast (featuring two brothers from Manchester) in the World, *Two Mr Ps in a Podcast*, in which we take a lighthearted look at life in the classroom from the viewpoint of those who work in it. Over the last few years we have seen how our podcast resonates not only with fellow educators but also parents of primary-aged children and anyone that fondly remembers their school days.

It is the special moments that make teaching the best job in the world and it really is true that no two days are the same. The impact you have as an educator, where you see a child use knowledge you have imparted, to make a positive choice, is incredibly rewarding; it provides a sense of fulfilment that most people will never be lucky enough to see.

The teaching profession is somewhat unique in that no two schools are the same, yet the experiences can be universal. Every school will have similar characters amongst their staff and pupils, the same traditions (that probably haven't changed in generations) and the same hilarious stories that make most teachers think, 'I should sit down and write a book about these.' So that's what we've decided to do.

As we repeatedly state on the podcast:

'This is an educational podcast where you don't actually learn anything.'

The same thing applies to this book; if you are expecting to come away from reading it with teaching expertise of the highest order, I would recommend choosing something else.

Reading this book won't result in teachers becoming better at their jobs, but we like to think it will give everyone a giggle as we share funny classroom stories, observations and absolute clangers from our time in education. Think of all the teacher lines you've heard, such as 'The bell doesn't dismiss you, I do!' There's no massive teacher convention each year where we all get together to share zingers like that. These are learnt sayings that are probably older than we are. One recurring theme in every classroom, however, will be that a wet paper towel can solve everything. Grazed knee? Headache? Sore eye-socket? Missing limb? Just shove a wet paper towel on it!

As far as we are concerned, the magical wet paper towel solves pretty much everything and it's probably the only medical advice we received in our teacher training.

While wet paper towels can fix many things in the classroom, one thing they can't remedy in the outside world is attitudes towards teachers and education in general. Jeremy Clarkson infamously once suggested that public sector workers, including teachers, protesting against their pay and conditions should be taken outside and shot in front of their families.

He was obviously joking, but we hope that the sentiment has changed over the years, especially since the coronavirus pandemic. When COVID-19 arrived in early 2020, the world changed massively. Amongst the huge disruptions of everyday life that were thrust upon the general public, a significant part was the closing of schools. Unless deemed a 'Key Worker', your child had to be educated at home; suddenly everybody was a teacher! On the first day of home-schooling, it all seemed like a bit of fun:

Monday: A beautifully prepared timetable was created on a spreadsheet detailing exactly when the children would be practising spellings, learning their times tables or following Zumba routines on YouTube.

Friday: Children and parent(s) in tears, lots of bottles of wine opened and the same long-division problem from Wednesday remains unsolved (half the page has been splattered with stray porridge).

After a few weeks of home-schooling shenanigans, social media became filled with GIFs, videos and memes professing newfound appreciation for educators and suggestions of 1,000 per cent pay rises (which is as likely as it is mathematically possible). It was a nice break from the usual teacher-bashing in certain media outlets, and while the love for educators obviously didn't last particularly long, the foundations for a bridge of appreciation and understanding were being laid.

If you are a parent and have picked up this book wanting to know why teaching your child to read is nowadays so different from when you were younger, you may be disappointed in your quest for answers. Almost as disappointed as when your five-year-old knew what a 'split-digraph' was and you didn't! This book won't help you to understand what a 'fronted adverbial' is, although the likelihood is, most teachers didn't have a clue until they had to teach it, either. We certainly don't blame parents for feeling a little confused by some of the terminology being used in modern teaching. If your six-year-old child comes home saying they've been learning about 'contractions', we've not been covering the miracle of childbirth during a Sex Ed lesson – it is another SPAG (spelling, punctuation and grammar) term they need to learn for testing purposes, which is every bit as ridiculous as it sounds. Worryingly, there are (at a push) only two years at primary school where the children aren't required to sit some sort of standardised test.

Regardless of your political persuasions, the sweeping (and, in our opinion, incredibly misguided) educational reforms in England since 2010 have made it much harder to be a teacher. For education staff, the pressure to meet unrealistic expectations while doing their very best for all the children in their care has never been more challenging. Sadly, the architects of the radical overhaul of our education system (who referred to teachers collectively as 'The Blob') have since moved on to bigger things, which include helping the trend of 'divide and rule politics' to become commonplace.

On a quite serious note, it's becoming increasingly difficult to teach equality and tolerance to primary-aged children when division and hate are apparent across the political spectrum. To top it all off, we are tasked with teaching 'British Values', which almost completely contradicts a lot of the tactics being used by leaders to stay in power. In spite of this, we do our best to prepare the children for a world where learning facts is important but spotting alternative facts can be even more so. It's hard to tell little Jimmy off for lying about the whereabouts of his homework when some of the most powerful people on the planet are routinely telling absolute whoppers and getting off scot-free. Amazingly, 'My dog ate my homework' is never seen as a legitimate excuse for students, yet we've heard a genuine story from a teacher whose dog chewed an exercise book they needed to mark! I think we can let them off on this occasion.

In this book we feel it is important to paint a realistic picture of a modern-day primary school. You will hopefully get an insight into the challenging yet rewarding job of teaching, so the next time you stumble across another teacher-bashing article in the press, you may think twice before deciding to quit your day job and seek one in education because it is 'easy'. We aim to put to bed those lazy clichés about finishing work at 3pm each day and why we should appreciate 'all those lovely holidays you get'. Teachers are very much human; we try our best to make a massive difference within a system that is set up to fail so many.

The importance of a solid primary education can never be overestimated. As on our podcast, we will be very honest in these pages about the pressures we face as school staff. One of our aims is to help anyone who might be struggling to cope with the pressures of the job and to make them see that doing their best is good enough. We want to inspire you to focus on the more positive elements of the profession that provide so many special and hilarious moments.

Our intention most of all, though, is to make you laugh and smile as we share some of the funniest, most random and downright bizarre things to happen to us during our time at school. As parents ourselves, Adam and I see how hard it is to bring up children in an ever-changing society. We hope you will enjoy a fun and sometimes nostalgic journey as we tackle every aspect of primary school from the classroom to the staffroom, from school trips to PE lessons and everything in between. We also hope this can be a wistful trip down memory lane, looking back to a simpler time. In the current world we live in, a distraction like this can be a very therapeutic way to escape the pressure of everyday adult life. This is exactly what we have tried to achieve with our podcast, and we hope this book is an extension of that mantra.

So, who's ready for today's lesson? I will be your teacher, Mr P, along with my teaching assistant, The Other Mr P, as we embark upon our learning journey, pulling back the curtain on life working in a primary school and why it can and should be the best job in the world.

And why the answer to every problem is to just 'put a wet paper towel on it!'

As a child, I liked school. I wouldn't say I loved it, but I had a pleasant experience. I would probably have loved it if I had been better at it. I was just ok.

I actually attended two primary schools. Within the first couple of weeks of Year 4 I was moved to another school. I never found out why. I can't even remember being that sad or upset about it. My move to my new school happened to coincide with my obsession at eight years old with the King of Rock and Roll – Mr Elvis Presley. My uncle was a DJ and had started adding his Elvis impersonation to the business he offered at that time. I remember spending two weeks in Year 3 writing, directing and performing my own play – *Peter Pan*. The funniest thing was that I was allowed to do it; I just said to my teacher at the time, Mrs McGrath (whom I later shadowed as a student teacher – absolute legend), 'I have just read this book, *The Play* (Oxford Reading Tree Level 4), and I'd love to do a play myself.' Funnily enough, that book would appear later in my career in the first real video that went viral. My teacher just replied, 'Yeah, go for it!' Go for it?! She literally allowed me to go to the hall to direct and perform a play for two weeks. TWO WEEKS! Nothing written in books, NOTHING! Can you imagine? There are some schools where just one lesson without work in a book would lead to a teacher on capabilities (see the last chapter), but here's the renegade Mrs McGrath allowing me and some other children to create our own play. Fair play to her – allowing me to live out my dream in Year 3 inspired me to do what I am doing today. It certainly started my interest in the performance arts, which continued throughout my childhood. Anyway, back to the King.

That Christmas, my grandma, who was a master at sewing, had given me my very own Elvis costume. It was one of the most precious gifts I had ever received. I started shadowing my uncle, learning the old hip shake, and performed at some family parties. I was in my element.

Cut to my first visit to my new school, being walked around by my new teacher, Mr Ellis (more on him later), before starting the next day.

'So, what sort of things are you into, Lee?' he asked, even though he probably had no interest in what a normal child would say – Game Boy, Sega Mega Drive, Man Utd.

My mum piped up before I had the chance to say anything. 'He loves Elvis. He has his own costume and performs at family parties.'

My face must have been a picture. Don't get me wrong, I loved performing, but I also knew this obsession with Elvis was not a mainstream interest in 1993. It wouldn't have been the first thing I'd have said, but my mum loved me doing it more than I did.

Mr Ellis's face lit up – it was like he'd just discovered a child prodigy. His whole demeanour changed to looking interested.

'How about you bring in the costume tomorrow and you can perform in front of the class?' Gulp.

My mum was buzzing ... I was terrified.

The first day at a new school is up there as one of the most intimidating experiences of your life. You are new, different and you're walking into a class that already has friendships, routines, labelled trays, books and table groups. There's something harrowing about having the only tray label in the class that is handwritten rather than printed. Having to deal with all of that would make the bravest of people nervous but now add in the pressure of having to dress as a music icon from decades earlier and sing a song that most, if not all, the other children would have no clue about. Mr Ellis made it worse by making me stand on a table in the middle of the classroom to do it. Without blowing my own trumpet, I must have been pretty good as Mr Ellis then made me go to EVERY other classroom in the school to give an exclusive performance. How the hell I wasn't crucified and bullied for the rest of my time at that school, I'll never know. I had the odd 'Elvis' shout in the playground, but I could handle it. The weird thing is I have since seen kids picked on for the most trivial and pointless things. A lad with ginger hair once ate a packet of Wotsits, so his name for SEVEN years at my second-ary school was 'stinky Wotsit'.

As much as I enjoyed school, I wasn't one of those people who have always dreamed of being a teacher. I have never met another teacher who did. I know there are some out there, but I reckon that hardly any child now would look at their teacher and think, 'I can't wait to grow up and be as stressed as you are!' or, 'When I grow up, I just want to prep kids for a SATs test,' or even, 'My only goal in life is to get an Ofsted inspector to tell me I am outstanding.'

I wanted to be an actor. Throughout my childhood I had garnered a number of impressive(?) acting credits. These included:

- Extra work on *Coronation Street* (walking behind Candice and Sarah Lou in a school scene, my face wasn't seen but my one-strap Nike bag was clearly visible).
- Playing the child of a murder victim in a *Crimewatch* reconstruction. (The reconstruction in question did end up solving the crime.)

- I played the baby daddy in a teenage pregnancy awareness video.
- I nearly played Ricky Tomlinson's son in *Mike Bassett: England Manager* but was told I was too good-looking. (Really, Lee? Did you really need to include this?)
- Was down to the last four for a part in *Hollyoaks*.

It was the last point of my overachieving resume that put a stop to my acting career. I was 15 or 16, the age where the most important people in the world are your mates and you know more than both your parents put together. I had got a callback from a *Hollyoaks* audition, which coincided with the biggest rugby tournament of the year. I had to miss the tournament and the lads hammered me over it.

I found myself with no real direction; I had fallen out of love with acting, and despite applying to do drama at university, I didn't get on a course. My girlfriend at the time had already been accepted on a teaching course at uni and suggested I did that. So I did. I went along for an interview. I remember being asked to prepare to talk about an issue affecting education at the time. I wish I could remember what I talked about as I would love to compare it to some of the issues we're facing today. I got a conditional offer, and after scraping the necessary results at A Level I was set to start my university degree doing a four-year BA (Hons) in Primary Education.

At the time of writing, my brother-in-law currently works in my school. He's been a TA for the past few years and is brilliant with the kids, and I mean BRILLIANT. He would make an amazing teacher. At the end of the first year, a senior colleague could clearly see his potential and asked him to do teacher training, but he said no. This has continued ever since. Just the other day, the same colleague asked me why he won't do it. I looked at him and said,

'Let's be honest, if we were in his position, would we do it? Yes, we'd get more money, but is it worth all the extra pressure, lack of trust, stress and workload?' He nodded in reluctant agreement.

I love teaching, I think it can be the best job in the world, but our system is broken. I am trying my hardest to fix it, but it is one hell of an uphill battle.

My university course was an interesting experience. One of the biggest things I learned was that there are some people in education who love faff. They love to turn simple tasks into the most over-elaborate things. Take the course itself: four years, *four* years, when most teachers do a PGCE in one!

This has just reminded me of one of the worst examples of how some teachers love to waste time on nothing. When I first introduced a digital learning journal – Seesaw – to our staff, we had a training session where I demonstrated the tool. When you upload an example of work, you can tag it with a subject, making it easier to search. The KS1 leader at the time then called a meeting to decide what colour each subject folder should be. I had to sit there for nearly an hour while the staff chose which colour should link to each subject!

Now, I will hold my hands up here – my attitude at uni wasn't the best. I was 18, straight out of school and had been given a student loan. I made the most of it. I joined the rugby team and was very much enjoying the social side of studying. That meant I did miss a fair few lectures, but as it turned out they were more like isolated SPAG lessons – pointless. Anything that was necessary I was there for, but the real learning always came on placements. I was lucky, most of mine were great. My first placement was a funny one since they did not do whole-class teaching ... at all. It was weird and definitely didn't work. It was a good job EduTwitter wasn't about then as they would have been hammered by the usual teacher trolls.

My biggest challenge at university came on my placement. It was my first experience of a truly toxic school. The school was in a period of transition as the head of 20-plus years had just retired. A new, younger head was trying to change everything – and I mean everything – in what seemed like a term. I was put with a really nice teacher who had a challenging class. On one of my visits before I started, I asked if I could swap one of my days so I could play rugby for uni. This simple request was my downfall. The assessing teacher told me within a week of the placement that under no circumstances would she be passing me. When I asked why, she simply replied, 'You're not capable of being a teacher.' I had ten weeks left.

I've never met someone who was so obsessed with paperwork. She once wrote a single literacy lesson plan for me that was FIVE PAGES! (FRONT AND BACK!) and because I wouldn't, or should I say couldn't, do the same, I wasn't good enough. I remember sitting at a computer at 11 or 12 at night desperately trying to pad out lesson plans to make them longer and more thorough, which had NO impact on the quality of my teaching. But according to the teacher, it was a must. An inability to plan an effective lesson would lead to poor delivery of that lesson. But here's the thing with me: I do what needs to be done. Life is too short. There will be no teacher on this planet who will lie on their deathbed and say, 'I wish I could have marked more.' Just because I wasn't willing to waste time on unnecessary paperwork didn't mean I was a bad teacher.

I really struggled with the class I was teaching, but so did the teacher; there was no support, no TA in a class where at least half of the children were on an IEP with no support. I always remember there was one child who could recite every Cypress Hill lyric but didn't know his number bonds to ten. Insane in the membrane, indeed. Despite the assessing teacher clearly hating me, I stuck at the placement, hoping to change her view. I initially thought she was saying it to test me; turns out she was just a bitch. Sorry, poor leader.

Halfway through that placement, the class teacher I was with fell pregnant. There's nothing wrong with that, apart from the fact it was a Catholic school and the teacher was not married, meaning the child would be born a 'bastard' (and if you read that in *Game of Thrones*' Jon Snow's voice, you're my kind of guy/gal). She had to confess her sins to the priest, which meant I became the least of the deputy's worries. The uni tutor who came to visit didn't know their arse from their elbow. Turned out, she was good friends with the deputy, so that was the nail in the coffin. I felt isolated, like I was rubbish and not cut out for teaching. I remember on the eve of my twenty-first birthday sitting on my mum's bed and breaking down. I'd had enough. What was the point of even finishing the placement when I was clearly not good enough? I remember my mum comforting me, telling me it wasn't that bad – 'think about Elvis on your first day at your new school' – and that I should contact the university to see if there was anything they could do. I am so thankful I followed her advice. Mums are just always right.

Within a couple of days the uni sent another tutor, who after spending an hour watching me teach and chatting, told me I was fine, the school was the problem. I always remember her saying to me that I was a decent teacher who would do the bare minimum, but that's not a bad thing. If a teacher works for four hours a night and you do half an hour, you can both be just as effective in class. But who lives the better life? Those words have stuck with me to this day. I finished the placement and, despite the teacher's every effort to fail me, the uni allowed me to do another placement. The extra placement was the complete opposite. I loved every minute of it. The class teacher was amazing, the staff were so supportive and I thrived, meaning I passed my third year.

But I will never forget how close I came to giving up. Stories like this now seem to be the norm and it shouldn't be the case. I am inundated with messages every day, not just from students but experienced teachers who are being bullied, mistreated and driven to quit. My advice is always the same: there are some toxic schools but there are also some incredible schools. No school is perfect. But if you find yourself in a position where you feel like joining the tens of thousands of other teachers who have already left the profession, please try another school first. This can also be flipped; sometimes you can take for granted the school you are in. Take my school – it is nowhere near perfect but there are so many positives and I love so many different elements of it: the staff (well, most of them; I'm not a fan of the mood-hoovers), the children and parents (again, most of them; some I would quite happily never see again in my life), the SLT and facilities. However, the vast majority of staff have only ever worked here, and the rest probably can't remember their previous schools as it has been so long. Now, while this might be a positive sign – in that staff retention is good – the downside is that the littlest problem can seem like the world is going to end. Sometimes I have to give some of my colleagues a little perspective – only because I've seen it myself since working in other schools – and share some of the messages I receive from teachers about the expectations and ridiculous micromanagement in their schools to make them realise that actually it could be a lot worse.

My final placement in the fourth year of uni was another amazing learning experience (it also helped that the school was walking distance from where I lived). The school was great and I loved the class I had – they're in their early twenties now and I will often see some of them out and about, and they usually let on. I love that. It was through that last placement that I managed to get an interview at the school where I still work. Once that placement had finished, I continued to come into the school to help with their football team. It was at a local area tournament hosted at my current school that I was introduced to the head, who made me aware of a position starting in September. I applied and was invited for an interview.

Now can we please have a quick word about interviews, because in the 12 years I have been a teacher, they have transformed into the *Krypton Factor*. My interview was with the head teacher and a couple of governors. I was asked a range of questions in relation to the teaching post I had applied for – discussions around behaviour, assessment, expectations and examples of when I had solved problems in my own experience.

Nowadays, the interview process looks something like this ...

See the advert for the post that will require you to submit an application form as a CV that seems double the length of the dissertation you penned back at university.

You can request to have a walk around the school. You need to do this; you will see the school as if it is the best that has ever existed. This can be the perfect example of what it is like to be hoodwinked.

> **Definition** of **hoodwink**. *transitive verb. 1: to deceive by false appearance: dupe people who allow themselves* **to be hoodwinked** *by such promises.*

This visit will give the candidate the opportunity to get a step ahead of all the other interviewees. So, asking the right questions is crucial:

How are you implementing Ofsted's new framework?

What are your expectations of behaviour?

In what ways are staff supported to improve?

When really most teachers want to ask:

Are you going to overwork me by making me do a load of
unnecessary paperwork?

Do people actually get time to go into the staffroom?

Is the staff 'Christmas do' a proper piss-up?

If you impress on that walk round and the application dissertation is hitting all the right criteria, you may be invited for an
interview. This will be a whole day, if you're lucky. If you're
going for a leadership job, the interview process could be an
entire week! This is where things are starting to get ridiculously
silly. Some of the things I have seen on social media or been
messaged about as far as what the interview process entails are
utter madness.

The briefing you receive may resemble this:

'You will be asked to prepare a 20-minute lesson for a group
of children from Reception to Year 6. There is a range of
abilities in the class, with one child the next Einstein and
others who think they are Donald Trump. You will be
completely blindfolded throughout the entire lesson. There
will be a TA in the class, however, they will not be able to
use their hands at any point. There will be a class of 38, with
children who speak 50 languages, none of which are English.
We want the focus of the lesson to be on the past
progressive subjunctive form and by the end of the lesson all
the children should have created a cure for cancer.'

And you see on all these Facebook groups desperate teachers pleading for some sort of inspirational idea or answer to this.

Alongside this observation, you may have to lead a whole-school assembly, cook and serve school dinners for the day, deep clean the entire school and sort the health and safety risk assessment form for the upcoming school trip. Then you have the interview. Your brain will be completely scrambled by this point, but now you have to test your skills and knowledge in the most intense round of *Mastermind*.

Name: Lee Parkinson
Occupation: Teacher
Specialist subject: Education

Ok, your hour of questions on Education starts now.

A parent complained that you didn't send the letter home, but you did, so how do you deal with this?

Explain that you sent the letter home and the child should take more responsibility in delivering it.

Oooh, incorrect. We were looking for take full responsibility and waste 20 minutes printing and photocopying another letter for said parent.

You get the idea.

Or, in the briefing email you get asked to bring an object that means something to you or that represents and symbolises you as a teacher. What a load of shit! How does that have any impact on the quality of a teacher? I know a friend who lost out on a job because of this. He brought a football as he loves football; the other teacher had baked a cake. What an absolute inspired choice: teachers and cake. There was only ever going to be one winner. The interview swung against my friend and he missed out. The kicker? The other teacher didn't make it to October half term. I don't know what I would bring: a dartboard with the latest Ed Sec's face in the middle, a can of Red Bull, a bottle of Xanax?

'So why have you brought this object?'

'What object?'

'The bottle of Xanax.'

'Oh, that's not my object, it is just what I have been on since preparing for this interview!'

The worst thing about the whole process, especially if it is a leadership position, is that you go through all of this to get the phone call or email that says, 'Thank you, but the position has been offered to the teacher who already works at the school who was always going to get it but we needed to go through the official channels before we kept it in-house.'

Anyway, I was offered the job of Year 5 teacher and was ready to start as an eager-to-please NQT as long as I got my degree. The only thing in my way ...? The dissertation.

In our third year of uni, we were all made to choose a specialism that we could focus on developing in our NQT year, of which we would eventually become subject leader. There were core subjects: English, Maths, Science, ICT (yes, this was a core subject at the time), SEN and a few others. I went for ICT. The dissertation had to have an ICT focus, so after much reading and research, I decided on ... drum roll, please ....

How interactive is an interactive whiteboard?

Wow, just wow. I know what you're thinking, that title deserves a first in itself. Exactly 15,000 words and tons of research later, it was a reading to be summed up by 'Not very'. I am sure you can guess from the writing you have endured so far that it wasn't a page-turner and quite rightly scraped me a 2:2, but it got me the degree, which meant I could spend the summer preparing my classroom. My journey into teaching had begun ...

However, I feel my story needs to be split into two parts, because my career took a very different path once I became a father. So, you've read the first bit, but how did I get to this point – from being a classroom teacher to now writing this book as the most-followed primary teacher in the UK on social media, and having worked with thousands of teachers and schools leading training and CPD over the past five years and starting a podcast that has now been listened to over three million times? God, that sounds really cringey! Sorry, like any of it matters. Don't get me wrong, I absolutely love the job I do now. I get to share my message, ideas and philosophy, and it is incredibly rewarding knowing that it is having such a huge impact on outcomes for so many children as well as helping teachers with not only their practice but their wellbeing. But the journey to this point was both interesting and difficult.

The Journey of 'Mr P'

'Have you been having any fertility treatment?' the sonographer asked us as my wife Claire lay on the bed with the ultrasound scanning her stomach. The nurse turned the screen away from us and stared at it more intently. I looked at my wife, worried. The nurse turned to us and held up three fingers. I was confused as Claire burst into tears. My six-year-old stepson, who was in the room with us, was just as perplexed. The screen was then turned towards us and the nurse pointed out three little prawns on the screen. We were expecting triplets.

We had married in July 2010 and were receiving the news on 15 November 2010 that we were expecting triplets. My whole life was turned upside down. Once my brain settled, my first thought was, how am I going to be able to pay for this? We needed a bigger house, car, trolleys, everything. I was in my fourth year of teaching, having had a TLR for ICT and, after discussing it with my head, I looked at applying for some leadership positions. I was very close to getting one job, but it was not to be. I look back now and think, maybe I didn't quite cut the mustard, or perhaps when I mentioned my wife was pregnant with triplets they thought twice. Regardless, I stayed at my school.

The triplets – Harry, Charlie and Lily – arrived in April 2011, on Mother's Day, and had to spend the first few weeks in the ICU as they were eight weeks premature. We couldn't have timed it better; it was the year in which we had the two-week Easter break, but Easter itself was the following weekend, followed by the Royal Wedding and the May Bank Holiday. All in all, it worked out that I was in school something like eight days in six weeks. Then, once all three babies had left the ICU, I took my two weeks' paternity leave. Before that we had an INSET day with legendary educational consultant Alan Peat (more on him later), and the staff had clubbed together and got me a hamper packed full of baby stuff, which was nice.

The first year of being a dad was one of the most challenging of my life. A lot of my friends who have since had children always ask, how did you do it with three? And to be honest, I can't remember. The whole thing was a blur. One tip that teaching taught me that really helped was routine. From day one, we had a strict routine of bath, bottle, bed, and by seven to eight months they were sleeping through. I will happily admit it impacted my work – I was trying my best but my priority was home. It completely changed my approach to teaching. I don't think I failed my class, and I still believe I was a very effective teacher, I just started to approach teaching differently. Things that I used to worry about quickly didn't matter as much, work that I had used to do that didn't have an impact on learning wasn't even considered. It gave me a new perspective that started my journey on working smarter, not harder.

A year later, I had a discussion with my headteacher. He knew that my situation had changed and I would be looking to move into a position of leadership. The head was great at supporting his staff this way, and he offered me the opportunity to come out of the classroom and cover PPA across the school. I had only been a KS2 teacher up to that point. It would give me the opportunity to gain valuable experience down in EYFS and KS1. The head also wanted me to focus on developing my curriculum subject, which was ICT. How did you become ICT subject leader, I hear you cry. Well, as an eager-to-please NQT I made a video for the Year 6 leavers' assembly of their time through school, with pictures set to some music – I think it was Green Day's 'Time of Your Life'. The head took one look and said, 'Right, you're the new ICT co-ordinator.'

At first, I wasn't sure of the proposal my head had given me, I couldn't imagine not having a class. I love the relationship you have with that group of 35, the journey you go on, the progress you see. Yes, it can be frustrating, and yes, it is hard, but being that person the children can rely on day in, day out is a special feeling. On the other hand, I knew this was an incredible opportunity to gain valuable experience that would help me when I eventually decided to move on to another school or a management position. I would have loved to move up within my school, but at my school no one leaves. After a discussion with my wife I decided to go for it, but I needed the school to invest in some updated technology for me to do it more effectively. At the time we had an ICT suite with around 20 desktop computers, 15 of which ran Windows 95 (it was 2012). I asked about investing in some mobile technology and, more specifically, iPads. He agreed.

My role that academic year was to cover PPA across the school, looking at how the technology could enhance and transform learning. I am not going to lie, there was definitely a novelty element to the iPads, for both myself and the pupils.

'Are we going to play with the iPad today?' was a regular question asked in those early days. It was bound to happen when pupils have only ever used an iPad to play with, or to watch or listen to content with. This is a view that I find is still held by a lot of school staff. I understand why, as most people only ever use the technology as a consumer: we watch films/TV shows/YouTube, we read ebooks, we browse the web, we play video games. This use of the technology has a place in the classroom, and there are some great tools that help us to know and understand different concepts. The problem with ICT and computing over the years is that this is the only experience we have had of it. If you're of my generation, our only experience of ICT at school was death by Microsoft Office. We would do a spreadsheet, animate a PowerPoint, or, if you were really lucky, use some WordArt. The ability to make your title curve in a semicircle in five different colours was something else. That is still happening in many schools today, which is why the change from ICT to computing was made. Not that I like to pay Michael Gove any sort of compliment, but if he got one thing and only one thing right as Ed Sec, it was that. The problem is you have a generation of teachers being told to teach something they've never really experienced before. So we're going from a death by PowerPoint approach to death by Scratch 3.0.

I soon focused on creating through the technology. I was looking at ways in which children could record videos rather than simply watch, write ebooks instead of just reading them, publish to the web, design video games, etc. I could see how this use of technology was making learning purposeful and empowering. The problem I faced was with all the work children were producing through the technology, none of it could be stuck in a book. I needed to find a way in which the work could be evidenced without wasting hours printing and sticking in books.

That's when I started our school blog. It was on separate site to our website, but it would be a platform where pupils could publish their work to the world. I was initially inspired by a lot of the work David Mitchell (@DeputyMitchell, a well-known education consultant) had done with blogging, and this helped us at the beginning. At the same time we started a school Twitter and Facebook page. This was linked directly to the blog, so as soon as anything was published it would tweet and post on the Facebook page. This created a really efficient workflow that saved me even more time. The blog started getting a lot of traction and views. This was extremely encouraging for both me and for my pupils, who were seeing their work being viewed, commented on and appreciated by people all over the world. I started to get more involved in Twitter discussions through the school account until Julian Wood (@ideas_factory) suggested I started my own Teacher Twitter, or #Tweacher, account. This was the beginning of the @ICT_MrP journey.

Alongside my social media accounts, I started a teacher blog. I worked tirelessly on this, writing and sharing ideas into the early hours. I explained how we had created the work being showcased on my school blog. This became incredibly popular, getting hundreds of thousands of hits within the first year. The socials started growing, too. I started to get involved in some virtual teachmeets where I would share projects that we had been doing in class. A teachmeet was a gathering of teachers from the local area in which a few would present and share some useful ideas to use in class. It doesn't sound much, but at the time it was some of best CPD you could get. Then I plucked up the courage to attend and present at my first teachmeet in Bolton. I remember I presented about how we had been using video games in different ways to enhance and support learning in the classroom. I was so nervous, but the feedback I received was fantastic and it encouraged me even more. Towards the end of that academic year, after many requests, I started doing after-school training sessions for local schools.

Soon after, I received a DM from Alan Peat. He was looking for someone who would work with him, focusing on the creative use of technology. At this point I saw my career taking a different direction. Alan Peat is a legend, with over 20 years as an educational consultant with some of the best resources to support teaching English in primary schools. When Alan had taken that INSET day, he had changed my whole outlook on teaching English. I was blown away, and I left that training more inspired than by anything I had experienced in four years of university. I started following Alan on Twitter and would regularly tweet him examples of work and he would always reply with fantastic feedback for the pupils. When he reached out and asked if I would be interested in meeting to chat about potentially working together, I was taken aback. I met with Alan, and his wife Julie came too, and he watched me deliver a session to a school. I knew he'd also met with a number of other people, so I was made up when he offered me the opportunity to work on behalf of his company and lead CPD sessions for schools. A few years later I asked Alan why he chose me over the others, and he said it was because everyone else he met with just talked about their 'journey', whereas I simply went in and talked about what the pupils in my school had been doing. To him, I was all about the children.

Anyway, the offer meant working part-time – two to three days a week at school, then leading training sessions on the other days. I so vividly remember sitting at the kitchen table with my wife and discussing the risk of going part-time, with no guarantees of bookings and the triplets running around in nappies. Claire had gone back to her job part-time, and making ends meet with three babies was already a struggle. She wasn't sure it was worth the risk, but I knew this was an opportunity I couldn't pass up. I said I had to give it a go because if I didn't I would regret it for the rest of my life. It was a really pivotal moment, as it could have so easily gone the other way.

My school was incredibly accommodating and I will forever be grateful for that. I know for a fact that many schools who would have just said either stay or go. I have always loved the way my school has made me feel valued; they seem to appreciate what I can still bring to them – even part-time. A lot of people would have used the opportunity I received as a way to get out of the classroom, but I never wanted that. What I think separates me from a lot of others who now lead training in schools is that I don't see myself as anything other than a teacher. A lot of feedback I receive from my training sessions will state that it is nice to have someone who is still doing it week in, week out and sharing tried-and-tested ideas to improve learning. I see the daily challenges that teachers face, which is why I am so outspoken about workload and wellbeing. I honestly believe you can be a really effective teacher and have a decent work–life balance (more on that later).

We spent that summer getting ourselves set up as a business. Mr P ICT Ltd was born. It was a steep learning curve trying to get my head around starting my own business, especially when all you've known is education. Luckily, Alan and Julie were so helpful with every aspect of the process and I am eternally grateful to them. Five years into this world of educational consultancy, I realise how different they were to a lot of other companies; they could have easily employed me on behalf of their company, limiting my opportunities to build my personal brand. Instead, they chose to work alongside me and help me create my own business. I learnt so much from them in those early days and don't think I would be where I am now without their help and support.

Technology can be an incredibly powerful tool if it is utilised effectively, but the biggest challenge is getting teachers confident and knowledgeable in using technology this way. This is what my training and later website has always strived to do.

One of the best examples of this was a project I did back in 2013. During the summer I had watched the film *Blackfish*, which told the story of Tilikum, a whale kept in captivity who had killed a SeaWorld trainer. Killer whales have been one of my favourite animals since watching *Free Willy* back in primary school. Visiting SeaWorld during a visit to Florida when I was 15 was a dream come true, but my view on the park changed after watching *Blackfish*. On the first day of the autumn term, I was working with Year 5. A child wanted to show a picture they had from their holiday in Florida. I couldn't help myself, and started to talk about the film once they mentioned SeaWorld. Sharing a few facts, I noticed the children were hooked, asking questions and offering opinions on the topic. I saw an opportunity and decided to go with it. One of the best skills as a teacher is the ability to adapt when an opportunity arises to take learning down a certain path. That flexibility has led to some of the best lessons and projects I have ever taught, with *Blackfish* being a perfect example. I had been asked by the class teacher to do some 'All About Me' posters. I could have stuck with that idea but I would have missed the opportunity to teach something the children clearly had a real interest in. That's not to say this happens every time the children show an interest in something. Can you imagine? It would have been a curriculum of fidget-spinning, bottle-flipping, flossing, *Fortnite* and TikTok dancing.

After sharing some more information about whales in captivity, my class were motivated to write about this topic. For a generation who follow and watch YouTubers and vloggers, I try to explain to pupils that behind every successful vlog, show or film is a well-written piece of text. Children never really make that connection as they don't often get the chance to do it. The fact that with an iPad you can easily transform a piece of text into a film, greenscreen project or other form of engaging media makes that writing matter. My class then performed their writing in a video, which we shared on our school social media platforms. Within a day it had thousands of views, and we received a message from Gabriella Cowperthwaite, the director of *Blackfish*. She was blown away by the children's work and offered to Skype with the class to learn more, along with a couple of the ex-animal trainers who were featured in the film. It was an amazing learning opportunity where the children could connect and speak to someone who lived on the other side of the planet and had experienced everything firsthand.

We continued to write, learn and publish work around this topic for the rest of that half term. The quality of the writing was phenomenal, mainly due to the fact that everything the children did was being published to our school blog for anyone in the world to see. We had letters sent to school from marine biologists in Australia, messages from the Born Free Foundation and towards the end of the term PETA awarded me their Compassionate Teacher of the Year award – even though really it was the class that led it all. I will never forget the moment, a couple of years later, when SeaWorld announced they were no longer going to keep killer whales in captivity. One child who had done the project came back into school to say, 'We've done it!'

This was a project I discussed and shared a lot in my training in the early days and I loved seeing how it inspired so many other teachers to do something similar with their classes. A teacher once said to me, 'You must love doing this job,' to which

I replied, 'I do, but what makes you say that?' They replied, 'Well, if you're in class full-time, you only get to inspire 30 kids. By leading training sessions for teachers you will end up inspiring thousands of children.'

The whole point of my training is to get teachers to use shared ideas in class to raise standards and improve outcomes, although you do get the odd person who will take an idea then claim it as their own. Teaching is a profession where we want to help and support each other, but not everyone adheres to that etiquette. One thing I have always prided myself on is having integrity. You can look back through all my blog posts from the moment I started and if I have ever been inspired by someone else's work I will always mention and credit them with a link into the blog post. It has never stopped me from getting to where I am by acknowledging others' work. I have seen people present, write books and even win awards using my ideas. It is disheartening and it used to really wind me up, but I have had to accept that imitation is the sincerest form of flattery.

My journey over the past five years has been incredible. Having the opportunity to work with so many amazing schools has been great, but it has also really improved my own practice in so many ways. I am so fortunate to have the best of both worlds – able to teach each week but also able to travel and work with thousands of teachers to help them improve their teaching. On top of all that, the growth of my social media has been amazing, too. I branched out of just sharing teaching ideas to making videos about life in the classroom. These have become a bit of a hobby now. I love the way these resonate with so many teachers, and nothing brightens my day more than receiving a message from a teacher saying they've had the worst day but watching one of my videos has cheered them up. As I always say on my training, we don't have a choice about using the internet, the choice we make is how well we do it. I like to think my social media channels do this – they show that we all have the same thoughts and feelings and go through the same struggles – and this is ok. The life of a teacher can be unique but universal at the same time.

Adam's Route into the Classroom

My route into working in a school; the up (notice the lack of an 's') and the downs. Perhaps I'm being too harsh, but it wasn't the easiest of journeys. In fact, it was quite the rollercoaster. Born the youngest of three brothers (everyone knows the third film in the franchise is always the best – just look at *The Godfather: Part III*, *Jurassic Park III* and *X-Men: The Last Stand* ...) I had some decent acts to follow and a few hurdles in my way.

There are plenty of stories on our podcast about some of the shenanigans I got up to as a child, but safe to say that after my two older brothers had passed through the school fairly unscathed, I often felt that my card was somehow marked. I was what you might call a child that (you'll read this plenty of times) 'didn't always make the right choices' or, as it would have been referred to at the time, was a 'cheeky little bugger'. Since my earlier school days, I have been diagnosed with asthma, type 1 diabetes and, to the surprise of none of my teachers, Attention Deficit Disorder. It's fair to say that I often found school to be somewhat of a challenge. Don't get me wrong,

I had a lot of fun, and as you read this book you'll find out why I still remember many things fondly.

When asked as a child what I wanted to be when I grew up (if I grew up), I was dead set on becoming a professional wrestler. Like many young lads growing up in the 90s and 2000s, I was obsessed with watching WWF (the wrestling, not the wildlife charity with the panda) or, as it is now known, WWE (World Wrestling Entertainment). I was hoping to be the next Undertaker, 'Stone Cold' Steve Austin or Dwayne 'The Rock' Johnson. Sadly, my ambitions of becoming a wrestling superstar were scuppered when I realised my ankles were made of glass; my dreams were 'shattered' (ahem). What else could a man of my many talents do?

I always liked the idea of becoming a fireman ... mostly because of sliding down a pole, but my asthma 'extinguished' that one.

Apologies, readers, just let him get these crap jokes out of his system...

My other interests included, well ... KFC, kebabs, Turkey Twizzlers (take that, Jamie Oliver), McDonald's, Pizza Hut, Indian, Chinese, Milky Bar yoghurts, ice cream, nachos and erm ... Burger King. A career in food-tasting or competitive eating surely beckoned ... that was until type 1 diabetes 'swallowed' that one up!

FFS! Once again, apologies, readers.

With my first-choice career paths out of the question, it was time to get real. My work life began with a part-time job at the high-street retailer Next. I'm confident in saying that my employment came as a result of my glowing CV, and definitely had ABSOLUTELY NOTHING to do with my two brothers already working there and being involved in staff recruitment. In a strange twist of fate, 14 of our closest friends were also hired and, in the process, the infamous 'Next Mafia' was created; this unexpectedly coincided with a sharp drop in customer service satisfaction levels yet a massive increase in Christmas party attendance. Remarkable!

The reason why Adam had 14 of his mates working there was because I was his youth football team's manager. At Under 17 level, I arranged for us all to go on a tour to Holland and we needed to pay for it, so I got the whole team a job at Next.

By the time I left Next, I was already five years away from my first job working in a primary school. 'So, Adam, what is your favourite film?' asked the interviewer at my local Odeon, my potential new employer. EASIEST INTERVIEW QUESTION EVER! Without hesitation I replied *Armageddon*, and with a beaming smile I could almost faintly hear Aerosmith serenading me with 'I Don't Want to Miss a Thing'. After that question came the more serious enquiry of: 'Which movie character would you say you are most like and why?' Naturally, I answered 'John McClane. Reason being, if terrorists descended upon the cinema complex I'd fight back!' I mean, the interview should have ended there; I knew I was in. Obviously, Odeon signed me up there and then, and before too long I was proudly donning my uniform and name badge, which displayed the member of staff's name and their favourite film. 'Adam Armageddon' was born. Perhaps Adam Armageddon should've been my wrestler name? Never mind, I had movies to see ...

Unfortunately, after my stellar performance during the interview, my tenure at the cinema lasted a measly four months. I thought I'd be able to watch far more films than I did and I spent way more time cleaning out the popcorn machines. But there were some perks; I was informed in the early days, while working a refreshment stall shift, that if the customer changed their mind or a 'mistake' had been made with an order, the product must be taken into the back and 'disposed' of. 'Disposed of?' Light bulb!

One quiet Tuesday morning shift, a mum and daughter approached the stand and ordered 'Large nachos combo with salsa – no jalapeños – and a large Fanta.' With no breakfast in my belly and my mouth as dry as the Sahara, I promptly made a large nachos with cheese and extra jalapeños, with a large Pepsi Max! As I approached the customers, they informed me that I had in fact made the incorrect order. What were the chances?!? With my head in my hands, I apologised profusely and swiftly prepared the correct order. Now I had to 'dispose' of my favourite nachos combo order, so I went into the back to feast like a king. I was being paid for this!

A few more places of work followed, including, ironically, a stint at the organisation all educators dread – the Office for Standards in Education, Children's Services and Skills – AKA OFSTED! You may think that I was a mole trying to infiltrate the system; a renegade sent to sabotage the 'powers that be' from within. John McClane returns in *Die Hard 5: Ofsted Armageddon* ...

Sadly, none of that happened. In fact, I worked mostly in one of their admin departments playing A LOT of *Minesweeper*. For any teachers reading this book, please don't judge me for turning to the dark side. I was young, I needed the money and I didn't know quite what I was doing. My eldest brother may have mentioned what he thinks of Ofsted a few times, but to me it was just a job. Another job that didn't really challenge me in quite the right way. I had a reasonably short stint at the Co-op next, and sadly I can't reveal how that ended – only attendees to our live podcast show know what went down before I departed. I certainly can't mention it here!

While I was at the Co-op, I started getting involved in running some rugby sessions at a local school with my old football manager. The volunteering was a really positive outlet and I enjoyed working with the kids. Not long after this, I had a phone call from my auntie, who had just started a job as a Behaviour Lead at a school in North Manchester. She said they were having some difficulties with a Year 5 child who was crying out for a positive male role model. She asked if I would be interested in volunteering with this child. I mean, I was a 23-year-old whose highlight of the week was being driven to the chippy on a Friday night by his dad; I checked my CV and sadly there was no mention of 'Role Model' (budgets were obviously tight there). Honoured to be asked, I gave it my best shot and struck up a fantastic relationship with this lad. It felt amazing to be able to channel my previous experiences of being 'a child that doesn't always make the right choices' and turn them into something useful. I think the lad really responded well to me, and by then I had been properly bitten by the education bug. My foot was in the door and I felt like I was starting to make the 'right choices' myself. I was finally on my way to turning my life around. Six months later I applied for a job as a teaching assistant, and I got it.

In the years since I started working in primary schools I have met some amazing kids, some brilliant parents and some of my most favourite work colleagues ever. Lots of these awesome folks make appearances on the podcast, although we have had to change their names to protect the innocent – and plenty of the 'not-so-innocent' as well. They are all legends, and I'm very grateful for the comedy gold they have intentionally and unintentionally provided for us to share with you.

From the first term of being a teacher I couldn't believe there hadn't been an *Office*-style sitcom called *The Staffroom*, which followed the escapades of a typical primary school staff.

During every placement I had as a trainee it was amazing that whichever school I was at, you would meet the same type of characters. Obviously, there are sweeping generalisations here, and these 'characters' may take different roles, but I reckon as we describe them you can easily think of a colleague that fits the bill.

We must also state that all these characters are completely fictionalised and are not based on any actual people. (More like a combination of people we have met over the years.)

Let's start with the most underappreciated member of staff:

Site-Manager/Caretaker

Despite the scowl, he's a top bloke.

School-branded baseball cap – to stop him pulling his hair out!

Liverpool F.C. scarf (despite living over 100 miles from Anfield).

To-do list – full of random stuff from the building's log

Mobile phone in extra-tough case – full of offensive jokes.

Paint stains on jumper from previous day's glossing job.

Drill/Robot sound-effect maker.

The largest bunch of keys ... EVER!

Steel-toe-capped boots that could break a Reception child's finger on impact.

He hates that one of the Year 6 kids is taller than him!

The image depicts some tell-tale signs of the 'typical' site manager/caretaker. They can be like gold dust – find a good one and they improve the school so much. However, I once worked with a site manager who probably had the worst fear for any person doing his job. No, he wasn't allergic to kids, or lazy, he was in fact scared of heights. I only discovered this after asking him to change a ceiling bulb in my classroom during my first two weeks as a student teacher, and it still hadn't been sorted by the summer when I returned to help out. He had managed to hide this fear well over the years. I think when it got to winter and the school was a complete blackout because there wasn't a single working lightbulb, everyone clocked on to the fact this guy couldn't handle being up a ladder. He would go to extreme lengths, like bringing the ladder into your classroom, setting it up in place and putting a new lightbulb on the table. He would then proceed to procrastinate to unseen levels. He would talk to you while you marked, 'forget' a screwdriver so he'd have to go back to his room, and he would wait until you had finished and left, then move the ladder back without stepping a foot on it. He had mastered this craft to the point that teachers would end up changing the bulbs themselves. He would explain he had a phone call with the gas company, a meeting with an electrician or he was putting up a shelf (another task that was only completed if the shelf was head height).

He was a fairly intimidating fellow to begin with, but once you were onside he was a good lad. Loved the gym, but also loved food. I sometimes felt that working at a primary school was not the best environment for him. He seemed more suited to a work site that would consist of non-stop lad banter and alpha-male shenanigans. I soon realised what made him stay working at a school and also motivated his gym addiction – MUMS. He would always be doing something in and around the school gates at prime drop-off and pick-up time. Flexing, winking, flirting, he loved it. And when that week in June came around when we got some sun in this country, his Gold's gym vest was proudly displayed while he strutted and sweated in front of mums like he was starring in his own Diet Coke advert. The funny thing was the parents were always completely oblivious, but that didn't stop him. I once joked that a parent was overheard saying they'd love a calendar with him as the model. The look on his face was a picture until he realised it was a wind-up.

You would walk past his room each morning and it would reek of rotten eggs; it could have been him boiling eggs to hit his protein goal for the day or it could also be just him releasing the gas in his bowels. His bowel movements worked like clockwork:

arrive in school at 6am but from 6.30 to 6.55 he would be taking his daily dump just before most teachers arrived for the day. This must have gone on for years until a new member of staff, who would arrive bang on 6.30am every morning, clocked on and reported this use of time.

He was spoken to sternly by the head, and he was fuming. I remember he once confided in me, 'I can't do my deadlifts if I haven't made a deposit at the porcelain bank.'

I admired his work ethic of not doing his work. I often think about whether he still works at the school, or in a school at all. He was the perfect example of the caretaker that would be great for the primary school staffroom sitcom.

NQT in September

Perfectly styled hair.

Hopeful eyes – full of enthusiasm.

Snazzy shirt and shoes combination that says, 'CBeebies presenter with brains'!

Glowing tan from post-university trip to Ibiza.

No marking to do – she did it all at lunchtime!

Facebook statuses – currently very positive!

Funky bag full of home-made resources.

Personalised mug with safety lid – a present from final placement school.

Beige trousers (pre-fingerpaint, clay and glitter-glue).

Brand new laptop case with 10-year-old laptop inside (budgets are tight).

NQTs (Newly Qualified Teachers), bless their little cotton socks. However you managed to get to the point of being an NQT – university degree, PGCE, school-based training – nothing will prepare you for that first year as a teacher. It has to be up there as one of the hardest years of your life. Obviously, it will be harder/easier depending on the school and the level of support you receive. It is often assumed that everything was covered at uni or on your placements, when in reality it wasn't. There are so many things you have to get your head around before you even think of the children. Timetables, routines, staff, procedures, expectations, school-wide policies, to name but a few. I meet so many NQTs who, dare I say it, are naive and have the ultimate dream of being the inspirational teacher they set out to be while still having a decent social life and relationships with their loved ones. They may spend the rest of their dwindling student loan raiding anything educational on Amazon, spending hours at home creating their own resources, and are freshly kitted out with a new 'teacher' wardrobe like they've just appeared on the catwalk showcasing the new teacher range for the autumn collection. I wish that enthusiasm would last, but for the majority it doesn't. I was exactly the same, in fact. While researching this book I went through some of my old files and folders that had gathered dust in a stock cupboard in my school. I was advised by my university mentor to keep a weekly diary to document my first year as a teacher, which would become a useful reflection tool.

NQT by February Half-Term

Hair tied back for convenience.

First grey hairs (despite only being 23 years old!).

'Fixed grin' to show she's still coping.

Pencil behind ear, which she misplaced an hour ago.

Incredibly heavy school laptop case (filled with books to mark).

Warm cardigan because her classroom is always <u>bloody freezing</u>!

Pockets full of school stationery to use as per the new marking policy.

Diet energy-drink – because coffee really isn't doing the trick right now.

Another 'Bag for Life' full of marking. This one is probably on its last legs.

'Bag for Life' also full of books to mark.

The comfiest shoes she owns.

BAG FOR LIFE (AS LONG AS IT LASTS)

Before long, I quickly resembled this:

I reckon I aged a decade in the space of a term. It seemed to fly by in an instant, but at the same time it felt like years. I remember fondly the outlook I had as I started my NQT year, how much I would make a difference, the impact I would have, the passion, the enthusiasm. I was on a mission to change the world, one child at a time! I reckon by the end of that NQT year I was a completely different person. Let's take a look at some of what I said in my NQT days and how things have changed over the years:

Staff Meetings

NQT: These staff meetings are so valuable, informative and inspiring. I am learning so much!

Now: Here we go, here's another hour of my life I'm never getting back.

Coffee

NQT: No coffee for me, thanks, I am fine with my water.

Now: What's that? No, this is my third cup. I know it's only half-eight.

Displays

NQT: I managed to get a few days off but I was mostly in school, sorting my classroom, creating displays from scratch, laminating, cutting and stapling. I actually really enjoyed it. It had to be perfect as I know how much these displays will support my class.

Now: The work up on display here, the children who did it are still in the school, aren't they? So I don't need to change it. What's that? They're in sixth form?!

The Curriculum

NQT: This knowledge-rich curriculum is fascinating. To be able to follow this innovative approach that is steeped in research is such a privilege.

Now: Yes, we had something similar back in the day when I first started like you. We called it TEACHING!

Behaviour

NQT: My approach is different. I am not going to be one of
these teachers who relies on using the typical cliche sayings.

Now: Right, class, this is your own time you're wasting!

Planning

NQT: It is taking a while, but it is so necessary to get these
lesson plans done with no stone unturned. I need to make
sure I have every possible scenario covered because if I
don't, there's no way I will be able to teach it effectively.

Now: What's the plan today? Good question, let's see what
Twinkl has to offer.

Teaching

NQT: I can't believe that didn't go to plan! After all that time I
spent planning it and it failed. Maybe I'm not cut out for
this. It's definitely me. I'm a fraud.

Now: Most of Year 6 managed to get the title down in their
book so I call that a success. The lesson can't fail if you
never planned it!

During Break Duty

NQT: What is the matter? Why are you upset? You've had a
falling out with your friend? Ok, let's sort it out. I will
dedicate as much of my time as I need to to establish why
you're both upset and work through this so you can be
friends again.

Now: You've had a falling out? Just go and find someone else
to play with!

Answering Parent Queries

NQT: I thought half-nine at night was late to email me but I replied straight away to ensure the parent's concerns were dealt with.

Now: No, I didn't reply to it. A wise old teacher once told me, you should never reply to the first email. If it is important enough, they'll always send another.

Longest-Serving Member of Staff

Started school as a cleaner in 1987.

Loves a bit of purple!

Proudly wears school-branded staff polo-shirt.

Became a 'dinner-lady' in 1994 and qualified as a teaching assistant in 2001.

Absolute whiz with phonics and an expert at laminating.

Follows a few questionable pages on Facebook.

Current mobile phone is a NOKIA 3310 (in purple, obviously).

'Bum-bag' from Lanzarote in 1991 holds paracetamol, mint imperials and her other set of glasses.

Known as 'Auntie Jean' to at least 30% of the children and 50% of the adults.

Has run the tombola and plant stall at the school fete since 1988.

The longest-serving member of staff. These are special people in every school, part of the furniture, the staff most likely to have only ever worked in one school. Wouldn't dream of moving. In some cases they started as a parent helper, or lunchtime assistant, and have moved up the ranks to be a teacher who has seen it all. I will say that these types of teachers are few and far between in primary schools today, where once they were a staple part of every school. They would nurse and care for those innocent NQTs, taking them under their wing and showing them the ropes. They would sit in staff meetings, rolling their eyes at the newest initiative as they claim, 'This is just like the other one the other year. All you've done is rename it with another catchy acronym!'

Hmmm, this is starting to sound rather familiar.

Well, yes, I will come on to that. But for years these no-nonsense, old-school teachers led the way for our profession. But I'd say over the past decade they have slowly been eased (or in some cases bullied) out through early retirement or 'budget restrictions'. In reality, these teachers were the last of a dying breed who would speak out against things that didn't make sense during a staff meeting. They would question the why, when what we did before was fine. Now don't get me wrong, you can go too far with this, but having someone who can at least question the validity of a new initiative is important. Without this, it only takes one busy leader to keep piling on more and more, and every staff meeting means a new approach to undertake while everyone nods along like compliant robots waiting until the staff meeting is finished to slag them off.

What is worrying is that I am currently in my thirteenth year at my school and, bar the headteacher, am the fourth-longest-serving member of staff. I am now that teacher who questions and speaks up.

I don't want to keep making sweeping generalisations, but the type of teacher we are talking about here can usually be my biggest stumbling block when it comes to my CPD training on

using technology. Whenever I visit a school to lead some training, there will always be a table of teachers (usually older, but
not always) who race to get to the hall to make sure they sit at
the back and then proceed to refuse to engage with the training
because they simply 'can't use technology'.

I always start patiently reassuring them, 'Of course you can!'

'No, you're dealing with the SEN table here.' A smile will
appear on my face.

Here's the thing that a lot of these teachers don't realise: I've
worked with these reluctant teachers and I know that most of
them just choose not to bother. It's funny how they will pretend
that they can't turn on an iPad in the training, but every night
on Facebook they'll be liking and commenting on every post,
'Don't you look beautiful,' 'Amazing, babes,' 'I can't believe it,
message me if you need anything.'

I can speak from experience with these teachers. Take, for
example, Dorothy, a TA who had worked at my school for
donkey's. When the TAs were asked to input some data for
some assessments we did in school she point-blank refused,
claiming she didn't know how to use a computer. I may add that
Dorothy, unlike the TAs in Adam's chapter, was one lazy 'so and
so'. She played a blinder with it and would carry on this charade
of being allergic to modern technology up until the point she
decided to leave teaching.

Two months later, and who has a thriving business online ...?
Bloody Dorothy. She had hoodwinked us all into believing she
was completely and utterly inept with technology, only to be
'excelling' (deliberate pun) with social media and office tools
enough to create her own online business. In the end I could
only sit back and respect old Dorothy for her efforts. But from
that point on, I refused to believe any teacher who said they
couldn't use technology because of their age.

Funnily enough, just after she left the school a couple of colleagues were on a hen do. They got on to talking about Dorothy and obviously didn't paint her in a great light. One of them went on a long rant about her laziness, unwillingness to do things and lack of ability in doing anything. Mid-rant she realised everyone was quiet and raising their eyebrows in an attempt to stop her talking. Turned out a friend of the TA's was also on the hen do.

Every school has a self-appointed 'legend'. The sort of dude, or dudette, that thinks life is one giant night out where the most important element is who had the best bantz (sic). A great example would

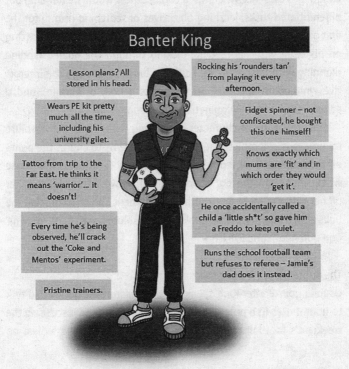

be the legend I worked with for many years that is Cockney John. That's not his actual name, but he is a Cockney and his name is John! He was a guy who lived by his own rules, never the official ones set by Ofsted or the school. Roughly 8.50am – five minutes before the children would be collected from outside (be on time at 5 to 9, and all that jazz) – he would blast Ibiza classics in his classroom to get him 'in the zone'. (All that was missing were some glow sticks and luminous face paint – he already had the whistle and sunglasses.)

Every day our head teacher would walk around the school to wish everyone a good morning. On this journey they would see some teachers writing dates on the board – long date and short date, obviously – and sometimes in French to tick off a bit of Modern Foreign Languages evidence where they could; others would be handing out differentiated tasks, learning objectives or searching calmly for the first glue stick lid of the day. But in Cockney John's class? He's sitting on his chair with his feet up, flicking through the guided reading planning with 'Insomnia' by Faithless blasting through the interactive whiteboard speakers! He manages a nod, a 'Mornin'!' and a salute with his 'Is it Friday yet?!' coffee mug.

How this type of character gets away with doing the absolute minimum is a complete mystery, but he seems to charm the pants off the management team before every book scrutiny. Is it because whenever he saw the loaf of bread (head) he would try to sweep her off her plates of meat (feet) with a compliment about her gracing the halls with a butcher's hook (look) of an absolute baked bean (queen)? Can you Adam and Eve it?!

The Banter King's Guide to Kids

Usually your Banter King speaks to the children like you would talk to your mates in a pub. He's there in the playground discussing the weekend's football and how nice some of the dancers looked on

Strictly. They live their best life every day, but sometimes they can overstep the mark, notably when they think they are at the point that they can have proper adult banter with Year 6 pupils.

April Fool's is always a classic day for the Banter King. I'm going to run you through a few examples of the typical things the Banter King would send his children around the school to ask for. To set the scene, he was teaching a very lively Year 5 class ...

The morning of 1 April arrived and different members of the class could be seen knocking on doors around the school. At one classroom door a child was asking for 'tartan-coloured paint'. At another, a child was asking for 'a left-handed screwdriver'. At many other classrooms lots of other left-handed apparatus was being asked for, including left-handed glue sticks, pens and rulers! But my all-time favourite was when the Banter King sent one of his boys to Year 6 to ask for a 'long stand'. The teacher was in on the joke and just said, 'A long stand? Yes, of course! Just wait there for a moment.'

Ten minutes passed – and it could have definitely been longer – but the headteacher, who was doing their daily rounds, noticed the boy stood doing nothing and upon closer inspection realised that this was a Year 5 boy in a Year 6 classroom. After questioning, the boy proudly exclaimed that he had been asked to do a special job and he was waiting for a long stand! It was at this point that all April Fool's Day jokes, including those amongst the children, were strictly prohibited. But the memories remain.

The Banter King's Guide to Parents

The Banter King has a simple guide to parents: when speaking to a father, hit them with some awful dad jokes, really play to the audience. A Year 5 girl was in panto practice and her dad came to pick her up. The parent said, 'Is Laura in the hall?' Banter King, as quick as a flash, replied in classic panto style ... 'Oh no, she isn't!'. The pair burst out laughing. Not to finish there, as Laura ran out to her dad, who was now in conversation with another parent, Banter King (from the other side of the playground) bellowed, 'SHE'S BEHIND YOU!' Now I have to take my hat off to the bravery of the man. I would be too scared to shout such cheesy jokes to a packed playground, but for the Banter King it was just your typical school day.

<u>The Banter King's Guide to Staff</u>

Now, when it comes to staff, the Banter King is always living it large, never more so than at the staff parties. Wow. Whether it's purposely getting the new teachers completely leathered (just to see what they would do in front of management) or doing shots with the younger, cooler members of staff, or slow dancing to a romantic ballad with the eldest member of staff, every school roster needs a Banter King.

For the Banter King I have mentioned previously, Mr Cockney John, staff parties were his playground, and my word did he like to play. During the good old days when John loved a bit of a drink prior to the actual shindig and rarely actually made it out, I always remember a famous summer party where every member of staff, including the management team, was attending. In a mass panic, we all warned John (due to the fact his language out of school contains expletives every other word) not to speak to the head-teacher, as we dreaded to think of the disaster that could ensue!

Roughly an hour into the party, the head pulled me to one side and asked me if John was ok. I assured her that he was but asked, 'What makes you say that?' She replied with, 'Because I just tried speaking to him and he just stood and stared at me without responding.' At least Cockney John was still able to take instructions on board.

In any job you will find a Banter King, and if you can't think of one, it's probably you!

The Entertainer

Acts as the announcer during the school fete and sports day (same jokes every year).

Clearly wants to be on the TV/radio.

Random parrot toy (Captain Reggie) that he uses as part of his lessons.

He's 'a bit of a character' to some people and an 'acquired taste' to others.

Disappearing thumb trick – nailed it!

Wears character ties most days (although he has no idea who SpongeBob SquarePants is).

Grass-stained knees from lunchtime football with Year 4.

His classroom is an absolute tip, but he can find anything within seconds.

Has the attention span of a gnat.

He fell off a table into a bush at the Christmas party.

Life and soul of the party, this guy is a joker, a clown and the funniest person you'll meet in the staffroom. King of the 'dad jokes', he can make anyone laugh, well, anyone apart from the mood-hoovers that hate his approach to life. He's the sort of guy that can start a conversation with a straight face, drag you in and then hit you with a punchline that you should've seen coming, but the rascal gets you every time, 'hook, line and sphincter'. (That's another one of his gags.)

Sounds like your mate.

Which one? I know plenty like this!

The Geordie PE teacher

Howay!

He did this one joke at my old school where he pretended to have read something in the news and looked rather concerned. He said to my friend in the staffroom:

'Did you see the news this morning?'

Concerned colleague replied, 'See what?'

'That celebrity actress who was killed in Hollywood. She'd been stabbed!'

'Stabbed? Which actress?'

'That blonde actress ... erm ... Reese ...'

'Witherspoon?'

'Naw ... WITH A KNIFE!'

The staffroom (including three people who had already fallen for the joke but played along anyway) erupted with laughter!

The Entertainer is the staff member that will always have an emergency assembly up his sleeve and really quite likes doing them. A born performer, he could grab the phone book (do phone books even exist anymore?) and make it fun for the kids.

If you've got a firefighter visiting in preparation for Guy Fawkes Night in early November, they quite often bring their uniform and safety gear to demonstrate to the children. One poor sucker is usually called upon to get dressed up in the firefighter's clobber. Most teachers are usually sinking into their seats to avoid being selected, but not this guy! He's on the edge of his seat, trying to make eye contact with the visitor, desperate to be picked. When he's not selected, as they decide to go for a particularly tall Year 6 child instead, he lets out a heartfelt groan and starts to sulk. This also applies when a touring pantomime, author or musical guest pops in to take assembly. He's pretty good with ad-libs, so if he needs to take an assembly at a moment's notice because a staff member 'accidentally forgot' it was their turn, he can whip out *James and the Giant Peach* and rattle off a few chapters while perfectly executing voices for Aunt Sponge and Aunt Spiker.

He's like Marmite – some staff will love him, others hate him. Most importantly, the kids really get a kick out of him and that makes him incredibly popular with the parents. When kids give him a 'World's Best Teacher' mug, they really mean it.

The mother hen is the traditional teacher, the one who mostly resembles pretty much every primary school teacher ever depicted on TV and screen. If you were to meet them for the first time and just look them up and down, you would all guess they were a teacher. The type of teacher who you just can't get rid of, who considered retiring but has stayed on as a member of staff because they are the only one that can play an instrument. In our primary school, both the head and deputy could play instruments: Mr Tyrell on the guitar and Miss Davies on the piano.

The Mother Hen

Has tried to retire twice but they keep bringing her back.

NQT and Student Mentor.

80% of the teaching staff have cried on her shoulder at some point.

Matching necklace and earrings bought with voucher she received at Christmas.

Green recorder — sounds as good now as it did in 1987.

She once farted in a staff meeting and blamed the deputy head.

Only member of staff that can play the school piano.

In some families, she has taught both the kids AND their parents.

Hasn't had a formal lesson observation since 2002!

Bite mark scar on her leg from 'difficult child' back in 1991.

Every assembly was like Sonny and Cher.

Yeah, it was special, no CD players, YouTube clips, just a live performance from two great artists performing their craft.

You knew as soon as Tyrell took the watch off, it was concert time.

He loved that watch, that was his thing, like his teacher's special weapon of choice. He needed to speak no words, but if he took his watch off and looked at it, you knew you were too slow, or wasting his time. It became iconic. I had a similar thing with my secondary school English teacher. On my first day, an incredibly nervous day for many, I don't know whether it was nerves or my first experience of eating undercooked sausage from that particular school canteen, but after lunch I had a particularly dodgy stomach.

You were going to sh*t yourself.

Nicely put. No, I felt sick. The next lesson was English. In strutted Mr Crawford, marching like an army sergeant with a gold ruler in his hands. He walked around the class dictating his expectations of us puny Year 7s while continuing to slap this ruler into his other hand where there was a gold ring, so every slap had an echoing ping. That first impression instilled fear into every single one of us. I must have looked like I was particularly scared as sweat poured down my face and all the colour drained away. I desperately wanted to ask permission to go to the toilet to spew, but fear of interrupting this teacher as he berated the class for no reason other than to stamp his authority on the first day prevented me. But if I didn't ask permission I could vomit all over the class. On the first day of secondary school, this would have been the end before I had started. Can you imagine the nicknames, the reputation? Something like that would live with you for the rest of your school life. I would never have been able to escape it. If I interrupted the teacher I could be singled out like in *Full Metal Jacket*, the victim for the drill sergeant to berate. And we know how it ended in that film.

I eventually put my hand up.

'What is it?' the teacher scowled.

'I really need to go to the toilet,' I said hesitantly.

The teacher could clearly see I was in a tricky situation. His whole demeanour changed, he broke character, encouraging me to go. I raced down the corridor looking like a squirrel with enough nuts to last a year in its mouth. I made it to the toilet and chundered everywhere.

Chundered, ha! Spewy Lewis.

Yup.

I walked back to class to silence as the teacher simply nodded. A nod of reassurance. That gold ruler became infamous throughout the school. Another example of a teacher's special weapon that made him iconic. I suppose mine would probably be an iPad. What would yours be?

Erm ... Turkey Twizzler?

That English teacher turned out to be my favourite teacher ever. Don't get me wrong, that first lesson was absolutely terrifying and for a while every member of the class was scared shitless of him. But once he had instilled that fear, he was able to relax and have a laugh with us.

During our GCSE year, Mr Crawford took ill with cancer. As we attended a Catholic school, now we were in sixth form we could go to Savio House for a religious retreat. In one of the sessions, we ended up talking about Mr Crawford, who at the time was very ill and we hadn't been told how severe it was. The priest leading the session alongside the teacher suggested we wrote letters to him about the impact he has had on us. As I knew this was private, I poured my heart out, I wrote about how he single-handedly made me love English as a subject and helped me achieve my results in GCSE. I talked about the first lesson I had, the laughs, the fear, everything. The letters were collected and we went to our next session. Soon after we found out he had lost his battle with cancer and passed away.

We were allowed to attend his funeral, which was the first funeral I had ever been to. Pretty much the whole school attended. We were just about able to squeeze into the back of the church. I'll never forget my dad handing me sunglasses as he clearly could see I was getting emotional and he knew I wouldn't want the whole of the all-boys school staring at me.

Big Mike. Legend!

Another teacher stood up to say a few words. He was also an English teacher but so different from Mr Crawford; I couldn't understand how they could be friends when they were polar opposites as teachers. He said that the day before Mr Crawford passed, he received letters from pupils and he would like to read one that Mr Crawford had in his hands as he passed away. The teacher read my letter, to the whole school. I tried my best to hold back the tears, but I couldn't. I am struggling now as I type this, to be honest. I was just overwhelmed to know that one of the last things he read before passing was my letter about how much I respected him.

I wonder if he was crying too. Not at the sentiment of the letter but how bad the writing was, the lack of ambitious vocabulary and erratic use of punctuation. I know we've had the editor of this book in the same state of despair.

I remember getting home, going to my room and just crying for ages. It was in this moment that I first realised the true impact of a teacher. The ability to connect and have such a positive influence on another person to the point that they still remember so vividly the positive relationship you had years later. It is something incredibly special. I often hope I can have the

Eco Warrior

Cycles to work in every possible weather situation.

Loves an 'eco-brick'. This one is going to make a whale sculpture.

Gets on with pretty much everyone ... until they quote mistruths from right-wing newspapers.

Head Teacher secretly gave her a day off to attend a climate protest but didn't expect she'd get arrested!

Prefers not to wear shoes unless she absolutely HAS to.

She brings in a vegan, gluten-free, taste-free baked item every Tuesday.

Classroom full of items she refuses to let go to landfill.

Her boyfriend is called Willow (everyone thinks he's a bit of a knobhead).

Eco council sold recycled craft items to fund new water-butts (decorated by the kids).

same impact on my pupils, I owe that teacher so much and I think he has had the biggest influence on me as a teacher. The fact that I am able to write this book and dedicate some of it to his memory is a real privilege. When things get tough, when I have one of those days, when I sometimes feel like it's too much, I think back to the moment I sat in floods of tears knowing how much I missed Mr Crawford, and it inspires me to keep going for my pupils.

Inspiring stuff.

The eco warrior is a staple of every school. A staff cannot be complete without their own adult Greta Thunberg on a mission to make the school as green as possible. It is a mission I admire

greatly and want to support, but there is a growing trend with these teachers. Yes, they run the eco council or eco club and have children scouring the playground every break and lunch with their own arm-reacher-grabber and a hi-vis vest. As far as school badges are concerned, let's be honest, the eco warrior badge is way down the list.

Can we just appreciate for a second how much badges were a huge flex in primary school. 'Flex?' I hear you cry. Yes, well, according to urbandictionary.com ...

Amazing that our first reference to a dictionary is Urban Dictionary. Really sets the tone for the type of educational book we are going for here.

Yes, according to urbandictionary.com, to Flex is to **show off your valuables in a non-humble way.**

Metal badges were a huge flex in primary school. Any old Tom, Dick and Harry could get a paper sticker that lasted minutes, unless you were particularly in the bad books with your parents and then a sticker had to survive the day so you could proudly share it with your mum and show her how much you were trying in school. The metal badges were desired by every pupil at primary, less so at secondary, but they obviously had different levels of flex. Badges that were given for different clubs were lower on the list. Of course, that would depend on the type of club. Eco club would be on a par with chess club or languages club.

I can imagine every MFL teacher in a fit of rage as they read this. I find, out of all the subject leaders within a school, the teacher who is in charge of languages can be the most passionate and cannot handle any sort of banter towards their subject.

An astute observation, my friend, I concur; a weirdly accurate observation that I cannot explain or reason with.

I think having a school council badge is a good one.

Yes, definitely more illustrious. I think it is because usually school councillors are picked from every class by your peers. It is like being your class MP. I've often let children prepare speeches, pledges and promises to the rest of the class in an effort to persuade them to give their vote.

Yes, but what happens if someone gets no votes?

You never take the vote in front of your class. You either get them to stand outside the class while everyone else votes with their eyes closed or you get them to vote on a piece of paper.

Have you ever rigged the vote?

Teacher confession time ... I know of teachers who have made the votes more rigged than the Russians did for the US.

I find the first student council meeting of the year a humbling experience for the newly appointed councillors. The pledges they make in class that win the votes:

'If you vote for me, I will abolish school uniforms.'

'We will campaign to have a four-day school week.'

'We will bring in a vending machine for snacks, crisps and chocolate.'

'A vote for me is a vote for a new swimming pool in the playground!'

I've heard them all and often chuckle quite loudly when the children confidently announce these promises to the rest of the class. Having won the vote, they head into their first school council meeting to be given their new badges and spend the rest of the meeting discussing how the £300 from the last bake sale will be spent after half of it has to be used to bulk up the glue sticks stock, as there isn't a single one throughout the school. Imagine the disappointment heading back into class:

'So did you pitch the idea for the swimming pool in the council meeting?'

'Sorry, no, I didn't get a chance.'

'Yeah, but you promised!'

'I will definitely do it next time.'

'So what did you talk about and decide?'

'We decided that instead of children bringing sweets in for everyone on their birthday, they bring in a book to donate to the school library.'

'WTF! Who suggested that?'

'Well, Miss did and we all agreed.'

'I'm starting a change.org campaign to reverse this decision.'

Prefect badges are more elite level.

Yes, only eclipsed by Head and Deputy Boy/Girl.

Team captains are elite-level badges but surely the top badge to wear at school is the one for representing a school sports team.

Agreed, biggest flex at primary, I believe. But I will just quickly run through my breakdown of the Top 20 Primary School Flexes. This hasn't been decided by a poll of thousands, it is just me, my experience when I was at school and my observations as a teacher over the past decade. This will certainly bring back some memories from your school days and remind you of a simpler time, but as a parent it will give you an indication of how to react if your child does come home saying they did one of the following:

20 Being recognised in class or in an assembly for sitting nicely. Usually the teacher will declare that they are looking for children who are showing the right example and displaying the right behaviour. Students will then sit, legs crossed, fingers on lips, straining their digits so hard to show how quiet they're being, hoping they will rise above their fellow peers as the perfect example. When it happens the sense of achievement is unreal, telling your fellow classmates, 'Guys, look at me, I am setting the example, I will lead you towards positive Dojo points.'

19 An early flex in your primary career – getting cast as a main part in the nativity play. Mary, Joseph or one of the wise men (the one who brings gold, as that is the only one the children can say) is a huge flex. But more on that in the nativity chapter.

18 When a pupil appears in the local paper – a rarity, but it turns that child into a celebrity for a day. It happened to me back in the day, TWICE. First, I was cast as a Lost Boy in *Peter Pan* at the Palace Theatre alongside Toyah Willcox and Frank Finlay. An open audition was put out to children in the area and I managed to make the final eight (this was well before the likes of *The X Factor*). The next time was when I organised my own car boot sale in conjunction with *Blue Peter*'s leprosy appeal,

back in the day. We managed to raise well over £500 and had so many donations, but I have to be honest, I wanted the badge. I wanted the badge so badly, but despite all the efforts it never did transpire. I did, however, have my picture on the front of the local paper for my efforts. I remember walking into Year 5 the next day to be greeted with, 'At least you're not on the front cover for your dreadful Elvis impression!' The fame lasts as long as it does for a *Big Brother* contestant; you're forgotten about the week after unless, of course, the achievement goes beyond local to national. But that has yet to happen to a child in our school.

17 When your sibling is acknowledged positively in assembly. Yes, this can only happen to students with brothers or sisters, but when your brother or sister is asked to come out to accept an award or certificate, everyone's eyes in the class are directed at you and you are accepting their praise as if it were the Oscars and you're accepting an award on someone else's behalf.

16 Having a parent working at the school – if your parent is also a teacher or school staff member there is a level of flex. It has its positives and negatives. You get the lowdown, an insight into what goes on. If you like doing jobs, you can come to school earlier, turn yourself into a mini TA. You tend to find out all of the other teachers' first names, which, as you know, becomes an obsession when you are at primary school. That knowledge is power in the playground, but with great power comes great responsibility. Personally, I never wanted my children to go to the same school I worked at. One reason was despite the fact I love the majority of my staff, there are a couple I don't rate. Sometimes knowing too much can be a problem. I wouldn't like the thought of sitting in a parents' evening having a teacher speak to me, knowing they weren't the best teacher.

15 When it is your birthday. For that day, you are king! You can get away with wearing a badge bigger than your head to ensure everyone in the whole school recognises it is your birthday. I've never really understood why you are then expected to bring a bag of sweets into school for everyone in your class, but having the power to give your mates the best sweets was always a flex. This gets completely flipped when you're at secondary school, where you wouldn't dream of wearing a badge to announce your birthday as it would lead to a day of getting birthday digs from every child in the whole school.

14 Breaking a bone. Yes, that's right, as a child if you were unlucky, or lucky for some, to have an accident when you were at school it was a different level of flex — especially if the incident happened at school. Off you go to hospital, while everyone whispers and spreads rumours about how you've broken your neck, then you waltz back into class with a cast on your arm and people flock like seagulls round a bag of chips to sign it. In primary it'll be lovely messages, whereas in secondary it's just cocks, a sleeve full of cocks. The ultimate here is breaking the arm you write with, as that is just dream stuff — a laptop all the way.

13 This links directly to number 14. If you have a broken bone, you get to stay in at break and lunch and can choose a friend to stay with you. Everyone in the class will suddenly become your best mate — apart from those football fanatics who wouldn't give up their lunchtime match for anything. If you are the lucky child to be picked to stay in — especially during the winter months when you'd otherwise be freezing your knackers off — it can make your day. Looking out the window from the warmth of the ICT suite seeing everyone turning to ice while you keep your mate company playing PC games for an hour is dream stuff.

12 Handing out equipment during a lesson. If your classroom role was handing out whiteboards or even whiteboard pens, this gave you a level of power most can only dream of. You decide which children get the pens that work, give a wink to your mates to sort them out with a clean whiteboard, while the child who wouldn't let you join in the game at break ends up with the broken pen and dirty whiteboard. Enjoy that! This classroom job was only topped by being the child chosen to take the register down to the office each morning.

11 When your parent is chosen as a helper on a school trip. More on this in the school trips chapter.

10 Being taken out of a lesson to do a music lesson. Missing normal learning time for a focused guitar lesson or learning the piano was special to say the least. This would never happen for every instrument; for example, no one is missing RE to practise the recorder, but having time away from class to learn how to be the next Ed Sheeran was a big deal. At some point you would then have the opportunity to perform to the rest of the class or even school during an assembly. This is your Woodstock and it goes down like a sell-out at Wembley.

9 When you go to pick up your younger sibling for school photo day. If you are going to KS1 from KS2 or even EYFS you are walking into the classroom like some sort of celebrity. The other children in reception flock to you like you are the most famous person in the school. Then when you rejoin your class, they are all making a fuss over your sibling. Even the teacher is joining in!

8 When you have the same name as a character in the class book. If your name is Charlie and you're reading the Roald Dahl classic *Charlie and the Chocolate Factory*, you might as well get a statue in the playground as that will put you on a pedestal over the rest of the class. Even better is when you've got the

same name as someone from a maths problem. We're talking about the questions that are ludicrous, where Dan is buying 49 pineapples. Everyone will look at you and ask you, 'Why do you need 49 pineapples?'

7 When you're chosen to go to the front of the line. If you are picked you have displayed immaculate behaviour, and the smugness as you walk to the front is brilliant. You might have the responsibility to hold the door open as you head to assembly, being able to report back to the teacher on which children didn't have manners to thank you for holding the door open.

6 Running the school office during lunch. This doesn't happen in every school but when the school office manager wants to have a natter and catch up with the other staff, they may trust some prefects to run the school office. That's right, answering phones, welcoming visitors, the lot. Imagine the pressure of answering the phone, knowing you are speaking on behalf of the whole school!

5 Controlling the lyrics in assembly. This has changed over time. Back in my day, it was moving the see-through sheets on the overhead projector whereas now it might be clicking the mouse on a laptop to move the lyrics on at the right time. It is like being the Calvin Harris of your school; if you're moving the lyrics at the right place making sure everyone stays on point when hitting the chorus of 'Sing Hosanna', it can be like being on the main stage at Pacha in Ibiza.

4 Being trusted to take a note from your teacher to another. Out of the 30 children in class, being chosen to take an incredibly important note to the other side of the school was made all the more important if the teacher said don't read it. A huge level of flex and a big deal. Just to clarify, the note is never that important; it is usually something along the lines of 'Chippy for Lunch?'

3 Sitting on benches in assembly. You have waited your whole primary school life – six years – to get to the point where during assemblies you have the luxury of sitting on the wooden benches at the back. The privilege of looking down on the peasants before you as you sit in the ultimate comfort of a wooden bench instead of a wooden floor is the pinnacle of a lot of pupils' primary school careers.

2 As mentioned earlier, it is having a badge for being part of some sort of group – prefect, eco club, school council, to name a few.

1 The ultimate flex at primary school has to be representing your school by being part of a sports team. Especially on the rare occasion you had to leave class early to go to a sports tournament, walk through the class, sign autographs, point and nod to your fellow classmates, chest pumping as you let them know you're about to go and represent your whole school. It's a feeling that has been hard to replicate throughout my whole adult life.

Another tell-tale sign of the eco warrior isn't the fact that their classroom is full of teddies representing all the animals they have adopted over the years, or the fact that they do the same term-long project on stopping parents from driving to school, which has zero impact on parents' desire to walk to school, or the fact their stock cupboards will still have every single curriculum document and resource they've ever been given or handed in a staff meeting. These teachers are dreadful hoarders – most teachers are, but these are on another level. It might be down to their refusal to allow anything to go in the bin as it might end up in a landfill. Here are a few examples of things teachers have found in stockrooms when clearing out or moving rooms:

Genuine Items Found in
Classroom Cupboards

- A stuffed owl
- Weetabix painted as sandbags for a trench
- A mouldy chicken sandwich
- Soiled underwear
- Rotten fruit in a bag on top of a cupboard
- A little pile of raisins that turned out to be poo
- A dead rat
- A dead mouse
- A four-year-old Batman cake
- A dried up human poo
- A disposable BBQ
- A dead bird
- Tarantula skins in an ice cream tub!

It is like reading the world's worst round of the *Generation Game*.

Didn't they do well! Actually, sounds like they didn't. Fetch me a bucket …

Eco warrior teachers also have the biggest photocopying bill of the whole staff. Oh yes, that's right, the teachers that campaign for a green school, who berate you for bringing in single-use plastic bottles, are the ones who use the most paper. They may also be known as Little Miss Twinkl. Not that there's anything wrong with Twinkl, but these teachers have printed every single worksheet that has ever been published on their site. After spending most of their lunch wearing a hi-vis vest picking up litter, they will then sit in the staffroom with a pile of photocopying bigger than them, bop their head above the mountain of worksheets to remind you to make sure you recycle your plastic tub.

The mood-hoover. You all know one – they thrive off negativity, spending each day focusing all their energy on sucking any positivity out of the staffroom. They usually have a face like they've sucked on a lemon sweet. In fact, they rarely enter the staffroom as they are too busy to have a break and they look down on other teachers who actually stop to take a minute and

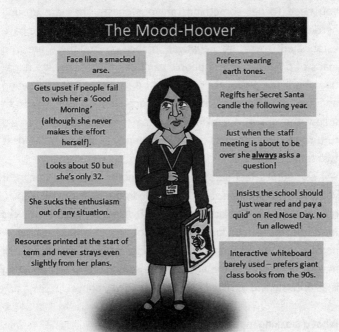

The Mood-Hoover

Face like a smacked arse.

Prefers wearing earth tones.

Gets upset if people fail to wish her a 'Good Morning' (although she never makes the effort herself).

Regifts her Secret Santa candle the following year.

Just when the staff meeting is about to be over she **always** asks a question!

Looks about 50 but she's only 32.

She sucks the enthusiasm out of any situation.

Insists the school should 'just wear red and pay a quid' on Red Nose Day. No fun allowed!

Resources printed at the start of term and never strays even slightly from her plans.

Interactive whiteboard barely used – prefers giant class books from the 90s.

gather their thoughts. They are definitely the teachers who coined the phrase 'Don't smile until Christmas,' although they never specified which Christmas, and if anyone actually had the patience to stay and listen to these buzzkills, the actual saying was probably 'Don't smile until the Christmas when you've retired.'

Now I am not saying people shouldn't moan. I love a good moan.

Yes, I think the fact that the longest chapter in the book is you literally moaning about all the bad things in education proves this point.

Having the odd moan can be rather therapeutic and it can be good to have that person on your staff that lends an ear when you need to get something off your chest. They are unsung heroes of the teaching staff. But there comes a line; as we have established, there are negatives in this job but there are also loads of positives. These people can't see that – they are negative about the positives. You could be sitting in a staff meeting and the head teacher could announce that no one needs to follow the drawn-out planning format and this teacher would turn round and moan as they have already planned for the next two terms.

I sometimes feel sad for these members of staff. I mean, if you can't find some aspects of the job in the classroom hilarious, how else do you find kicks in this life?! Unless they get their kicks from the more mundane elements of the life of a teacher – perhaps a book scrutiny gives them goosebumps, a learning walk makes them weak at the knees and a safeguarding staff meeting is as entertaining as *The Lion King* Broadway show.

What a cracking musical.

Up there with the best.

These people can be the worst for SLTs unless they actually become the SLT, in which case, God help us all. The way to deal with these people is to get them on the Christmas do. Of course, the biggest challenge is to get them to actually come out. They may well use every excuse in the book to avoid it, including that they are too busy updating their tracking sheets. But if you can manage to get them away from their never-ending to-do list, get them on the Jägerbombs. You'll quickly see a different side to them and hopefully the alcohol will encourage them to step outside their comfort zone, even doing something they might regret in the morning. Make sure you have evidence of it so the

The 'Miss Honey'

KS1/EYFS teacher mostly. Hasn't taught higher than Year 3.

Reminds people of 'Miss Honey' from Roald Dahl's *Matilda*.

Annoyingly sweet and adored by the children she teaches.

Her class displays are infuriatingly amazing.

Very quiet during staff meetings.

Class guinea pigs live with her during the weekends/school holidays.

Has only raised her voice twice in seven years.

Manages to incorporate her favourite yellow cardigan into most outfits.

Got drunk at the Christmas party and showed everyone her knickers.

Listens to AC/DC and drinks snakebite.

next time they start mood-hoovering everywhere you can remind them to wind their neck in otherwise the footage of them straddling the headteacher, shirtless, while re-enacting Peter Andre's infamous 90s banger 'Mysterious Girl' might make it onto the staff WhatsApp group. Isn't that right, Adam?

I have no clue what you are referring to, mate. I am always a true professional, even on the staff night out.

Ah, the 'Miss Honey' staff member. I get that reference, because I've read *Matilda*; it's my favourite book!

Favourite book?

Alright, it's the only book I've read. Still, I know exactly who Miss Honey is.

Well, the 'Miss Honey' in a school is your typical primary school teacher; the staple of every school and a valued member of the team. The teachers who just love teaching, with no real aspirations to go into management. There is nothing wrong with that; I hate the expectation in education that if you are a really good teacher you should go into management where you do less actual teaching. It's weird. The thing is, sometimes the best teachers don't make the best leaders and the best leaders can sometimes be poor teachers. The job of being a really effective leader has very little to do with how well you can teach. A headteacher's job isn't about looking after the kids because, if we're completely honest, most heads rarely see the children. Their job over the past decade has transformed into more meetings, budget handling and, most importantly, people management. They need to have an understanding of education and a respect for teachers, but their job isn't about the kids, it is focusing on the people who look after the kids. If a leadership team can create an environment where teachers and staff feel valued, trusted and appreciated, they will take care of the rest. My favourite quote for this has always been, 'A person who feels appreciated will always do more than is expected.' Trust is the best way to show that appreciation.

The Miss Honey is an all-round lovely person who just wants the very best for their pupils. Yes, they are frustrated at the fact that the job is increasingly different to what they dreamed it would be when they were in school themselves, playing their own game of classroom in the continuous provision area, but that doesn't stop them carrying on and being a trooper, because they know the difference they make to their pupils.

I hope the one thing you can take from this chapter is that teachers and school staff come in all different shapes and sizes. They each have their own unique quirks, and they all bring their positives and sometimes negative elements to the team. These positives need to be embraced and celebrated, as this weird obsession in so many schools to try to squeeze every teacher into the same box and mould them through non-negotiable policies is wrong and needs to be stopped.

The individualities of staff members should be a huge factor in the success of a school. It should reflect the vast, diverse and wonderful world we live in. A collective approach to diverse personalities is surely only going to have a positive impact on the children's experience and social skills during their time at school.

The Classroom

Despite popular belief, teachers don't have the whole summer off. I am not going to start this chapter by having a go at the majority of people whose only experience of teaching was from their own school days or ridiculous TV shows like *Waterloo Road* where teachers would leave school at the same time as the pupils at 3pm. I can assure you that no teacher has EVER left school at 3pm.

Unless you've got a 2.30 appointment. Life lesson: always book a 2.30 appointment. That way you'll need to leave around 1.30 to avoid traffic and lunchtime ends at 1.15 so you may as well call a half day! I once had a 2.30 asthma appointment. I left before lunchtime and sat in Abdul's Kebab House to eat a full mixed kebab – that was a lunchtime to remember. Although the appointment didn't go too well! My peak flow (the thing you blow in to see how quickly you can blow air out of your lungs) was at a record low and it's never a good sign when a bit of doner meat exits your mouth and gets stuck in the mouthpiece!

Wait, are you telling me you're allowed to book appointments during term time? I thought school staff would just spend most of the half-term break catching up on all the hospital and doctor appointments they should have had during that term.

Here's some advice for any teachers or school staff who might encounter one of these narrow-minded, clueless, 'those who can, do; those who can't, teach' people. A simple five-step approach to dealing with anyone who thinks teachers have it easy:

1) When in conversation with the person, make sure you interrupt them every 5–10 seconds to replicate what it is like to try to speak to 30 children. You can go easy and start by raising your hand but then quickly start blatantly interrupting them. To make this even more authentic, make sure you interrupt with a statement, never a question, and ensure it is completely unrelated to the conversation you are having. The more random the better. Keep doing this to the point that the person leaves or gets so angry they shout at you. At that point, kindly remind them that they should really keep their patience.

2) Whenever they tell you something, refuse to believe it is true unless they can prove it by showing you evidence in an exercise book or allow you to observe this thing happening. If this can't happen for some strange reason, explain that you need them to prove the point through endless amounts of data and spreadsheets and, if all else fails, you can then spend a couple of days doing an

intense inspection to check that what they have said is actually true.

3) If they tell you a story, ask them to repeat it, and to repeat it, again please repeat it, one more time can you repeat it? In fact, just for good measure, ask them to repeat it again. After that, ask them a question that clearly demonstrates that they are going to need to repeat the story once again.

4) Every other day send them a letter of complaint, blaming them for something that you probably should have done yourself. Make ridiculous requests about how you need more time, more space or as many special allowances as you can think of. If they refuse to do that and/or bend over backwards to do something you should be doing yourself, ask to speak to their manager or, better yet, take to social media to slag them off for being crap at what they do. This will give them a taste of what it is like to deal with some parents.

5) Finally, this one is probably hard to do but if you can do it it will really prove a point. Find out what job the person you are speaking to does and then apply to become the CEO, president, director or top manager of that business, job or career. Then just start making ridiculous decisions knowing you're completely out of your depth as you have never worked a day in your life in this job or industry. When that person starts to moan about how bad and tough the job is, tell them to shut up, stop moaning, they don't know how good they have got it. This will hopefully make them realise what it is like to have a Department of Education making all the decisions about education even though not a single person within it has ever worked a day in a classroom.

Follow those five steps and you will have certainly proved a point.

And tell them that when they're on a break at work to not get a drink, to not go to the toilet but instead stand outside freezing your bits off while supervising the best part of up to 200 children!

The point I am making is that teachers usually work some of the holidays — especially if you're moving classrooms, moving schools or starting as an NQT. When you go on a school-based placement, the classroom is already sorted, everything is in the right place, all the displays are done for you. This is just one of the 8,653 elements of teaching that you never learn in your teacher training.

The moment you inherit your first ever classroom is a special one in every teacher's career, as this is when things get real. When I got my first teaching job, I had also been accepted in a role to travel to the US and do some football coaching. I remember at the end of the interview, the head asked me if I had any questions. I asked him about going over to the States for the summer and he looked at me with a look of sympathy at how naive I was. He explained I would probably need to spend some time over the summer sorting my classroom. I was taking over from a teacher who had been at the school longer than I had been alive.

My God! No wonder that teacher retired, they must have been an absolute fossil. I bet the cupboards were full of random textbooks from the 80s and those old register books and probably the odd VHS tapes and empty cassette cases.

The scope of designing your first classroom should never be underestimated. Of course you have seen plenty of other classrooms before, but this one is *yours*. You have to make every decision about the layout and design. I remember heading into school for a day in the summer before I started. I just sat there with every intention of stripping (as in the displays, not myself, as that would have ended my career before it started), but was hit by an overwhelming sense of responsibility. At the time I thought classroom displays actually added to learning and were a necessary tool to support children. Turns out they're not. Well, they can support learning but nowhere near as much as you'd imagine considering the time and effort teachers put into them. That's always been the thing with me: is the time I'm spending on this task worth the impact it will have on learning? I believe that displays are more about the teacher than anything else.

I have to admit, I was lucky when I designed my first classroom. Within the four walls, one had windows so there were strictly 'no displays on the windows' allowed, but some crafty teachers got around that with some string and pegs and created a washing line across the window to further display work. Another wall was taken up with the interactive whiteboard and a general noticeboard that had the textbook birthday display with every month and the pupils' names written on the relevant month.

For the other two walls, I knew we were required to do a literacy, a numeracy, a science and topic display. Now, before we crack on discussing displays, I first have to check what type of teacher you are, as this will determine whether we allow you to continue reading.

Quick question. When you take down a display do you:

a) Keep the staples in?
b) Remove the staples with a staple remover to ensure an even and smooth surface for the next teacher who will be putting up their own display?

If the answer is A, I am sorry but you're going to have to stop reading now, I cannot have you enjoying this book when you're a 'staples-in person'. I don't care if it means taking this book back and getting a refund. I can't stand you people, you are everything that's wrong in the world – lazy, inconsiderate, selfish tossers. The hours, literal hours, I have spent picking out staples. As mentioned earlier, my first classroom was inherited from a teacher who had taught at the school for almost 30 years. Guess what? She'd never removed a single staple in that time. I spent almost a week picking out staples from every display in that classroom.

To be fair, with the evolution of staple removers, there's no excuse nowadays, but back in your day you would have been using the scissors nobody really cared about ... the yellow and green left-handed scissors!

I'm a lefty, so I actually did care about those scissors.

Do you remember the ones that used to look like a python's mouth? Now they are those stick ones that slide under the staple, remove it and keep the used staple in its grip. Whoever invented that deserves some serious dojo points.

Why didn't you just leave up the displays from the previous teacher? I hear you cry, but as I have stated, she was at the end of her career, and as you will soon see, the enthusiasm towards displays quickly diminishes the more years you teach. Can you imagine the amount of effort and detail put into displays in the classroom of a teacher at the end of her 30-year career? It was a sight to behold. (This has no reflection on her as a teacher, by the way.) I can only use the analogy of the year 2020. Take the first three months, these represent the first three years of a teacher's career – full of promise, attention and detail. Then as the year progresses and the pandemic ensues, the level of detail starts to dwindle. Don't get me wrong, you get the bare minimum done as far as displays go, similar to how you did your Zoom quizzes, attempted home learning and kept in touch with family and friends. As the months progress, just like the years of teaching, the amount of effort put in to anything diminishes to the absolute bare minimum in order to survive.

The expectation for me at the time by my school was simply to make sure the displays had a border and didn't use yellow as a text colour on a white background. Common sense prevailed. However, fast-forward a few years and schools now have in-depth display policy procedures to follow, and displays will be inspected by bosses to ensure they are up to the defined stand-ard. I've had more than one message on Facebook from teach-ers who have had displays ripped down in front of the class as the staples didn't all line up vertically! And we wonder why so many teachers are leaving the profession in their droves? In what world does it matter whether staples are stuck in vertically, horizontally or diagonally? Is that really going to have any bearing on the quality of learning happening in the class? It's complete and utter bollocks. Another question I have to ask is: HOW IS IT HUMANLY POSSIBLE TO DO IT? Have you tried putting up a display by yourself? Having to measure the backing paper and hold it at the right angle while being perched on a ladder trying to reach the top corner to correctly staple it in according to the policy? I was just happy to get it stuck up; the least of my worries was the direction of the bloody staples.

Then, once the backing paper was up – and this could take a while, trust me – in order to comply with said policy, you had to put a border around that bad boy. Which do you go for? Do you go for a wavy design or pointed? Smooth or corrugated? Decisions, decisions.

I just want to give a nod to all of the TAs out there who are heavily involved in displays and often give up some of their holiday to help out their teacher BFF. Life lesson for all my beautiful TAs who can't stand doing displays: do a really bad one! That way you will never be asked to help with a display ever again. Teachers are perfectionists and won't want to hurt your feelings, so instead of being asked to back a board you'll be back to the less-responsible jobs. In other words, jobs you can eat, drink and sit down for, like sticking book labels on or pushing stuff through the laminator.

New teachers will spend too much time considering the blend of colours, whereas for more experienced teachers, any border you can find will do a job. All of this and you haven't even considered the content of the display yet! I remember all the different phases we had to go through. The early part of my career was all about VCOP – Vocabulary, Connectives, Openers and Punctuation. I think it was the Big Writing approach. I was a fan at the time, but then I discovered Alan Peat and his approach to teaching writing and the penny dropped for me. The display would have some sort of WOW word aspect, sharing some great vocabulary children can use in their writing. You would try different designs to make it as hip and cool as possible to your kids. My favourite was the McDonald's one I had for one year. It was 3D! I had collected a few empty chip boxes (which justified my excessive trips to Maccys) and I then created laminated chips (threads of yellow paper with an 'ambitious' word written on them). On each chip box I would write a 'boring' word – happy, sad, said. Each chip would be an alternative word that would uplevel children's writing. Did it work? No, for one, every time the children went to the display to get a chip, they would be told off for getting out of their seat. If they did the right thing and put their hand up to ask to go to the display, I would usually say no as it would disrupt the rest of the class and I would then ask them the word they wanted to improve and give them some ideas myself. If at some point the children did take something from the display, they never put it back in the right place and the next time a child went to find another word for 'big' they would be given words such as 'ecstatic', 'distraught', 'bellowed', and the writing made less sense than it did by just using the word 'big'.

God, I'm glad that my teachers didn't have McDonald's packaging on their display boards (not that I ever looked at the displays) as I would have definitely tried to make my mates laugh by eating a WOW word or dipping one in PVA glue pretending it was mayo.

Then you would have an openers and connectives part of your literacy display, which again just offered some examples of openers and connectives. The punctuation part had the infamous punctuation pyramid, which started with a full stop at the top, followed by question mark, comma and then exclamation, eventually working down to include every possible punctuation mark. These at one time were even printed and given to the children every time they had to write. The problem with these displays was having all these words with no context is only slightly more useful than having nothing there at all. The best display I ever had, again after attending an Alan Peat training session, was to put an extract of text in the middle of the display. Within the text, there would be examples of words that could be improved, openers, conjunctions and punctuation. The display would then highlight these examples, and to the side of the text there would be an explanation followed by alternatives that could be used. I felt this gave children context with their choices when it came to writing.

A maths display just needed to try to include as many elements of the maths curriculum as possible. A times table poster is a must until you see every child trying to get a cheeky glance during the weekly times tables tests. Get something in there for shape, conversions and, of course, something relating to problem-solving. The problem with the problem-solving displays? None of them help children with problem solving.

You know what really grinds my gears about displays? The only time that kids pay attention to or even notice a display is during SATs, when they are covered up terribly with random sheets of faded, dusty old paper – that was always my job, hence the 'terribly'.

I am also a fan of mainly using displays to showcase children's work. Children do buzz from that, they always have. However, I have found that buzz has wavered in the internet age. This is something I talk about all the time in my training. The internet is a platform that allows you to share, publish and celebrate children's work with a truly global audience. Yet most schools don't use it. We still expect children to do their best possible piece of writing by saying:

'Ok, class, today is the day. We have been working for three weeks to get to this point. Today is our BIG WRITE DAY! You are now going to do the best piece of writing you have ever done in your life and you know I mean business as I've lit a candle and I have put Mozart on!'

'Why does it need to be the best piece of writing, Mr P?'

'Well, I will take it home tonight and spend three hours marking it in three different colours for you all to completely ignore, and then it'll go on the shelf and we will never speak about it again. In fact, no, sorry, we need to update this display, so some of you lucky devils will have your writing on a washing line for some of the other children in class to see.'

What incentive is there for children to do their best possible piece of writing if the only person who is going to read it is you? Older children realise the only reason you're taking the time to read and mark their work is because that is your job and what you're paid to do. Whereas now, within minutes we can share children's work with the world, and once it is online, it'll be there forever and anyone from anywhere at any time can read it. It is an example of how technology can make learning so much more purposeful.

But I digress. Let's explore some of the other delights you'll find in every classroom.

Now the displays are sorted, how are you going to line up your desks? Traditional rows or grouped tables, or do you think outside the box and go for a horseshoe approach? It's like a football manager deciding on the formation to play for the big cup final. It changes as the term goes on as well. Depending on what happens in class, an early sending off (child making the wrong choices) will make you adjust the formation. After moving the tables for the umpteenth time, you turn in the Mike Bassett 'We will play Four Four F*****n Two'. Once you've had your class for a couple of weeks, you make the decision about the children who don't always make the right choice, like when a football manager always says about a particular player, 'They are always the first name on the team sheet.' The children I am talking about here are the ones who are always on the seating plan first. You have to decide, do you have these children sitting at the front with you, in your eye line so you can catch them at every opportunity? The problem with this approach is that sometimes the children in question see sitting at the front as their stage and so this can encourage them to perform more, hoping to get a reaction. An alternative is to sit them at the back so they are not able to distract anyone and will leave you to be able to actually teach without being interrupted every ten seconds to remind them of the classroom rules.

The classroom rules is a late addition to the display as it is usually an activity you do in the first couple of days to try to make your class feel involved in the process and to hopefully make them take ownership. Be careful with this task, as what starts as a simple exercise can become a list of 150 rules. The typical list would look something like this:

OUR CLASS RULES

Try your best.

Listen to your teacher.

Be kind to each other.

Look after your belongings.

Have Fun!

These classroom rules will always be placed somewhere at the front of the class for you to reference when needed, maybe next to your whiteboard. The whiteboard is a staple of every classroom. Give me a classroom where all the walls are whiteboards and I would be happy. The only problem – and this happens every single time I want to write something on the board – is that whenever I pick up a marker to write, I always, ALWAYS pick up the marker that doesn't work. That packet of new whiteboard pens you receive in September will be used in the following order: black and blue straight away, and if they make it until October half term you've done very, very well. Brown and red are next, followed by orange. Then by spring term you are left with just the yellow one.

Yellow whiteboard pens have a similar life expectancy to a white pencil crayon – infinite, as no one ever uses them. They are always perfectly sharpened and glistening like a new penny. Even those people who claim to use them on black paper are liars, because they don't even work that great on black paper.

Since the turn of the century, most classrooms have had their whiteboard upgraded to an interactive whiteboard; a large touchscreen device that connects to your laptop or desktop and displays your screen. The potential of this groundbreaking technology was massive, and millions were spent installing these devices in classrooms all over the UK in the belief they would transform teaching and learning. And did they? Not really. Again, it wasn't the technology, it was the lack of adequate training. They do have their benefits, though, and I would take an interactive whiteboard over an overhead projector any day. (There is bound to be one of these some-where on the school grounds, gathering dust. RIP the over-head projector.)

Next to the interactive whiteboard will be the teacher's desk. There are only two types of teacher's desk. First is the 'neat and tidy' – everything in its place, not a loose Post-it note anywhere. Each drawer is labelled and filled with just enough equipment so the drawers easily slide in and out. There may be a picture of the teacher's family in a homemade frame, which was given as a present. Other ornaments that highlight how amazing the teacher is will border the desk. There might possibly be a small plant on the corner of the table, too.

Then you have the other type of teacher's desk – the one that looks like a bomb has just hit it. Debris all over the shop. There is paper everywhere, random stationery dotted around the table, the surface hidden beneath random Post-it notes and reminders. The drawers can't be opened as they are packed full of junk and random things you have confiscated from children over the years. (See the classroom crazes chapter for what would fill these drawers.)

The only thing in common between both desks is the trusted sweet drawer. This is a must in every classroom. When you need that quick sugar fix during a long afternoon trying to explain to seven-year-olds the difference between igneous, sedimentary and metamorphic rocks, a quick nip in the sweet drawer to scoff a handful of Haribo can save the day. You must make sure you write something on your board while you desperately try to chew and swallow the gummy bears before any of your class clocks on to what you have done. It is one of the many examples of how hypocritical teachers can be. The number of times I've berated my pupils, 'How dare you come into my classroom chewing food. This is not a restaurant, go and spit it out now!' Yet there has been the odd occasion (most days, around 2pm) where I will subtly reach down to look like I am tying my shoelaces by my desk, only to be devouring some cola bottles.

This is just one of many examples of how teachers can be the biggest hypocrites. Other examples include:

To the child who forgot their PE kit:

'What do you mean you've not got it? There is no excuse, you should have your PE kit in school every single day!'
'Are you joining in, Mr P?'
'Not today, class. I was so busy this morning, I forgot to bring my trainers in!'

When you hear a pupil use inappropriate language:

'Please say I did not just hear what I thought I heard? A swear word in my classroom? How disrespectful. How dare you think about using such vulgar language in my class!'

'Mr P, do I need to underline the title?'
What I think: FFS! Of course you do, it's something you've been doing for every lesson since the start of f*****g September, why the f*** would I now, in May, expect you not to underline the f******g title?
What I say: 'Yes, please!'
Five minutes later: 'Mr P, I've not got a pencil.'
What I think: WTF! Are you f*****g kidding me? What the f*** have you been doing for the past five minutes?
What I say: 'Why don't you get one from your pencil pot and get on with your task.'
'Mr P, my pencil is broken, what should I do?'
What I think: Go and f*****g sharpen the b*****d pencil then!
What I say: 'Grab the sharpener from my desk and sharpen it quickly. Well done.'

There have been a couple of occasions when a swear word has slipped out. The hardest period of my career in the classroom came when the triplets had just been born. I find that if I am extremely tired, I often have a problem pronouncing my words, sometimes slurring them. Part way through the lesson, I was about to give the clear instruction to the class of picking up their sheets and sticking them in their books, but what came out of my mouth was:

'Right, Year 4, pick up your shits and stick them in your books.'

Luckily, I was dealing with a class who rarely listened at the best of times, so I was able to pass it off by quickly repeating myself with the correct pronunciation. Bullet dodged.

After hearing about some of your class spreading rumours and gossip about each other:

'Now, class, it has come to my attention that during break
and lunchtime there are some of you who are gossiping
and talking about each other behind each other's backs,
which can be another form of bullying and we can't have
that sort of behaviour in our school. If you're not willing
to say something to someone's face, don't say it at all.'

Running to my teacher BFF as soon as I hear some juicy gossip:

'Miss B, Miss B, you won't believe what I've just heard about
Jenny. Wait until you hear this!'

Teaching e-Safety:

'Children, you all need to understand how important your
digital footprint is. Once you put something online, it is

there forever and you never get it back. This can have a huge impact on so many areas of your life, including job prospects.'

Just spend about half an hour on EduTwitter (following other teachers on Twitter) and you will see how hypocritical this is.

When a pupil forgets their homework:

'Everyone has managed to get their homework in on time apart from you, you've had enough time, there are simply no excuses. You will have to stay in at break to finish it.'

Also me: 'No, I've not managed to mark all your writing yet, I've had a lot on. Played footy with my mates the other night, walked the dog too and there's this brilliant true crime documentary on Netflix that I am obsessed with. But I'll get it done soon.'

My most common hypocritical expectation is the one where you explain to the children why water is the only drink that is allowed in school because water reduces fatigue and helps learning. I'm giving this lecture while cracking open a frosty can of Dr Pepper Zero that has been cooling in the staffroom fridge for a couple of hours!

Over the past couple of years there has been a growing trend of cornering off part of your already packed space to create a dedicated reading area. This is where you really can unleash some teacher's creativity. Don't believe me, just type 'reading areas' into Pinterest. Actually, don't. Pinterest is a one-way system to guarantee you feel like the most incompetent teacher when you compare your classroom with those you see on there. My advice is to either stay away or constantly remind yourself that the likelihood is they are crap teachers.

This reading area obsession seemed to coincide with when Michael Gove (Pob), who was Education Secretary at the time, made a speech in which he said he expected children to read at least 50 books a year. At the same time his government was on a mission to close every single library in the country. Which meant that schools were left to pick up the pieces and create reading areas in the classroom with a shelf or small library. So you try to make the reading corner as welcoming and comfortable as possible, even though the children hardly ever get a chance to actually use it. Instead, they tend to use it to have their own pillow fight or, as we had in our school, their own toilet. Yes, that is correct. One child once left a huge turd right next to *Billionaire Boy* by David Walliams. It was quite the review.

So here is a list of some of the random things you only find in primary school:

Glue spreaders – These little plastic tools would be found near a sink in the classroom, in a plastic cup, most probably all stuck together from the last time they were used in the 90s. If they're not stuck together, they are stuck to the pot. You then need Eddie Hall or The Mountain to visit your school to prise them apart so you can use them again. The best use of these was to spread PVA glue over your own hands and wait for it to dry so you can peel it off for ultimate satisfaction. I'm not going to lie, I still do this as a teacher, subtly though, so as not to be seen by the pupils. It has also been a welcome distraction during the third risk-assessment staff meeting I have had to endure.

The class set of scissors – Well, I say a class set, but maybe it covers half the class due to budget cuts, and of those half, the majority will be the left-handed green/yellow pair, which as a left-hander myself I couldn't use. You spend lesson after lesson explaining the importance of carrying the scissors the correct safe way around the room, even though they are that blunt they barely cut through paper.

The print dryer rack – I don't know if every class has one of these. To be fair, I spent the majority of my NQT year trying to work out what it was and what I could use it for. Every single piece of artwork would go on the window ledge and dry that way but the corners would rise and start curling. Eventually I learnt the use of this life-changing device and have loved it ever since. Alongside the paint drying rack there will be a basket of old school shirts that pupils can use to stop paint getting on their uniform. The little cherubs still manage to get their sleeves caked in poster paint alongside snot, glitter and half of their lunch. A collection of old newspapers will be stacked in a corner ready to cover your tables during an art lesson, too. Please make sure you check the papers you use; there's nothing worse than setting the class up for an afternoon of art to be disturbed because your pupils have spotted a Page 3 model smothering the table.

Multilink – Multilink cubes are a staple of most classrooms. There will be a tray somewhere in the class full of these. They are a great resource to help with so many elements of the maths curriculum, from counting to fractions to data handling. Despite having the best intentions to include these multicoloured blocks as a useful manipulative tool to help children visualise and represent numbers pictorially, the children spend most of the lesson using them to build the biggest sword and then have a full-on duel with their partner during the lesson.

Mini whiteboards – The most useful resource in a classroom has to be the mini whiteboard – so handy, so useful.

'Right, class, write your answers on your whiteboards, show me in 3 ... 2 ... 1.'

A game changer when you have a parents' evening and you don't want another page in the exercise book to mark, some whiteboard work will do for today's class.

Despite being really useful, they are a nightmare to maintain. There will always be some whiteboards that are beyond dirty. No matter how hard you wipe, they will not clean at all. Children run through whiteboard pens like they are going out of fashion. Pressing as hard as they can to ruin the nib, just colouring in the whole whiteboard for no reason other than shits and giggles. Children seemingly mistake whiteboard pens for permanent markers, too, or want to see what the whiteboard pen tastes like, sucking on the nib and turning their whole mouth a dodgy shade of black. As budgets continue to diminish, teachers try every trick in the book to make the whiteboard pens last, including pulling out the nib and swapping the end or just letting children use a whiteboard pen with absolutely no ink in, trying desperately to make out what they have written and then assuming they have it right or wrong and awarding a team point.

Paper towels – Having a batch of these in your classroom is a must for any teacher. These blue, or sometimes green, paper towels are the go-to for most classroom issues. If a paint pot of water for washing the brushes is knocked over ... paper towels. If a child turns a shade of white and chunders all over the floor ... paper towel. A child bangs their head during break time ... put a wet paper towel on it. Got yourself a headache? Put a wet paper towel on it. Cut your finger? Wet paper towel. Broken arm? Wet paper towel. Twisted ankle? Wet paper towel. I honestly think that the WHO should try putting a wet paper towel on the coronavirus and we might be able to sort it out.

Despite its miraculous ability to sort any ailment, the reason wet paper towels are used in this way is purely down to the fact that us teachers are clueless when it comes to any medical issue. We are teachers, that's what we are trained to do – teach and impart knowledge, not diagnose illnesses. We have two choices: give them a wet paper towel and crack on with the lesson or send them down to the office/medical room for them to be sent back to class five minutes later with a bump note or cold compress, and now you have to repeat that part of the lesson for the child who was missing.

I can only imagine what state the NHS would be in if I were a GP, based on my answers to pupils who are feeling under the weather:

'Mr P, I feel sick!'

'Oh dear, let's just see how you get on. If it gets any worse, just let me know.'

'Sir, I really don't feel well.'

'Well, it is near break time. Let's see how you get on during break once you've had some fresh air.'

'I'm not feeling 100 per cent.'

'We are just about to finish for lunch, so let's see how you feel once you've had something to eat. I think you might be a bit hungry. I know the smell of the cheese whirls will surely make you feel better.'

'I've got a really bad headache.'

'Why don't you go and have a little drink? Go and have a sip and see if that helps.'

'My head is banging.'

'So is mine, I get headaches too. I know how you feel but we'll work through this together.'

'Mr P, my arm hurts when I do this.' (Child moves arm up and down.)

'Well, just don't move your arm like that then it won't hurt.'

'I really don't feel well.'

'Why don't you take your jumper off? Might cool you off and make you feel better.'

Then when it comes to any physical injury, the simple flow-chart on the next page usually does the trick:

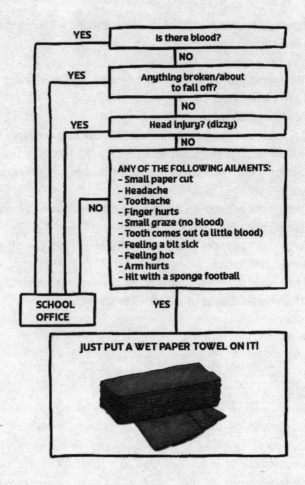

Well, after all that, the classroom is where most of the amazing, crazy and unbelievable things happen. If those four walls could talk they would probably tell you most of the things we have just told you!

For most people, their only reference point for a teacher's working life is what they see on TV or in a film. I can't think of a single movie or TV show that truly captures it accurately. A simple scene that involves a classroom scene can completely ruin the whole film for any teacher or school staff.

Here are a couple of examples:

During a scene in the 1996 film *Matilda*, adapted from the only book Adam read when he was younger, Miss Honey is welcoming Matilda to the class, clearly asking her to put her hand up to share an answer. She then starts giving the class some times tables to solve, and with all the class answering correctly she jokes that the way they are going they'll be able to solve 13×379. To which Matilda shouts out, '4927!'

Now, if on a child's first day they come out with an answer like that, any teacher will be completely flabbergasted. You will also be excited at the prospect of a child being of greater depth or in the top set. That is likely to take your class average up a few points, which can certainly help with your performance management if you're trying to move up the pay scales. My problem, however, is the fact that Miss Honey clearly stated that if Matilda wanted to speak she needed to put her hand up. Matilda completely ignored this instruction and instead shouted out her answer. Miss Honey then failed to acknowledge this, which I am sure would be against the desired procedure in the school's behaviour policy. I can only imagine the depth and length of the behaviour policy written by Miss Trunchbull, but I would have expected at the very least a warning.

Here's how that situation would have gone down in a real classroom:

'Ok, Matilda, thank you for sharing your answer, however, I clearly stated that if you want to share something you need to put your hand up. Now, I will only say this one more time: if you shout out like that again, you will need to step outside and have some time to think.' Remember, you need to set your stall out early, or else before you know it Matilda will be walking all over that classroom.

I think you are clutching at straws here, bro.

Ok, how about *Finding Nemo*? First, when Mr Ray appears to take the class on a school trip, he rocks up late. I can't imagine ever rocking up to school after the children have entered the classroom. Then he takes the children on the trip with no hi-vis vest, no sick bucket and no health and safety form. I mean, where is the risk assessment?!

Again, scraping the barrel here.

Next, the classic 90s film, *Jack*. The one where Robin Williams plays a 10-year-old who has a condition where he ages four times quicker than a normal person. This means when he is 10 years old, he looks like a 40-year-old. He then decides to go to school and his teacher is Jennifer Lopez. That's right, Jenny from the block. Believe it or not, that's up there as one of the most believable elements of the film. At one point Jack asks his teacher to go to the dance with him, and when she tries to stop his advances, he kisses her. While on screen that looks like a 40-year-old is kissing a teacher, in the film's reality it is a 10-year-old planting one on a teacher. The teacher just allows it, then asks him to leave. No repercussions, no reporting it to the leadership team, no reporting it on CPOMS (an online safeguarding tool that schools use to log any incidents). How this was allowed into the final cut of the film I will never know.

Ok, no arguing on that one, it is dodgy.

Ask most teachers and they will tell you that the working week usually starts on Sunday evening. You have every intention to get an early night to be as prepared as possible for another full-on, exhausting week. The vast majority of teachers will have used a huge chunk of their weekend to do some school work: plan lessons, mark work or update a progress spreadsheet. This can make it almost impossible to switch off and relax. Most weeks I go through the same Sunday-night routine.

10pm: Head to bed, try to relax so I can get a full eight hours ready to attack the week.

11pm: I've clearly left the heating on. It is far too hot. I'll just put my arm out. Nope! Too cold. What about my leg? I'll put that outside the cover. But what about the monster under the bed?! Wait, I'm over 30 and a teacher. I can't still believe in monsters under the bed. Even so, best not chance it.

Midnight: Wait, is it a twilight staff meeting tomorrow? Will I need to sort childcare while I sit in the staffroom doodling away and get told something that is either a complete waste of time or going to add even more to my workload? I'd best just WhatsApp the team to check. Ooh a notification. Yes, I suppose I do want to know who the Man Utd manager is interested in signing and it definitely cannot wait until the morning.

1am: Did I email in my planning? Yes I did. Even if I didn't, I can do it first thing in the morning. Why can't I sleep??? Come on, don't think about school, you can still get a full six hours' sleep if you set your alarm for 6am. Did you set your alarm? Let me check, 6.15am because those extra 15 minutes will really make a difference. And relax, you can get a full five hours here ...

2am: I forgot to respond to that parent who complained, so I'll have to do that in the morning too. Why are they so angry? What if they go to the head with their complaint? I'm probably going to get sacked! (Most teachers will lose sleep over complaints, observations, worries about children and their home environment, knowing there is little they can do about it. I find it very difficult to switch off. Teaching is one of a few careers that never has an end point. Once the bell does ring, that can usually be the end of the easiest part of your day. The marathon of marking, planning and preparation for the next day, which might come after a staff meeting, after-school club or PTA event – before you then start to think about other concerns – can truly become overwhelming.)

3am: (Slowly drifting off to sleep.) Your class will love the lessons you've planned tomorrow. A lesson on subordinate clauses is going to go down a storm. Even if Ofsted were to come in and observe, they'd love it ... (Sits up in a cold sweat.) OFSTED!

4am: I think rearranging my tables from a row into a horseshoe might help the children engage more effectively in the discussions.

5am: You didn't glue in the worksheets from Friday. There's a book scrutiny this week, you'll get a right telling off!

5.30am: Finally drifts into a deep sleep.

6.15am: Alarm starts to ring, instantly hit snooze.

6.30am: Finally drag my zombified body out of bed ready to attack the week.

Well, at least when you get into school you'll have time to sort everything so the day will go exactly as you plan. Yeah, right! If you ever wondered why your teachers at school seemed to be pissed off before any of your lessons actually started, I am about to explain why. The painstaking process of the morning routine is the stuff of nightmares for most teachers. Let me talk you through it.

You arrive at school around 7am so by 8.15 your laptop will have finally logged on – and that is if it isn't doing an update. You then jump onto the resource site where you can download your worksheets for the day. Labelling parts of the digestive system, BINGO! CTRL + P, off it goes to the printer on the other side of the school. You then follow it down the corridor, doing what I like to call the Morning Walk. This consists of putting the biggest fake smile on your face as you walk down the corridor, letting on to every staff member with 'Morning! You alright?' even though you are dead inside because you've not had your morning coffee.

You arrive at the printer and what is there? Not your work-sheet, that's for sure. In my 13 years of teaching, the worksheet has never been there the first time. The wifi has dropped out, someone has clogged up the spooling, there's no ink, toner, paper or the phantom jammer has struck again. There is a teacher who seems to get to the printer/photocopier, sort them-selves out, then break it and do one without being caught. We've had to install CCTV in the reprographics room to try to catch the culprit.

You finally get your worksheet printed by 8.30am and you have 20 minutes before your pupils arrive, but now you need to get your 30 photocopies. But who is hogging the photocopier at half 8 every morning? Yes, you guessed it, YEAR BLOODY SIX, who decide to photocopy 90 full SATs papers, oblivious to the fact that all the other staff are slagging them off behind their back. 'They're there again, hogging that photocopier, 90 SATs papers. They don't sit the tests till May, and it's flipping September.'

You get the photocopies minutes before the bell rings for the start of day. What do you have to do now? Yes, that's right, trim them. It amazes me that we have the technology to print body parts and help people walk again but we have not yet been able to design exercise books that can fit a sheet of A4 paper. So now I am on the hunt for the guillotine, AKA Houdini – I leave it in my class for one minute, next minute it has disappeared.

At last your sheets are ready just in time for the bell to go for you to welcome your cherubs into class. To continue to build a positive relationship with your class, you now have to stand at the door and greet every child as they enter. Not a problem with this; I think it is great for the children to see your smiling face greet them even though behind the mask is a teacher already on the brink of a breakdown. As with most things in education, there are always schools who have to take this a step further and a number of them now have a protocol where outside the class door is a small display of three options – usually a high-five, a hug or a dance. This seems to be an initiative imported from the US, as there was a video doing the rounds online where a kindergarten teacher had learnt 30 individual dance/handshake routines, one for each child in the class. I'm sorry, but it takes me a good few weeks to remember all the names of my class.

I am not a fan of the hug, high-five or dance greeting. I am not going to lie, I don't want to be getting that close to the children. Can you imagine seeing mucus Matty walking towards you with snot coming out of every orifice, snail trails all over his sleeves, and asking for a high-five? You begrudgingly hold out your hand, only for it to stick to the child's hand and you can only imagine what the material is that's sticky. Or there's the child who only declares their parents found nits in their hair after they have hugged you! All I can say is, thank God for Covid. That quickly put a stop to the greeting-at-the-door shenanigans.

Next, you get your class settled, which depending on the class can range from 10 seconds to 10 minutes, all so you can take the register. The register is always the tell-tale sign of how your morning is going to go. As you start to say 'Good morning, (insert name)', the reply you receive gives you an instant idea of who is awake, who is asleep, who is going to engage and who isn't going to make the right choices. Once that is done, the register monitor steps up to take the register from your class to the school office. What a job! Bounding out of the classroom like Bilbo Baggins about to go on another adventure, not knowing when you'll return to the class. It is usually around Year 3 or 4 when pupils can do this job independently. Before this, they will always, always ask if they can take a partner, which is fine, except the child then takes half the lesson deciding which of their friends will be the chosen one to hold hands or hold half the register as they walk all of 50 metres to the school office. The lesson suddenly turns into the *X Factor* judging round where the register monitor is giving reasons for and against choosing another child, just waiting for Dermot O'Leary to appear and say, 'Sorry, Sarah, we're really going to need to push you to choose one to take through to the school office.'

Once the register is out of the way, we can start the lesson, but first we need to stick the worksheet in our books.

'Ok, class, first things first, can we open our books on the next clear page?'

For most primary school children, this seems to translate as, 'Wherever you fancy, do it there. You're going to leave five pages, why not go for ten?!'

'Can we very quickly but neatly stick our worksheets in our exercise books, just like we've practised every day so far this year. Just a little dot of the glue stick in each corner, and then place it nice and neatly in the middle of the page. Just the middle, nice and neatly. John! John! Why is it hanging over the edge? You're pushing me to the edge!'

If it is any time after September in the year, you're most likely to only have one glue stick in the whole class, so you then end up saying things like, 'Well, what can you be doing while you wait for the glue stick?' Again, a mix of budget cuts thanks to a Tory government who don't care about children and children who feel like they need to cover every inch of the back of their worksheet with glue whenever they need to stick something in their book leaves us glue-less.

Ten minutes go by, the worksheets haven't been stuck in, and you've still got guided reading, SPAG and a mental maths test to get through before break! A few children seem to be causing quite a fuss at the back of the class, so you go to investigate.

'What's all the kerfuffle? You've lost a lid to the glue stick? RIGHT, CODE RED, LOCKDOWN! We are not leaving this class-room until we've found the lid. I am not losing another lid to the Bermuda Triangle of this classroom!'

If you are a parent reading this, you will know how having a young, inquisitive child can be a blessing and a curse. An average of 5,823 questions asked by your little angel a day can quickly become annoying. Now put yourself in the position of a teacher who will be asked this number of questions by 30 children at the same time.

Let's take a typical scenario. Say it is the Halloween disco tomorrow and I make the announcement to my class. The rest of the day might look something like this:

'Ok, class, just before we start the lesson, very quick reminder that tomorrow is the Halloween disco and you are more than welcome to dress up. But just to make sure you remember, there are to be no weapons and no masks, make-up is fine but no masks. Ok, let's get on with the lesson ...'

Pupil raises hand.

In my head: Oooh a question, do I open the floodgates? It is only one so if I answer quickly, I can nip it in the bud and that will be that done.

'Yes, what is it?'

'Mr P, what about the mask I have made of a unicorn?'

'Unfortunately not. As I just said, the school rules state no masks are allowed.'

'Yes, but I made it with my mum!'

'That's great and I am sure it is a great mask and you'll be able to wear it when you go trick or treating. Just think, the horn is big and pointy and can be dangerous. Come to think of it, are you sure a unicorn is the best costume for Halloween?'

'It is a zombie unicorn! Mr P, my mum won't be happy! She's probably already posted her frustrations to the WhatsApp group.'

'What WhatsApp group?'

'The one where all the parents moan about you.'

Another child then asks, 'Mr P, is a knife a weapon?'

'Yes, a very dangerous one at that!'

'What about a plastic one?'

'No, that would still be considered a weapon.'

'No! It hardly penetrated the skin when I used it on my sister the other day!'

'How many times have I got to tell you, you should not be trying to stab your sister!'

Another child chips in: 'Can I wear my Freddy Krueger mask?'

'How do you even know who Freddy Krueger is? You're six!'

'Can I just bring my mask and carry it?'

'No.'

'What if I bring it in my bag and just leave it in my bag?'

'Again. No!'

'It's not fair! Why is it Miss Burns gets to wear a mask every day but we don't?'

'Miss Burns doesn't wear a mask, that's just her face.'

'Really? Why is it so scary and so old?'

'She's 24! She's an NQT. That's just what the stress of the job can do to you!'

'Mr P, what's tomorrow?' asks another child.

Sighing heavily: 'The Halloween disco. Don't worry, I have put a letter in your bag for you to take home, the letter that you are now chewing.'

Seeing another pupil crying in the corner of the classroom: 'What's the matter? Why are you crying?'

'I won't be able to come to the disco.'

'Of course you will, I've just given you your ticket.'

'No, because the other night I dropped my dad's phone and smashed the screen and he called me a right weapon. So if I am a weapon it means I won't be able to come!'

'No, you're fine, your dad shouldn't have really called you that, it isn't very nice. But it isn't the type of weapon we're talking about.'

'What type of weapon is it then?'

'We've not really got time to talk as we need to start the lesson. Right, let's just get the register done!'

The bell goes for break!

This is where the favourite teacher line of 'Is it a matter of life or death?' becomes a lifeline. This can be used to ensure that only relevant questions are asked.

The other day in the school calendar that always causes chaos and utter confusion for both staff and children has to be school photo day. No matter how much organisation goes into making the operation run smoothly, the struggle is real.

One point I will make is how flipping expensive it is to buy school photos. I would like to state, these prices have nothing to do with the school. If you have to remortgage your house to afford a keyring picture of your child, take this up with the photography company.

My favourite story linked to school photo day has to be this one that a teacher shared, it didn't half give us a laugh:

It was picture day at school and our kids who have pictures in family groups go separately. One of our families was new so our P3 teacher sent one of the girls from the class to take this family to the assembly hall for their picture. They had their photo and came back down to class, escorted by the girl. Cut to a few weeks later when we get the proofs in for parents to look at and choose to buy the pictures or not. This family photo arrives and, unknown to the teacher or any member of school staff, the girl who had escorted them up to the hall had decided to go in the picture as well. There she was, standing proudly with a family of girls who had no idea who she was. The photographer apologised and offered the parent another photo session and we had the photo put up in our staffroom to give us a laugh when we came in for break times.

Despite these regular occurrences where you question your own sanity, inside the classroom there can be comedy gold. Like proper, completely unexpected hilariousness from the kids, particularly when they don't even know they are being funny. Adam's wife had a brilliant example involving some children being newsreaders.

With little Adji? The accidental comedy genius?

That's the one.

Well, sometimes, as a teacher, it must feel like you have FOOL written on your forehead.

This is highlighted when it's group work time. You ask the class to pair up, and you may even throw a kicker in like, 'Choose someone you know you're going to work sensibly with.' As a result, almost by the power of magnetism, you know that the two 'wrong-choice' makers are going to find each other. They know their pair will achieve a grand total of zero work done and almost certainly cause maximum disruption.

Unfortunately, this is where you're faced with a dilemma: do you split up the WCC (Wrong Choice Crew)? By doing this it will mean you have to disrupt a perfectly pleasant and compliant partnership (Sensible Sallys) and one of them is going to have to be torn away and stuck with some doughnut that is bound to cause her a head-ache. You may issue a challenge to the WCC: 'Go on then, prove me wrong!' In some cases you will be proved wrong (annoyingly) but in most cases you've got four unhappy kids stuck with a less-than-ideal workmate.

If you're looking for an example of good, sensible work, you have to choose the right child; the child who you could easily depend upon, not the child who just talks a good game. The classic 'all fart, no poo' kind of kid that will give it the big one but when they're put on the main stage, they freeze. Even when you think you've landed the right child for something, it can still go awry. A wonderful example involves my wife Kim teaching an English lesson where the children wrote news stories and performed them as a broadcast to the class. The kids seemed to be quite into it and a few of the children asked if they could name their news anchor. Kim thought that was a fair idea and agreed. Obviously she had to deal with the potential threat of an inappropriate name, the sort you'd hear on *The Simpsons* when Bart prank-calls Moe's Tavern asking for names like 'Al Coholic', 'Amanda Huggen-Kiss', or the always hilarious 'Hugh Jass'.

Once she'd made it quite clear that 'Dabby McFloss' was not a viable option, she started looking around the class to see who could be a good example to deliver their news report. Kim's attention was drawn towards the perfect good-choice maker. She thought to herself, '*Winner winner chicken dinner*'. And this is where we meet our lovely Hungarian lad, Adji. He would be classed as an EAL (English as an additional language) child.

'Are you happy to share your report, Adiji?' asked Kim.

'Yes, Miss!' he replied.

'And you have a sensible name for your newsreader ...?'

'I do!'

Kim was satisfied that Adji wouldn't let her down and that she'd definitely made the right choice. Adji began: 'Welcome to the *6 O'Clock News*, with me ... BOB MARLEY!'

Kim's smile turned to a grimace. A few sniggers in the class followed and my wife used all her professionalism to not break down in laughter.

'Oh no, Adji, you can't use Bob Marley, we all know who he is. Can you go away and have another think, please? Choose a name we don't know.'

Adji looked disheartened and a little upset. Kim was desperately trying to keep it together and not spend the rest of the session dropping Bob Marley puns to make her TA laugh. A short while later, she decided to invite Adji up again for a second go, he didn't seem as keen, so she said, 'Adji ... get up, stand up, you will get it right!' With the joke flying straight over his head, Adji then stood up ready for a second bite of the cherry:

'Welcome to the *6 O'Clock News*, with me ... RICK ASTLEY!'

Kim had been 'Rick-rolled' in front of the entire class, but rather than stop his flow, she held it together and let Adji crack on. He actually delivered a super news report, but all that time she was secretly hoping his story involved two people that were 'no strangers to love' or that Dabby McFloss would interrupt so she could tell him, 'You know the rules and so do I.'

Good old Adji!

Another staple of the school day is Show and Tell. For anyone reading this who never experienced it when they were at school, what weird school did you go to? Show and Tell usually happens towards the end of the day. This is mainly so teachers can use it as a bit of a carrot to dangle to keep some pupils in line. 'If you don't get your work finished, there'll be no time for Show and Tell.' Just the classic type of bribery that most parents use with things like dinner: 'If you don't eat your vegetables, there'll be no dessert.'

As most parents will admit, Show and Tell is their worst nightmare. The things children reveal have literally split up families! During these sessions, the teacher will encourage pupils to come up to the front of the class and either share something they have brought in from home (show) or some news that is important to them (tell). I love Show and Tell when the children reveal something that they shouldn't, although it can also be tedious. There are only so many drawings you can see that the children have done that, let's say, wouldn't be displayed in the Tate Modern.

Another skill of the teacher is being able to treat everything that is shared in class as a big deal to make the child feel valued. The tedious bit really comes when a child has finished sharing their news, and you allow their classmates to ask some questions. They are always the same and usually consist of:

Do you like it?
When did you get it?
Where did you get it from?
Did you like it?
Was it good?
Do you like it?

To be fair, 95 per cent of what the children share or talk about isn't worth mentioning as it is very run of the mill – football trophies, dance certificates, new pets, etc. But every so often a child will bring in something that is not what they think it is, which is followed by a rather awkward discussion with a parent. The most common inappropriate items brought into school for Show and Tell tend to be either furry handcuffs or a sex toy. But that is just the start of some of the weird and rather disgusting things to have been brought in to be proudly showcased. We have had so many stories from teachers and school staff on the podcast, and here are some of our favourites:

A verruca in a pot.

'My cat had kittens yesterday. But don't worry, Mummy drowned them in a bucket.'

A photo of their dad wearing a mankini 😂😂. Dad came to collect, too.

I have had tonsils from a pupil's recent operation, which inspired another child to bring in their recently removed foreskin after their operation.

One of my girls last year shared a dead animal with us that she had found. Utterly speechless.

A hairdresser's daughter told the whole class with great delight that her mommy dyed her 'downstairs' hair blue for her 30th birthday 😄 I moved swiftly on to the next child! I also had to keep it together at the next PTA meeting.

A five-year-old told the class about a great game of hide and seek he and his family played one weekend. 'We played hide and seek with a policeman. He didn't find us because the door was locked and me, Mummy and Daddy hid behind the sofa. He gave up.'

I had a boy of six come up and tell a joke. Said joke was, Why can't Ken and Barbie have babies? They come in different boxes.

A dad's cockring.

One child brought in her Cypriot grandad to speak about our Greece topic.

A dead pet tarantula, which was followed by a complaint from another parent because their child was not allowed to bring in their pet. So the next week the child and parent were allowed to bring their pet horse onto the school field.

A tortoise. In a Sainsbury's carrier bag, hung on a peg in the morning.

A Reception child once proudly presented a very large lump of Blu-tac. No words of explanation, just held it up with a smug look on his face. It was all from where he'd helped himself from the backs of classroom displays.

One of my little girls in Early Years told us that her tooth came out the night before and the tooth fairy brought her £100! Do you mean 100 pennies?, I asked. She said no – see? She then pulled two £50 notes out of her tights to show us! Her mum was mortified; apparently her dad spoils her!

Pictures of a mum's new nose.

A boy brought in his umbilical cord one week and the following week the ashes of his dead dog.

But our favourite story that we've heard has to be this one, which funnily enough, happens more often than you think:

Late one week, a child told me he had something in his bag for Show and Tell. He'd asked every day and for one reason or other we didn't have time to do it until the Thursday. I finally agreed to let this child share his item and he was so excited he raced to his bag and returned with a Tupperware box. I was sitting at my desk half paying attention when he returned. I wasn't really listening to what he was saying until the smell hit me. One of the worst smells I'd ever smelled in a classroom and, trust me, as a KS1 teacher I've had all sorts. I stepped over as the child said, 'Jellyfish'. Panic set in. The school was nowhere near a beach or sealife centre, so I knew it was not a jellyfish. This child had brought a condom in a Tupperware box to school. That's not even the worst part. The worst part was that it was USED!!!

I grabbed the box, put the lid on and told the pupil to sit down. I allowed someone else to share a tell while I completely panicked and lost my shit. So many questions went through my head, the worst being the fact he'd had it in his bag all week! I then had to get my head around speaking to the parents, which I convinced myself would just be a quick 'This happened, don't worry.' Turns out it became one of the most awkward parent interactions of my career so far!

Dad came to pick him up, for the first time that year (he works away a lot). I started by making pleasantries and then explained what had happened. The dad's face turned white. I asked if he was ok. He didn't say anything, just standing there for what seemed like a lifetime before taking the box and leaving. I'm not great with awkward silences but it seemed like a Guinness world record attempt. No apologies. I put it down to embarrassment, especially the fact that it was the first time we had met. I was embarrassed having to explain, so I can only imagine how the parent felt. What didn't make sense was the fact he just took the box with him. Why? Why not just ask us to dispose of the 'jellyfish'? God only knows what he did with the box. I imagine once he was able to come around from the cringe-induced coma he binned it. Needless to say, I never saw the dad again. As far as Show and Tell goes, I don't think that one can be topped.

The Real Superheroes of Primary Schools

I want to ask you a question, Lee.

Shoot ...

What is the most valuable thing to a teacher?

An unlimited amount of Pritt Sticks, and I mean the good stuff, not the cheap own brand that's more like lip balm.

No.

Adequate funding so teachers are well equipped to teach and support their class.

Again, no.

A Nespresso coffee machine with George Clooney putting the pods in.

George Clooney?

He's on the adverts.

One last try …

An educational system that is set up to trust teachers to do the job they are very capable of doing instead of an obsession with accountability that leads to so much unnecessary paperwork and workload.

Right, I am stopping you there, you'll get your chapter to vent and rant and put the world to rights. Listen, the most valuable thing to any teacher that will have the biggest impact on a pupil's learning and progress is … ME!

What?

A TA or LSA.

Couldn't agree more, I knew that straight away. The only reason I didn't say it was that I thought that witty bit of banter would eat up even more of the word count.

Ah, clever.

I know!

Fantastic!

Yes, I thought I would try to employ some of the age-old tactics from back in the school and uni days where you have a 3,000-word essay and so you would tactically fill up the word count by essentially writing nonsense that was oh-so-vaguely linked to the initial idea.

Yes, or when you wanted to copy something to avoid any plagiarism, you would simply change the order of the words in the sentence.

What's funny is that now you are a teacher it is so blatantly obvious when a child has just copied something from the web.

So obvious, even I can spot it.

Now it's Google. Teachers will be the first to tell you how that is not always the best idea. Here was a recent example another teacher shared, which summarised what can happen if children simply copy what they see on Google rather than digesting and thinking about the content they engage with.

A teacher had set the children a homework question: what is the message of Greece? The child had misspelled the word Greece and so her answer was:

'In 1959, America was about to "grow up" sexually and into full sexual adulthood in the 70s (*Rocky Horror*). Too many people believe that the message of *Grease* is that to win the man you love, you have to be a slut.'

The slightly worrying thing with this is that the pupil had handwritten this onto paper to submit to the teacher. I can understand a quick copy and paste job into Microsoft Word but to handwrite it and at no point think, well, I am sure Greece is a country in Europe so why is America getting involved? Or even, I wish I lived in Greece if all the women are sluts.

One last point on googling if you are a teacher or student teacher. Please be careful when asking children to search things online. Most teachers will have at least one example of a time where innocent little Johnny (in fact, please don't google that phrase) typed something into the World Wide Web to be greeted by images that would even make the other Mr P blush.

I have experienced this myself. During a task in our Victorian topic, the children were learning about Queen Victoria and her husband Prince Albert. After asking children to find some interesting facts about the monarchs, one child shouted, 'Why is there a picture of this weird snake?' I dashed over to see a picture of a male member with a piercing through the urethra. My career flashed before my eyes. It was a tense situation, and that was just the image! I quickly removed the device from the child.

And booked yourself in for one?

No, I stopped the children and followed our procedure of online safety where I shared some appropriate websites with the children. Luckily the parents were very understanding, but it was a lesson learnt that day.

Yeah, here's something in the book that might actually help you in the classroom.

Here are some things that teachers have googled that have presented worrying results:

Granny pics or friendly grannies – When searching for pictures of families, the term 'granny pics' brought up plenty of cougars, MILFs and GILFs.

Wait, let me check ... Lee, I'll be back in 10 minutes.

Stockings – Hoping to get pictures of Christmas stockings can easily lead to suggestive pictures of lingerie.

Daddy Bear – When looking at the story of Goldilocks, be very aware not to google Daddy Bear.

The letter D – That's phonics out of the window!

String – Again, more lingerie.

Exotic birds – The sort or term you'd hear Sid James use in a *Carry On* film!

Brazilian – As you can imagine, lots of links for waxing.

Rabbits – Even without the word 'rampant' in front, you will get said sex toy in the image results. Also be aware of Magic Wand, as this is another sex toy, I believe.

Black holes – No words, simply no words.

I am sure there are plenty more, so please feel free to email us and we can warn the rest of the teaching profession on the next podcast episode.

Anyway, Adam, as you were saying, the most valuable thing to a teacher ...

A passionate, hard-working TA is:
50% teacher
20% first aider
15% superhero
15% behaviour guru
100% underpaid!

Hold on, that's 200 per cent, Adam ... and therefore, mathematically impossible.

Dammit! That is 200 per cent.

But I do get your point and I completely agree with the 100 per cent underpaid bit. There are people returning trolleys in supermarket car parks that earn the same as some incredibly hardworking teaching assistants. No disrespect to the trolley guys, but if you are looking for value for money in your school, then a good teaching assistant is worth their weight in gold.

Damn straight!

You must be worth a hell of a lot of gold, Adam ...

Oi!
    The teacher/TA relationship, when done well, is a thing of beauty. Some years there might be a combination that fails to click, but if you can REALLY make a connection with your 'classroom partner' it will result in a fantastic year and, most importantly, the best possible experiences for the children.

Almost like a classic double act ...

Laurel and Hardy ...

Ant and Dec ...

Kenan & Kel ...

Batman and Robin!

I suppose many would perceive this to be potentially a 'Batman and Robin' dynamic but I think that's unfair ... teachers are surely better than Robin and I've never known a TA wage to stretch as far as a Batmobile! The best double act I can compare this unique relationship to is Paul and Barry ...

Who?

The Chuckle Brothers.

Of course. Going for a sophisticated approach with this one, are we?

You bet! Think about it; when deciding on which group you're going to be working with it's quite often a case of **'to me, to you'**, and when you finally mark the children's work it's probably more of an **'oh dear, oh dear'**. But throughout the madness of the school day, you're always there for each other as you face every obstacle together. Even though I've never seen an episode of the Chuckle Brothers where Barry and Paul played rock, paper, scissors to see whose turn it was to clean up the sick!

Grim!

Can you imagine Barry going arse over tit in a pile of regurgitated rice pudding?

Even more grim! I know from some of the brilliant TAs I've worked with, you don't get nearly enough credit for what you do.

Hell no! I'm sure existing opinions of teaching assistants may only stretch to photocopying and tea making!

To be fair, my old TA did make a brilliant cuppa!

No doubt, but while school folklore suggests that TAs are the best brew-makers, in reality that takes all of six minutes out of a

480-minute day. A decent TA is a godsend to any teacher. Communicating tasks to a wide range of abilities in the class with zero prompting from a teacher.

> Need 30 worksheets? Piece of cake!
> Stapled? Easy!
> Back to back? Boom!
> A3? I can do that without looking at the buttons!
> Yes, TAs can whip up a classroom display in a matter of minutes …

Did I ever tell you about my *Kensuke's Kingdom* display?

I think everyone who has ever listened to the pod has heard about your one and only (literally) *Kensuke's Kingdom* display!

Well, it's definitely the best display I've ever seen, but I digress … back to dropping some truth bombs about the heroic job of a teaching assistant. Teaching assistants recognise the crazy, intense job of a teacher and, yes, we may not have the mounds of planning or marking to do but a good teaching assistant will do whatever is humanly possible to ease the stress of a teacher and, in my case, keep them smiling all day.

That you do! Tell you what, Adam, talk us through your typical school day.

Warts and all?

Definitely warts and all!

Off we go, then …

BREAKFAST CLUB

Some TAs rock up at the same time that the children arrive or just before, depending on their contracted hours, but not me; I'm in at 7.45am to help at the school's breakfast club. This is the place where children are dropped off up to an hour before school starts in order to help their parents get to their place of work. This is where we try to give lots of children a great start to the day. Some positive activities and putting something filling in the children's tummies is the name of the game, and the extended hours of care offered to working parents can be a godsend. Just before school starts, there's a rapid turnaround that almost requires military precision. A quick tidy, matching children to coats/lunchboxes/book bags and lining them up ready to be distributed to their correct class, all in the space of five minutes!

CHILDREN ARRIVE

Due to going from my role at breakfast club straight to the classroom, I am given a quick time briefing by the class teacher about what will be happening during the day. If you work with an ultra-organised teacher, they've often asked you to copy resources for the next day before you leave the night before. If you work with Cockney John, then it's bedlam!

Braving wind and rain, I'm often tasked with bringing the class in from outside. It ranges from jolly smiles kicking up autumn leaves to shuffling kids in under a torrential downpour. Snowy days where it's freezing cold but it hasn't been snowing enough to close the school are usually when you need to wear your thickest coats, as waiting for you will be at least three lads with a plethora of pre-made snowballs with your name on them. It's all fun and games until one genius launches an ice-missile at the back of your head, nearly giving you a concussion, but don't worry … you'll get your revenge at play time!

While I grab the class from outside, the teacher writes the date and LO on the board – that's a learning objective, not a lunchtime organiser! We do not condone sticking a 60-year-old dinner lady under the date on the board. At this point I'm feeling like I'm on the front line of a *Braveheart*-esque battle sequence, facing up to parents approaching in pyjama pants and flip-flops explaining that their child might be tired because they didn't have a good night's sleep, but the Malibu on the mum's breath gave the game away straight off the bat. It's always worth lingering outside as you know that Bed-Hair McGee would be upon us any minute before reporting back to base with the troops to begin another day of learning.

Is it just me or have you ever been taken aback when you find out a child's middle names? I've genuinely seen middle names of 'Kris Jenner', 'Katy Perry' and 'John Lennon'!

Interestingly, I can honestly say I've hardly come across any worth mentioning. This may be due to where we have both previously worked. For you, inner-city Manchester has the advantage of more creative names and possibly more creative spelling.

While the teacher is doing the register, you're being bombarded with tales of the night before. 'Sir, did you watch *Love Island*? I can't believe Olivia recoupled!' As shocked as I was at the recoupling, I remain professional and tell them to save their conversation until break time. As I quieten down the rest of the class, I start to collect in your classics – planners, homework, reading records and permission slips. Talking of permission slips, I feel more detail is needed on this subject. Here's a breakdown of the types of permission slips that I genuinely have been handed over the years:

<u>Different Types of Permission Slips!</u>

-The tea-stained one that reminds you of those treasure maps you used to make as a kid.

-The wet ones... the less said about those, the better!

-The 'perfectly cut along the dotted scissor line and folded to fit neatly in an envelope' ones.

-The tiny handwritten one.

-The one that smells like 20 Marlboro Lights.

-The one that contains traces of last night's lasagne.

-The one containing none of the required information.

-The one that was returned 3 days after the deadline.

-And the one that has clearly been forged by the child.
(At least the slip was returned in time!)

SESSION 1

After the whirlwind of registration, it's now apparently the best time to impart knowledge to the little cherubs. Mornings usually consist of the core subjects – Literacy and Numeracy. Oh no, it's actually English and Maths again. Why is that? Why did they change it?

It came with the changes of the curriculum in 2014 thanks to the greatest Education Secretary in living memory … Michael Gove.

For me, the idea of literacy is something that evolves and changes. Technology has always been at the heart of that, defining the way in which we communicate and access information and stories. The Gove approach wanted the curriculum to focus on English as it was taught in 1876, it seems.

The role of a TA during these lessons can vary. Sometimes you can sit in a full class with a group; other times you have your own little spin-off session with a chunk of the class and, much like TV spin-off shows, it can be difficult to recreate the magic. But by hook or by crook you do your best. In my case, if the teacher has taken the time to plan, differentiate and simplify the instructions … for me … Do you think all teachers do that for their TA or am I a special edition?

You definitely are special!

Well anyway, simplification or no simplification, by the beard of Zeus I will get the job done and swiftly move on because it's time for assembly.

ASSEMBLY

Assembly time – Thank goodness!

BREAK TIME

Now break time is the name of the slot for the children. For TAs it is definitely not a break. The only break I can liken it to is *Prison Break* because it's 15 minutes of making sure everyone is safe, present and accounted for in the yard. I use break time as a time to prove to all the doubters that I've still got it. Whether it be hopscotch – I'm the only person on the playground who can get from 1 to 9 in one hop – or that complicated pat-a-cake thing that the children do – '2, 4, 6, 8, Mr P is really great' ... yes I know, thanks, smashed it!

Surely the children should do the chanting rather than the 18-stone idiot. Question is, can you skip and chant at the same time?

I'm a skipping master – as long as the holders of the ropes are strong enough (although it has been known for me to come a cropper on the unforgiving tarmac). As for that massive parachute where you ruffle it elegantly until that one fool takes it too far and shakes it quicker than anyone else can and ruins it for everyone ... sorry, guys!

You again?

Quite probably. Something else I always get involved in is 'tig'. It's easy because you can pretend that you're not playing but secretly pat a child on the shoulder ... I've still never been 'it'. Hide and seek - I always find them because I blow my whistle and they think it's time to line up ... amateurs ... it's only been 10 minutes of your 15-minute allocated break time!

GUIDED READING

Guided reading is about as enjoyable for the children as it is for the adults. Enough said, really.

SESSION 2

If you did maths first thing, then this is English time. If you did English as your first lesson, then you'll be doing maths. The only exception is usually a session dedicated to the class topic or potentially PE, as your class were the last ones to sign up for the PE timetable and so you get the crap slot!

LUNCHTIME

In my role as an HLTA, I will also be involved in lunchtimes.

The following events have all actually happened to me or my colleagues when on duty:

 And it begins! Only 2/3 of the school are outside as the others are eating in the dinner hall. Things are far too calm and sensible. That will change very soon.

 Game of tig causes argument because Kieron said that he'd tigged Caleb. Caleb says that Kieron hadn't tigged him and Zoe saw everything so ask Zoe.

 Zoe saw nothing. Zoe and friends, however, have prepared a performance for everyone to enjoy. Their dance troupe is called 'Sparkle Unicorn United'.

 Max called Isla a 'poo-head'.

Squirrel in the playground. Everybody loses their sh*t!

Caleb and Kieron have had a fist fight over the disputed game of tig. Both children sent to the wall and tig is banned for the rest of lunchtime.

Child discovers a spoon. You tell them to take it to the canteen and they nod and smile before walking in completely the opposite direction of the canteen.

Child A gets a ball stuck in the tree. Hopefully the wind will bring it down soon enough.

Child B throws hoop into tree to get the ball down. Hoop gets stuck so I'm off to get a broom or a metre stick.

Child C, trying to be helpful, throws their shoe in the tree. Broom not long enough so I'm off to get a ladder.

Child that found spoon has been digging for nearly 20 minutes with two of his mates and they are now caked in mud.

For some reason. With approximately three minutes left of their lunchtime, about 40% of the class will get into a number of fights, scrapes, arguments or disagreements. Why? Nobody knows!

AFTERNOON SESSION

I have changed the famous saying of 'Upstairs for thinking, downstairs for dancing' to fit into a TA's school day so that it's 'Mornings for learning, afternoons for surviving'. Once you have crawled through the trenches and reached the promised land (otherwise known as lunchtime), you are hit with a huge reality check when lunch is done. These are usually the 'wing-it' afternoons. The morning core subject lessons are intense, usually taking a lot out of the children, and the staff! Primary school afternoons are a time when you take your vitamins, say your prayers and hope that it's one of those dream days like when a clock in school hasn't been set properly and it's much later than you thought. Afternoons now are made up of lessons like RE or PE, PSHE or SRE ... I mean, what a difference a single letter makes.

GETTING READY FOR HOME TIME

Now this is a time I truly believe would be impossible for a teacher without their trusty, noble TA. You can always tell when a teacher has dismissed the class on their own at the end of the day, as they look like they've fallen out of a tree and hit every branch on the way down! The only people happy with teachers dismissing their class without any support are the supermarkets, whose wine stock will be attacked even on a Monday evening!

Let's talk through a typical end of day for a TA ...

First, handing out letters. Now this sounds like a simple task, but you give a child at the front of the line a letter and by the time you've made it to the end of the line 'that child' at the front is no longer holding a letter but the classroom has gained a new doormat.

The order of 'Take home your PE kits!'. Now, if anyone is telling me that everyone in their class takes their PE bag home, your pants are on fire! Why, you ask? Because you're a liar! No matter how many times you say to the class, 'Don't forget your PE kit,' when you check the cloakroom there is guaranteed to be a Tesco carrier bag swinging from the peg.

<u>HOME TIME</u>

When you finally exit the building and it's time to ship the kids off home, the life-size version of 'Guess Who' begins ... Is your adult wearing glasses and a hat? Do they have bright purple hair? Are they called Alfred? All the children have been matched with an adult. Game over!

<u>SEARCH FOR THE MISSING SCHOOL JUMPER</u>

Well, I thought it was 'game over' but what I actually mean is, onto the next game. Crystal Maze - a fiendish challenge of trying to find a school jumper (with no name on it, obviously) that has been put in the lost property box with a dozen other nameless, yoghurt-stained jumpers. Once you have rummaged through and rescued the jumpers within the specified age bracket, the only identifiable feature is said child's signature scent. The pressure is on, so you rely on your team member (for the third time this week) to sniff 12 jumpers in as many seconds before the gate closes. You begin to waft a continuous conveyor belt of lost jumpers under the nose of an eight-year-old child ... 'No, Sir, that's not mine' ... 'Nope, but I think that's Jimmy's' ... 'Yuck, no that's deffo not mine' ... 'Oh Sir, I've just remembered that I put it in my bag!' In my mind I'm effing and jeffing (still no clue who Jeff is) but to the child's face I find the positive ... 'Thanks so much for helping me find Jimmy's jumper!' Instead of leaving with a handful of gold foil, I'm leaving with a handful of hand sanitiser after sifting through those manky jumpers!

to

AFTER-SCHOOL CLUBS/ACTIVITIES

A word that used to mean banging tunes, double spirits for a quid and a kebab to finish. Now the word 'clubs' means spending another hour or, in the majority of cases, longer than an hour, hosting an array of after-school activities. Some of your finest being: Scrabble club, baking club, drama club, gardening club, French club, film club, photography club. Basically, anything goes as long as it has the word 'club' after it. Instead of double vodkas, it's a drop of cheap squash and a biscuit. At the start of the year, a club is usually well planned and morale is high, with enthusiasm flowing through the veins. By week three, there is no plan. For example, at gardening club, when the weather is wet and windy, an old YouTube clip of *Garden Force* will suffice! Scrabble club, when most of the vowels have gone missing due to wet play at lunch, basically turns into a guess-the-missing-letter club.

In the role of TA you can feel undervalued and underpaid, but one thing I feel that we can all agree on is that we are not underappreciated by the people who matter the most – our wonderful children and their inspirational teachers.

From Dennis the Menace to Horrid Henry to Zack Morris from *Saved by the Bell*, there are loveable rogues in every school. Your perspective on behaviour as a child is often very different to when you are a teacher.

You were always a flippin' 'goodie-two-shoes', Lee!

I wasn't!

Yeah, you were. Mum says she never had any phone calls about your behaviour, just requests for your Elvis impersonations.

Leave it out! I definitely was up to no good plenty of times; I just wasn't stupid enough to get caught.

Fair point!

Behaviour is and always will be one of the trickiest areas of teaching.

Especially if you taught me!

Very true! Ultimately, there is no golden nugget that every school can implement to ensure every child will always behave. At the end of the day, we are dealing with humans, and every human is different. This is why behaviour policies will differ from one school to the next. In fact, despite policies, behaviour management will differ from classroom to classroom based on a teacher's view. There are teachers I work with who treat a whisper as equivalent to a child 'flicking the Vs'. Every teacher has their own boundaries on what behaviour they find acceptable. I can tolerate some low-level noise as long as the children are semi-engaged in what they are supposed to be doing. I think the one tip I can share with any teacher or trainee teacher that has helped me is consistency.

Consistency is very important. I know job-share classes where Monday to Wednesday is like boot camp and Thursday/Friday is chaos city!

Absolutely! Children thrive on routine and consistency. If you can be consistent with your behaviour expectations, sanctions and routines, you don't tend to go far wrong. That's not to say there won't be challenging days, weeks or even terms where you feel like you're going insane because certain pupils are starting to boil over and pushing you to the brink. The reason for this is not always clear, and for some children your presence may well be the only consistent thing in their life. I try not to take certain children's actions towards me personally. It is hard at times, but children always deserve a chance to redeem themselves and grow.

There are days when I feel like I'm banging my head against a brick wall and often speak in a completely different language. For example, one time, just before a lesson observation:

What I say:

> 'Ok, class, today we have a special visitor coming to join us today. They want to see how hard you work and how well you behave.'

What my pupils hear:

> 'Someone is rocking up to see who can be the biggest class clown. Feel free to show off by chatting, messing, fidgeting and ignoring everything I say; it is a complete free for all. Oh, and whenever I ask a question, please make sure you put your hand up to either ask to go to the toilet or say something completely unrelated to the question.'

Ah, man, I know classes that pull those shenanigans during Ofsted visits.

Yikes! And that's far from the only time the class have selective hearing. Here's more examples:

What I say:
'Right, class, we now need to come and line up nice and quietly, please.'

What my pupils hear:
'Right, class, I want you to all do your best impression of a flash mob but each and every one of you has learnt a completely different choreographed dance. Off you go.'

What I say:
'Please can you underline your title in a nice straight line.'

What my pupils hear:
'Wavy lines, zig zags, come on, kids! Be creative. Make sure it is anything but straight.'

What I say:
'The head teacher is going to pop into class, children, look at some of your books and ask you a few questions to check your learning.'

What my pupils hear:
'If you dare tell the head anything about what we've been learning over the past few weeks, your birthday will be cancelled.'

What I say:
'We need to walk down the corridor nice and sensibly.'

What my pupils hear:
'Did someone say CONGA???'

I think there is a universal truth in teaching that no teacher will ever publicly admit, and this may well be the most controversial statement I make in the whole book. Teachers have favourites.

Hell yeah! Of course we have favourites. Anyone that pretends otherwise is talking rubbish!

Of course they do, we're human. It is only natural to find some children more likeable than others. The biggest test of how successful you are as a teacher is making sure no one knows you have favourites. Again, this comes back to consistency.

There are some bona fide knobheads out there. A scroll through Facebook and Twitter – especially the comments on most news stories – will quickly reveal they are everywhere!

Even with your colleagues, there will be some you like more than others. That doesn't mean you can't be respectful and tolerant. I once made the mistake of trying to use this mantra when dealing with a lunchtime falling-out that happened between children in my class. After a group of kids had been nasty and called each other names, I went on to explain that in every stage of your life there will always be people you don't necessarily get on with, but that doesn't mean you can't be respectful and treat them the way you would like to be treated. At this point, I should have left it. I felt that what I had said was clear, it had addressed the point and given the children some-thing to reflect upon. However, sometimes I can labour the point or, as my wife calls it, 'turn it into a bloody sermon'.

Amen, brother!

I followed this useful and precise information with, 'You know, there are some teachers in this school that I wouldn't invite to my birthday party or call them my friend. But I can still treat them respectfully, you know, how I would like to be treated.' Unintentionally, the rest of the lesson turned into a game of Guess Who? The children solely wanted to know which members of staff I wasn't a fan of. I overheard one child say, 'It's defin-itely Miss Wilkes, she's horrible!' (not her real name. I can't reveal that because I still work there). I managed to redeem the situation by making the point when I said, 'The fact you can't work it out shows how much I treat everyone with respect.'

Nice save! Although the kids are right, you've told me many times that Miss Wilkes (definitely not her real name) is a pain in the arse!

That is the point, though; whether staff, children or parents, being an effective teacher is being able to make sure people can never accuse you of having favourites. Favourites are pretty damn obvious in the staffroom, though. So many discussions revolve around which children you really like having in your class and which ones you'd happily offload if there were a January transfer window, like in football.

I'd have ended up at Mansfield Town if my teachers had had their way!

Definitely! Although, what's wrong with Mansfield Town FC?

Nothing, they were just the first non-Premiership team I could think of.

I'm always amazed at how different teachers have different views on which type of child they like having in their class. Some like the ones who are impeccably behaved, never step out of line and just get on with it.

Your 'Sensible Sallys'.

Others find them boring. Some don't like children who have a bit of a laugh, have a bit about them and are streetwise. Others can't handle the fact some children have a better sense of humour than they do. You might also prefer some children who remind you of what you were like when you were younger.

My job would be so boring without those kids. You need a bit of craic to get you through the day. I do my best work with kids like that.

I've worked with teachers that were picked on terribly at school and as a result they really struggle with any child that reminds them of those bullies. That's not to say they were hard on these kids and therefore a bad teacher, but it would just be discussed within the safe four walls of the staffroom. It's human nature to have those feelings but it is important to make sure you are always fair with all your pupils. This can be incredibly challenging if the parents of a particular child are out to make your life a living hell. The professionalism of teachers when they have to bite their tongue if they are being accused or blamed should always be respected. It is a hard act to master to make every child in your class feel that you like them. The nicest person in the world would struggle to treat a child who tried their best, listens to everything you say and shows exemplary behaviour equally to one who swears at you every two minutes, refuses to engage and seems to be on a mission to disrupt every lesson you teach. But that is the art of teaching. Actively trying to find common ground between you and your pupils so you can talk to them about things they are interested in will always help them feel valued and unique.

There is, however, a collection of phrases and sayings that every teacher has in their arsenal for whenever you need to control the behaviour in your class. These teacher one-liners are almost passed down from generation to generation. Obviously, some haven't lasted; you'll never hear teachers shouting, 'Right, that's it, I'm getting the strap!' Nowadays, that despicable practice has quite rightly ended. Despite these typical sayings never being formally taught at university, they seem to be learnt by osmosis. The number of trainee teachers who proudly state, 'I'll never be that teacher who spouts the same old lines, I'm different!' Two weeks into the term and they've got the teapot stance down to a tee while uttering, 'It's your own time you're wasting!'

In the majority of cases, these ultimate teacher one-liners will help maintain behaviour in class, although teachers know they won't work with every child. As trained professionals, teachers are well aware which children will respond to these lines and which won't, and they will then have a range of other strategies to use when dealing with children who have more specific learning needs. Unfortunately, due to the severe lack of funding in primary schools, especially when it comes to SEND children, it can often feel that we, as teachers, are failing them. If schools were funded adequately these children would all have their own one-to-one learning support assistant catering to their specific need. In the meantime, teachers have to just try to do the best they can. I am sure there are some parents reading this who feel like their children have been failed by the teacher and school, and, in the rarest of cases, this may be true, but I can guarantee the teachers will have done everything in their power to support and help the children in their care. They just don't have the necessary resources to ensure the child's needs are catered for in a way that both teachers and parents would want.

Back to the one-liners. These are worth sharing as they may well help if you're a parent and need some go-to phrases when your little ones just need a reminder. If you're a teacher reading this, we can have some fun with it; almost treat it as a little drinking game – take a drink every time you've said one of these lines either today, this week or ever (it depends how drunk you want to get).

'Ok, class, we've had a great morning, let's not ruin it.'

'Four legs, two feet. Have I not told you about the child in my class a few years ago who was swinging on his chair, fell back, cracked his head open and DIED.' To this day, I have never actually heard that this story is true, but I will continue to lie if it means children sit on their chair properly.

'It is your own time you're wasting!' This is a classic. Every teacher uses this once they have exhausted all other avenues of trying to get their class to be quiet. I use it often even though I know it's complete bollocks. It isn't their time they're wasting, it is mine. If I don't get through everything I had planned, I am going to have to waste more time re-writing my plans to cover what wasn't completed in the lesson. The children lose no time as I am not the type of teacher who will keep them behind during break. Why? Because that is my break time too and I need it. Some teachers thrive on this sanction; walk into their classroom and there will be a huge list of initials of children who are staying behind to either finish work or reflect on their behaviour choices during the lesson. It has to be something really serious for me to do this, mainly as it backfires later in the day — students need their break and lunch, they need the fresh air, to run around and burn some energy.

'I don't care who started it, I'm finishing it.'

'I'm not angry, I'm just really disappointed.' In other words, I am beyond angry but I can't express the levels of anger as I could potentially end up saying something that would lead me to face disciplinary action. Usually, that phrase is a replacement for 'You have got to be f***ing kidding me, what the f**k are you doing?'

'Would you do that at home?' Always a risky question to ask and often the pupil will say yes, leaving you in an awkward position wondering what to say next.

'Who do you think you're talking to?' 'Who do you think you are?' 'Who do you think you're dealing with?' These aren't examples of teachers having amnesia and short-term memory loss – we are trying to help the kids. We are trying to remind them of the etiquette and dynamics of the situation. In other words, let me remind you that by saying this to me, the teacher, a person in a position of authority, the punishment is going to be more severe, so maybe take a moment and compose yourself.

'I'm sorry, it seems some children in this class are being incredibly rude.' This has to be said with your eyes wandering around the classroom, then glaring at the culprit on the word 'rude'.

'What time do you call this? The bell went five minutes ago and you're just swanning/waltzing/floating in here!'

'Ok, I am going to count down – 5, 4, 3, 2, you really don't want me to get to 1!'

'No, it's fine, I've got all the time in the world. I'll just wait for you to be quiet.' How this works I'll never know. Again, it is a complete lie! I don't have all the time in the world. I need to get stuff done.

'Oh I'm sorry. I'll stop what I was doing as it wasn't very important and leave you to finish off your conversation. Go on, carry on.'

'No, class, that is not a fire detector, it is a camera that I can check to see who was telling the truth!'

'Ok, Jacob, would you like to repeat what I just said? No, why not? I'll tell you why not, because you weren't listening, so turn around and give me your full attention.' This is always a risky one as there is nothing more humiliating than saying this for a child to answer with exactly what you said word for word and you're left awkwardly saying, 'Right, well then, let's carry on.'

'Is it a matter of life or death? No? Right, get on with your work then.'

'Why are we having a mother's meeting by the bin? Just sharpen your pencils and get back to your desks.'

'Seeing as you're choosing not to listen, do you want to come to the front and teach this lesson?' Luckily, I've never had a child answer this with 'Yeah, ok', as this would make for a very awkward moment where I have to backtrack and tell them to just listen.

'I assume with all the talking, we've all finished?'

'I am not your slave!'

'I'm sorry, am I keeping you up?'

'Don't come in here shouting the odds!'

'I hope I've not heard what I think I've just heard, because if I did hear that you would be in serious trouble.' This is always my go-to when I hear a child swearing and I'm only 99 per cent sure. I will give them the benefit of the doubt as it means I don't need to then deal with the severity of a child swearing.

I think the ultimate teacher line has to be the short but sweet, 'Excuse me!?' Teachers have a knack for delivering this in such a way that it becomes a thing of beauty. For example, adding an 'erm' at the start can enhance the sentence. Imagine a scale of 1 to 10 based on how shocked and appalled you are at what you have just seen. Taking the number on the scale, that is how long you are going to drag out the 'erm' in seconds before hitting the 'Excuse me?'. Your eyebrow game needs to be on point, with eyebrows as high as possible to show the shock of what you have just seen. To hit maximum effect with the 'Erm, excuse me?' we need to make sure our chin is pushed as far back into our neck as possible. This makes your turkey as prominent as possible. In fact, your double chin has to be displayed proudly to show your pupils how disgusting their behaviour is by how disgusting you look.

Again, I want to emphasise that teachers will always be cautious around using these go-to behaviour lines as it will always depend on the child/children. But, generally speaking, these are the phrases that if someone was to write a book on teaching, would definitely feature ... oh wait.

Challenging behaviour is part and parcel of being a teacher, and in lots of ways it would be dull and boring without these challenges. Although these can be draining, and in some schools potentially dangerous, violence towards school staff is on the rise and is never acceptable. For the average teacher, these don't tend to be the issues that cause the most frustration. The things that frustrate me the most have been and will always be having to repeat myself or the questions children ask that literally make me question my own sanity, such as:

After delivering my input, which has been on point, clear and precise, with questions to check understanding and clearly explaining what the children are about to do, I'll say, 'Ok, class, so we all know exactly what we need to do, any more questions? No? Ok, fantastic, off we go.'

Ten minutes later ... 'Mr Parkinson, I don't know what we're doing!'

Cue Simon and Garfunkel's classic 'Sound of Silence' as my internal monologue starts: He can't be serious, he's been waiting 10 minutes. What has he been doing in those 10 minutes? I asked them all, clear as day. I said, did anyone have any questions? I waited and no one said anything. Why is it now, 10 minutes later, he's stating he doesn't know what he is doing?! I mean, maybe it's me, maybe I didn't explain it clearly enough. The two hours I spent planning, putting the resources together, simply weren't enough.

'Right, ok. Let me go through this one more time ...'

Welcoming the class back after lunch: 'Welcome back, class, I hope you've had a great lunch. We've got a busy afternoon planned so we need to jump straight in. Let's get the register done so we can start. Yes, what is the matter?'

'Can I go to the toilet, please?'

In my head: Really? I mean she's had a whole hour for lunch! That's 60 minutes or 3,600 seconds. She's got half of her lunch plastered all over her face so she didn't take her time with that! What has she been playing at? I said before lunch to make sure you go to the toilet. She's left me in a no-win situation here; if I say yes, I am opening the floodgates. Every other child will want to go and that's the afternoon wasted. If I say no, I'll either have a doctor's note saying they can go whenever they want or we'll have an accident, and with our budget meaning we've a short supply of paper towels it could spell disaster.

'Ok, off you go, be quick, and next time make sure you go during lunch.'

'Right then, class, I am working with this group at the front. You all have your worksheets in front of you. I want you to try to work through these questions on your own, trying your best to apply everything we've learnt this week.'

'Mr P, I've finished the first question, do I need to do the others as well?'

My internal voice: Are they really asking me that question? Are they REALLY asking me that question? It's not like I spent an hour last night making the worksheet based on the vast range of abilities in class to then waste another hour this morning going back and forth from the computer to printer to get it all ready for them to do one of fifteen questions that I've created? Come on, work with me here, what are you expecting to do? Stare at the other 14 questions. Breathe ...

'If you can have a go at the other questions, that'd be fantastic!'

These are just a fraction of the internal thoughts that go through a teacher's head during a single lesson. No wonder we need the holidays ...

I know a lot more about getting on the kids' level from working with some children that really had issues conforming and sticking to the rules.

But it's amazing how much you appreciate what it was like to be a child when dealing with behavioural issues in school. Many schools nowadays have behaviour policies that will clearly state which crimes require a verbal warning and which call for parents to be involved. Big crimes like swearing, violence and stealing will be at the top of the severity stakes, but minor misdemeanors ...

Miss Demeanor? Was she at the school before I joined?

No, you chimp! Like small violations of the behaviour code: swinging on your chair, constantly chatting, telling fibs ...

... I know plenty of kids who were very liberal with the truth!

Oh, here we go.

In every classroom, in every school, there is a child who often struggles with the truth. A child that is quite partial to telling a few 'porkie pies'. Not hurtful, nor harmful, but plenty that are so ridiculously absurd that you struggle not to laugh in front of the entire class (hopefully).

On one occasion, when the class were asked what they did over the weekend, one child gleefully declared, 'I went to visit my family in Africa!' A wonderful excursion, no doubt, had it not been for the obviously white, British boy whose family are clearly born and bred in North Manchester making the claim. The joys of being a teacher mean that you can't call him out on his lie, so you kind of just have to accept it ... this is until he starts talking about the animals he saw on his 'Safari in Kenya' that were clearly on David Attenborough's programme the night before.

Daily classroom falsehoods turn teachers into expert detectives as they search for the perpetrators of infamous 'white lies'. One break time, I heard the familiar call of 'Sir, Johnny just kicked me!' Upon hearing such a claim, my reading glasses are removed, an 'S' appears on my chest and my cape ripples majestically in the wind. As my superpowers tingle, I gaze over at Johnny (who would normally look like butter wouldn't melt). On this occasion, he looked like a very guilty man. Cue the agonisingly slow teacher walk: arms crossed; eyebrows pointing diagonally towards the top of the nose – the classic angry face ...

'So ... Johnny, did you kick Sam?' A straightforward question, but before he had a chance to reply, you can hit him with, 'Remember, if you're honest now we can sort it. But if you lie, it's going to make things ten times worse.'

(I've always wondered what is 9x worse, or indeed 11x worse?!? Sorry, I digress.)

Johnny had been caught out, cornered and had nowhere left to run. Turning towards his crew, he hoped one of his posse would take the rap on his behalf. Sadly for him, they were already off playing a game of rough-house 'tag' ... you know, the one that's supposed to be banned! Taking a huge breath, Johnny replied, 'No, I never touched him!' Tempted to burst out the classic 'Liar, liar, pants on fire!' I fortunately remembered that I'm a 31-year-old member of staff, so instead I went with my go-to 'disappointed look' (you cannot lose with an 'I'm not angry, I'm just really disappointed' face in these situations). In a very friendly and reassuring way, I responded, 'Ok, I believe you ... BUT ... did you kick him a little bit?'

(The trap is set.)

With a cheeky grin, Johnny falls for it. 'Yeah ... I kicked him a little bit!'

BOOM BABY! Just call me Sherlock Holmes!

Go and stand by the fence, Johnny, I've got a game of illegal tag to put an end to!

Now, little Johnny and David Attenborough Jr were masters of deception, but they weren't a scratch on the King. There are fibbers, falsifiers and 'fake news' merchants ...

... then there's David.

David, AKA 'The Fly', as a result of the number of times he's been caught in a web ... of lies!

Having worked with young David from Year 2 and through the rest of the school, I learnt about his uncanny ability to bend the truth. My favourite example of this came in Year 5. To set the scene, I used to run all the school sports and primarily worked in Year 6, where I also had the responsibility for the school football team. David's passion was definitely for football, so I decided to use this to try to improve his behaviour and hopefully help put him on the right path moving forward. I decided to make a deal with him that if he could steer clear of any silliness, especially avoiding telling any lies for a period, he would be selected to play for the school football team.

After a few good weeks, I said to David, 'Listen, David, I'm going to put you in the school football team' (cue HUGE smile). 'But you've got to promise me, David,' I continued, 'you can't tell any more lies. And IF you can cut out the lying, you will be wearing that brand-new football kit.'

Sounds like a pretty fair deal to me.

Exactly!

Hand on heart, David solemnly vowed:

'I promise, Mr Parkinson, I won't tell any more lies.'

'Well, I believe you, David, I really do,' I assured him (hoping this could possibly be true).

David was literally jumping for joy at the prospect of wearing that new football kit and representing the school. He gave me a massive hug.

Driving home that night, I was feeling like I'd make a real difference to this boy's life and this approach was going to work.

You've inspired him!

I've inspired him. He is never going to lie again ...

... 9.14 the following morning...

... we hear 'KNOCK KNOCK KNOCK!' as I'm covering a Year 6 reading lesson. 'Come in!' I politely called. I genuinely thought it was going to be the classic, 'You've forgotten to save your register' or, 'Eva's mum is here with her packed lunch that she's forgotten for the third day running.' Yet no, it was our Year 5 teacher and our good friend David. I could already tell by David's face that this wasn't good news. I wondered what he had managed to do that required a visit to my room after only 14 minutes (10 of which was hanging coats/bags and taking the register). What on earth could he have done in four minutes?!?

The Year 5 teacher started explaining the reason for David's visit.

'Mr Parkinson, I've been informed that you spoke to David about the possibility of him representing the school football team, as long as he doesn't tell any more lies.'

I replied, looking somewhat concerned, 'Indeed I did, Sir.'

He said, 'Go on then, David, go and tell him what you've been telling everyone this morning.'

A sheepish David slowly walked towards my desk with half the class of Year 6 pupils pricking up their ears; something juicy was about to go down! Just as his teacher was leaving, he turned and said, 'Oh and Sir, just ask David what he's got in his garden.'

'So go on then, David, what do you have in your garden?'

I waited with bated breath; 32 pairs of eyes, fixed on David. Not a head in a book nor pen in hand, waiting for what was supposedly in David's garden. I mean, this could literally be ANYTHING! David looked all around before finally stating:

'A DONKEY!'

A DONKEY?!?!

The class had hands over their mouths. I also had to tweak hairs out of my legs to stop myself breaking down laughing. I just about pulled myself together to reply:

'But you haven't got a donkey, have you, David?'

'NO!' replied David.

I then went on to remind him about our deal and his responsibilities. You can call me soft, but I didn't think this minor fib could quite justify our deal being called off. David and his donkey were definitely skating on thin ice, though!

Skip to 9.45 the following morning. I'm with the same reading class, working faster due to the interruption of yesterday's lesson. A knock at the door again, 'KNOCK, KNOCK, KNOCK'. The door slowly opens and there he is, in all his glory, DAVID!

He looked happier this time around and I spotted a book in his hand. So excited and elated he shouted, 'I've brought good work to show you, Mr Parkinson!' Date, LO (underlined, of course) and a great couple of paragraphs produced in his morning lesson. You could sense the disappointment from the Year 6 children that there wasn't an elephant or a cheetah in his garden this time around, but with pride in my heart and near tears in my eyes, I said, 'Well done, David. I will be round later with your permission letter for the football if this continues.'

As David skipped joyfully through the class to the door, I had to enquire:

'DAVID! What happened to your donkey ...?' After a brief moment of silence as he went through the door, David popped back in and replied with a Cheshire Cat grin:

'IT DIED!!!!!'

Safe to say that was the end of my reading lesson; the class were in fits of laughter!

Well, I'm glad David managed to turn that around.

I have to share the story of the biggest lie one of my pupils ever told – it literally nearly killed him. We're going back a few years when my school was one of the leading schools in Manchester for sport. We'd be competing in as many competitions as possible and were successful in a lot of them. It was a

real team effort, I was PE subject leader and a passionate one at that.

You had to get that one in there.

No, I am saying the staff were really dedicated, I couldn't do it all on my own. I did a lot, don't get me wrong, and I did win the School Sports Practitioner of the Year Award; that I will mention. Anyway, the head would always allow staff to have a free school dinner for every after-school club they did. This had no bearing on my interest in this area, I swear. It was just an added bonus, the fact that I didn't have to pay for a single school dinner in five years.

Towards the end of the year we entered a swimming gala competition. I was keen to take the team but I had already had quite a lot of time out of class because of sporting competitions, so it was offered to another member of staff. An NQT at the time jumped at the chance, and even though they weren't as sporty as some of the others, they certainly were enthusiastic. As we didn't have the opportunity to take the pupils down to the swimming baths and do trials, the teacher asked the children whether any of them swam at a local club. To our surprise a lot of hands went up, including Keane's. Keane was in my class at the time and on first look you wouldn't describe him as athletic. But he was really keen and explained to the teacher he swam at his local club. The teacher had no reason to doubt him and so went about sorting letters for permission.

Keane's letter came back signed by his mum, and the day came when the teachers and students went down to the local swimming baths to take part in the gala. The team were doing brilliantly, coming first overall heading into the last race – the relay. Finish in the top three and the trophy would be ours.

Keane was second in the relay; the first child got off to a great start, ahead by a length. When he touched the wall, Keane was ready for his big moment. In he jumped, a rather unorthodox entrance to the water, the teacher thought, but not to worry, we've still got this in the bag. The only problem was Keane didn't then resurface for a while ... a long while. Long enough for the teacher, referees and lifeguards to become concerned. Eventually, Keane surfaced, arms flailing all over the place. He was literally drowning. In went the lifeguard and Keane was saved. The race and consequent championship were lost, which was a huge disappointment for the rest of the pupils who had worked so hard and done so well. The teacher received an earful from the parent who coached as she couldn't believe we'd let a child who couldn't swim take part in the competition.

The teacher had to explain we could only go off what the children said, and despite saying in the assembly that we only wanted children who were really competent swimmers and ideally swam at a club, Keane had convincingly duped everyone into believing he was capable. Hindsight is a beautiful thing – just the mere look at the lad would have made you doubtful – but the fact he turned up in Bermuda surfing shorts with no goggles or hat, compared with all the other children kitted out like they were Michael Phelps at the Olympics, was another tell-tale sign.

I had received a number of reports from other children in the class that Keane was in fact keen on embellishing the truth. Imagine a 10-year-old Jay from *The Inbetweeners*. I had previously laughed off his claims that he had invented Facebook and his dad was the brains behind the Crazy Frog phenomenon that was popular many moons ago. But the teacher had been given written consent from Keane's mother, so surely she wouldn't have allowed him to put himself in such a dangerous and potentially embarrassing situation? It turned out the parent hadn't bothered to read the letter, which as a parent I can understand to a degree, as letters from school are usually as entertaining as *Mrs Brown's Boys*. She had simply asked the lad, who said it was to go swimming, and she signed it. It was a valuable lesson for the NQT who, despite being disappointed the team didn't bring back the trophy, counted her blessings that the first sporting outing didn't end up in a death.

However, David and Keane look like angels compared with a certain young Adam Parkinson. If the kids at your school knew what you were like when you were their age, they'd never behave again.

What do you mean?

Have any of your kids been sent to the head teacher for a lewd act?

Fair point ...
I think it's fair to say that if you were to ask my teachers, especially during my years at primary school, to describe me, there would be a range of replies. Some liked me; some (many) didn't. Some would actually celebrate if I wasn't in, but the general consensus would be that I was a child that 'DIDN'T ALWAYS MAKE THE RIGHT CHOICES' – a polite way of describing cheeky little sh**s! For anyone that works in education, or even just someone that can remember their school days, I bet you can name five of the little blighters almost instantly. By all accounts, I was probably in most teachers' top fives at my primary school. It's not a badge I wear proudly now, but it helps me in my approach to children that fit that description in my own classes.

As the youngest of three brothers, it's safe to say that I was probably the least academic of the siblings.

He's not lying!

The other two were always willing to take their time to earn the best results, while me, well, I would charge through my work like a bull in a china shop, hoping for some doodling time at the end.

Kids during the 90s were really lucky, in my opinion. We grew up when some of the most fantastic TV shows and toy lines were available. My passion above anything else for a decent period was professional wrestling and, in particular, the WWF/WWE. I was a fully fledged wrestling fanatic, and being one of the bigger lads I was always able to perform the moves on others (despite always being told not to copy them by WWE). This landed me in hot water more than a few times. We were certainly warned about the dangers of 'playing wrestlers' during one assembly by our infamously strict head teacher and man-mountain, Mr Tyrell.

Tyrell was a monster of a man, but facially he looked like the evil food critic from the Disney/Pixar film *Ratatouille*; Anton, Ego!

Ah, Mr Tyrell, or 'Tyrell' as he was affectionately known, was definitely one head teacher you shouldn't get on the wrong side of. If you got sent to his office, you knew you were in for a world of trouble.

Tyrell's assemblies were always pretty scary, but on this specific occasion the whole school knew something serious needed to be talked about. Aiming his wrath at the Year 5 and 6 boys in particular, the big man made it very clear that after a few incidents we were NOT to perform any of the moves we saw on WWE TV wrestling shows like *Raw* and *SmackDown*. During this essential briefing I was clearly paying no attention whatsoever, and this was evident at break time on the very same day. Within seconds of being sent out to play I had jokingly kicked my friend Kristian in the gut and placed him over my shoulder in preparation to deliver a 'Tombstone Piledriver' – which for the uninitiated wrestling fan is a devastating move where the victim is dangerously dropped on their head.

Definitely DON'T try this at home, kids!

As I strutted around the playground with Kristian's upside-down carcass, his head dangling dangerously close to the concrete play-ground, I revved the crowd into a frenzy; this was until I saw a tree in the distance. The tree was surprisingly moving ... walking towards me. As the tree came closer, I saw that the branches were actually human arms and, strangely, the brown trousers weren't bark ... it was Tyrell! He lifted Kristian to safety and took me by the arm. I was tempted to reverse the move and perform a counter-attack on my headteacher, but that would have almost certainly guaranteed I would be in even more trouble and, more importantly, NO chippy tea for me that Friday! One visit to Tyrell's office later and I was defi-nitely aware that wrestling moves were NOT allowed on the play-ground or anywhere in the school for that matter. Did I take heed of this advice? Of course not, but I tried to be a lot more careful not to get caught in the future. Sadly, that wouldn't last ...

Wrestling was my life back then. From superstars like 'Stone Cold' Steve Austin to 'The Rock', the WWE 'Attitude Era' was all about being anti-establishment. No group personified this mantra more than D-Generation X. These were a bunch of outlaws with no respect for the rules. D-Generation X, or DX as they called themselves, stood up to authority and loved to 'stick it to the man', which is all well and good in the world of professional wrestling, or 'sports entertainment' as they like to call it, but in the real world, waving the middle finger to the powers-that-be definitely had consequences. We copied their swagger, their moves, their catchphrases and, unfortunately, their hand gestures. One of these gestures was a rude one ... one I would find out the hard way was not safe for school.

The offending hand gesture was affectionately known at the time as a 'crotch-chop', where the person performing the move would form an X-shape on their groin, insinuating where the opponent should direct their attention (yes, I was only 11 at the time but all the cool kids were doing it and so were my heroes on TV). Not only did the person performing the offensive gesture make an 'X' above their private parts, but they completed the move by calling out one of DX's most famous catchphrases of 'SUCK IT'! Yes, back in the late 90s it was perfectly normal for young lads to motion towards their reproductive organs and instruct another human to 'SUCK IT!'

1 a) Lift arms above head in a 'Y' formation.
  b) Prepare to bring the hands down just above the pelvis in an 'X' shape.

2 a) Stick your tongue out.
  b) Yell 'SUCK IT!'

Being in Year 6, I clearly didn't understand it. I just thought it was a lighter version of swearing; simply my way of showing people in positions of authority that I was a rebel and not to be messed with. One infamous incident happened when I was outside my class and Mr Ellis knocked on my classroom door, then stood there talking to my teacher, Mrs Callaghan. She was definitely not one of my biggest fans, and as I looked through the window from my table outside I caught the eyes of my trusty compadres inside the class. I could see on their faces that they were wondering what the big man (me) was going to do next. Time to cement my legendary status, methinks. I stood behind Mr Ellis, put my hands in the air, then slammed them down towards my 'special place' in an 'X' formation with my tongue out. Take that, Ellis! The joke absolutely slayed my crew inside the class, but unfortunately the laughter from inside the room caused Mrs Callaghan to peek around Mr Ellis and see me loving life, mid-DX salute, with my tongue out. 'Get to Mr Tyrell's office now, Parkinson!' yelled Mrs Callaghan. BUSTED!

Nearly at Tyrell's office, I approached the door, but it felt like I was walking in treacle. A more confident version of me would normally be singing the Tyrell song that the boys and I made up – 'Mr Tyrell is a squirrel and he has no nuts.' Today was definitely not the day for that sort of tomfoolery – this was serious. I tried to distract myself, but all I could think of was being so upset that I wouldn't be getting a Dr Pepper after school; I knew my dreams of a KFC or a McDonald's were dashed, too. I was almost certainly in for the big one!! The school secretary indicated that Tyrell was ready to see me, so I knocked quietly on the big brown door. 'COME IN!' he yelled, and I sheepishly made my way in to face the music. I was greeted by a scowling Tyrell and my old enemy ... that damn blue chair!

'Well, what are you here for, Parkinson?' asked Tyrell.

Bottom lip quivering, I replied, 'Er, Mrs Callaghan sent me here for doing something rude behind Mr Ellis.'

'Well, go on then, Parkinson, show me what you did,' Tyrell requested.

Uh-oh!

I'm not going to lie; this was the stuff of nightmares. I lifted my hands with great trepidation before slamming them (less enthusiastically than before) towards my crotch.

'Well, what does that mean?' asked Tyrell.

Now in hindsight, any normal child would say: 'It just means "D-Generation X", Sir.' Which Tyrell wouldn't have had a clue about and I could have just got away with a minor telling-off. But with me being me, thinking that honesty is the best policy and with tears in my eyes, I told Mr Tyrell to (ahem):

'SUCK IT!'

Tyrell lost it. His face went bright red and I thought he was going to throw that blue chair at me. He grabbed his phone and rang my mum (was my home number on speed-dial?) to tell her that I was going to be in isolation for the rest of the day. When I saw the lads the next day, they all asked me about what went down in Tyrell's office.

Rather than recall the fact that I nearly soiled myself, I had to save face. I carefully looked around to check that neither my head teacher nor any of his minions were in earshot. The coast was clear, so I turned into 'Billy Big B****cks' and declared: 'Yeah, lads, not only did I give Ellis the DX crotch-chop, but I told Tyrell to "SUCK IT" as well.' In my own mind and theirs, legendary status was cemented.

The difference in opinion about what constitutes an essential purchase between adult me and six-year-old me is vast. The gap created could be filled by collecting up every Happy Meal toy in history and placing it in that gap. Amazingly, there would still be plenty of space left over. That's how HUGE the gap is!

We used to drive Mum and Dad up the wall wanting stuff from the shop!

The ridiculous change of tune can be illustrated using the classic staple of any childhood ... the Kinder Egg.

Love them!

A younger version of me would look upon the beautiful red-and-white, foil-wrapped object of destiny, glistening under the supermarket lights, tempting my senses with not only an edible treat that would tantalise my taste buds but also provide much-desired entertainment. I not only wanted it, I needed it! That was then, obviously. Now I'm a parent, they are just random crap toys surrounded by an amount of chocolate that would struggle to sustain a gnat.

Kids go crazy for the most random things; the must-have items that determine whether you are the cool kid on the playground or not. Stuff that our dad, Big Mike, would deem 'A bloody waste of money!'

I mean, he was completely right. I haven't played with my laser pen keyring in years!

That's because Mum donated it to the school jumble sale.

I wondered where it went. Hold on ... I think I bought it back for a quid. Damn you, mother!

As kids that grew up (mostly) in the 90s, we were really lucky to experience all the amazing stuff at the tail end of the 80s and into the technological advances of the 00s as well.

So true! You know, when I look back at the classroom crazes from my day (wow, I really am getting old) compared with the craziness of today's popular fads, I'm just happy that I lived through a simpler time when my success wasn't determined by likes on a screen but by crowds in a playground. There are so many crazes that I was lucky enough to experience, and what's brilliant about them is that they keep repeating themselves. They keep coming around again. What's the word, Lee?

Cyclical?

Exactly, cyclical! Stuff like sticker collections were such a huge part of so many children's glory years. Stickers – whether it was football, wrestling, cartoons, movies or TV – there was usually a Panini sticker book for whatever your heart desired. Now the only panini I hear of is one filled with cheese and Cajun chicken ... Mmmm ...

Stop drooling and continue with the stickers, Adam!

Sorry! With stickers, I remember standing there with a huge wad ...

This isn't going to be filth, is it, Adam?

... of spares or what we'd call 'swaps'. Scouting through people's piles of swaps repeating the legendary 'Got, got, got, got' ... until the moment arrived ... 'NEED!!!' At this point, it depends on the desire of the person as to whether they wish to offer you a deal or not. You'd start off small, trying to catch yourself a David Dickinson Bobby-Dazzler of a bargain, until you worked your way to the deal you wanted. Sometimes 10–20 stickers could be coughed up in a swap for one sticker - more than likely a shiny! If you had a holo-gram Bushwhackers logo from the 1993 vintage WWF/WWE collec-tion, that would set you back a shedload. The more streetwise the kid, the better the deals they could make. Also, exploiting the naivety of a younger sibling was all part of the game.

'What do you mean you swapped an ultra-rare Ronaldo for only three Emile Heskeys and a Shaun Wright-Phillips!?! You FOOL!!'

There was always one kid that either had significantly more disposable income than the rest of us or he'd clearly been stealing from his parents. That kid would brandish his stack of stickers like an absolute boss while children sucked up to him, hoping to get first dibs on his duplicate David Beckham. Similar to the football stickers, Pokémon cards were a huge hit by the late 90s, early 2000s, and let's be honest, way beyond. Clever marketing meant that children really believed the slogan that they literally had to '... catch them all!' Whether their parents' income could sustain coughing up at least £10 a week on packs of cards was another thing altogether. Clearly, brightly coloured hybrid fire-salamanders that could only say their own names were big business.

Plenty of crazes go out of fashion, but they soon rear their heads again a few years later, and one of the biggest comeback kids of them all is clearly the humble yo-yo! Even our dad remembers having them at school. Back when health and safety was encouraged but not particularly enforced, yo-yo enthusiasts could boast such tricks as Walk the Dog, The Elevator, Rock the Cradle and the ever-dangerous Round the World (where you swing the yo-yo like a madman and it would definitely strike anything inside a 1-metre radius). The thought of children busting out a 'Round the World' in a packed playground would fill any staff member with dread nowadays.

While crazes can be cyclical (see, Lee? I used that word again), crazes can also be seasonal. The absolute daddy of seasonal crazes must be the humble game of conkers! According to our dad, these were better than a yo-yo; mostly because they didn't cost a penny.

Back when conker battles were commonplace in schools, they could be epic! Dad was right, and all you needed was a conker, screw-driver and shoelace. This could provide you with hours of fun, starting with the task of finding a strong, thick, butch conker to compete in the games at school. The talk of the school would be about the person who put their conker in a bowl of vinegar all night to really strengthen their challenge. There was a lot of posturing about who had the alpha-conker! I also remember a boy in my class coated their conker with 10 fresh layers of Tipp-Ex – the lengths children used to go to to become the conker champion. It's been easily 20 years since I have seen a competitive conker game and I'm not going to lie, I still think there is a place for it – maybe not on school grounds, as there could be some serious parental complaints. The potential for me causing great harm has increased significantly, as well as a much greater chance of a child nursing some bruised knuckles for not paying attention.

Then there were Pogs!

Pogs, yes ... remember what they did? No, neither can I, but I'm sure they were popular for a reason.

I googled it and they were based on the American game of 'milk caps'.

What's that?

Still no idea!

Well, Pogs made an appearance in the 90s and they were basically little discs with pictures of cool characters of the time that you'd smash with a bigger, more dense one. If my memory serves me correctly there was another version called 'Tazos', but these also had little grooves so you could link them together. I remember some of them were available in packets of crisps. There's something you rarely see in the present day, free stuff in crisp packets. It used to be one of the most exciting things about dinner time, that and trying to find Monopoly money in a bag of Walkers crisps.

Didn't they come in little blue packets?

Yeah, but once I found one and forgot I was eating some 'Salt & Shake' crisps. No winning prize in my blue sachet ... only sodium chloride. At least it improved the flavour of my crisps.

One thing you wouldn't want to find in your crisps was an alien birth pod. You know, the little plastic eggs filled with slime and a mini baby alien made of rubber. These slimy alien eggs were rumoured to give birth. My classmates tried to keep theirs warm, putting them next to another alien as they bathed in their own slime. Sadly, these theories were defeated with science and facts and common sense. Me, I just used to launch them so they would stick on things. All I know is, they were one of the only affordable things you could blow your school trip money on when you used to visit the local museum's gift shop. You could buy either an alien birth pod, a keyring of a cannon/tank or a wooden bow and arrow that would almost instantly be confiscated when you tried to hit the bus windows with the sucker thingy.

But now we move on to look at more recent crazes. Personally, it may be an age thing or it may be the fact that I'm on the other side of the teaching curtain now. I'm no longer in the middle of the action as a competitor, I'm now (supposedly) the peacekeeper and the role model. But with all that being said, I'm hardly impressed with the current crop of classroom trends. The new crazes don't make me particularly wish I were a 10-year-old again.

The first big new classroom craze that came into circulation when I began working in schools was ... loom bands. If you don't remember these, they are very small, colourful, elastic bands (almost identical to those rubber elastics that dentists put in braces to make them stand out just that little bit more). When you used some wizardry or a plastic board, I suppose you could make quite impressive bracelets alongside other designs. Perhaps it's my lack of patience or ability to sit still, but I much prefer the noisier bracelets that took our school days by storm: the old slap bracelets! So loud and so annoying, but so much fun (until you slapped it too hard that it broke slightly and you never quite got the crisp snap again). That wouldn't stop you attempting to slap it on the back of your mate's neck ... which would also result in a teacher confiscating it.

I'm starting to notice a theme here, Adam.

Erm ... anyway. Loom bands! They are still loved at our breakfast club so they must be here to stay. They turned your most unsuspecting girls and boys into master designers, who would show off amazing, heartfelt, colourful and most importantly, wearable masterpieces. Personally, back in the day, I used to wear the odd loom band on a night out, as in my single days, my go-to chat-up line was that I was a primary school teacher. So when this amazing rainbow-coloured bracelet caught the eye of a pretty lady, I would say, 'Love this bracelet? This is a loom band one of my school children made me because they think I'm such a great teacher!' In truth, I may have confiscated that certain loom band, but the chat-up line worked 80 per cent of the time ... all the time.

Loom bands had mixed reviews from school staff. Cleaners absolutely hated them. At the end of a school day there would be tiny bands all over the classroom, and these were not Henry Hoover's friend! Alongside the mess they made, children quickly cottoned on to the fact that, like elastic bands, if you tactically put the bands on your fingers, they were terrific firing material; you were able to flick them from one side of the class to another. I still have a rainbow loom band bracelet tucked away, though, just in case things go south with my wife and I need to bring back my classic night-out material. Perhaps loom bands weren't too bad; just flipping annoying!

Speaking of 'flipping' and 'annoying' ... BOTTLE FLIPPING! Actual bottle flipping became such a huge hit with children across the world as a result of YouTube. The basic challenge involves throwing a plastic bottle, typically half-full, or half-empty (whichever you prefer) of liquid into the air so that it rotates, in an attempt to land it upright on its base. Suddenly, every child had an old plastic bottle, and whenever they had an opportunity they would be flipping it and trying to land it.

Early doors, I wasn't too fussed about this new craze. No one was getting hurt; playtimes had gone from a tense football game to children taking it in turns throwing their bottles in the air. The problem came when children became unable to stop the flipping and became 'flipping addicts'! We're talking about before school, after school, in class, sitting down at dinner and even during tests! Anywhere a child had a bottle, it would flip. To add to the increasing level of annoyance, most of the children were not very good at it. The sound of constant bottles dropping was a headache you just didn't need, but the misery was compounded when children wouldn't screw their bottle lids on properly, so the noise of bottles falling was swiftly joined by splashing, screaming and work ruined!

Another item that was up there on the 'brilliant for the first few minutes then bloody annoying' stakes – FIDGET SPINNERS; two words that will strike fear into any adult that faced this hugely popular craze. If a toy has a name with the first word 'fidget', it's more than likely going to annoy the living hell out of you. Growing up, I was constantly asked to stop fidgeting, but now a popular toy that spins on its axis was encouraging children everywhere to fidget. They were highlighted as a good toy for children with ADHD, obviously to help with focus and allow them to stay calm, but most children had one. I was properly diagnosed with attention-deficit issues as a child so I definitely feel qualified to comment.

Either way, plenty of kids would feign neurological issues to do with concentration, purely to justify having a light-up, glitter-covered Pikachu (or possibly Minions) bad-boy with them at school! Funnily enough, the rise in the presence of fidget spinners in class coincided with their increased confiscation during assemblies. By the end of some days, a teacher's drawers would have two Pritt Stick lids, three non-working biros and sixteen fidget spinners! I will always remember when fidget spinners became extinct in a school I once worked at. One day, a fairly street-wise child managed to conceal his spinner under the desk with minimum fuss. Due to the majority of the class already having had theirs sent to their teacher's drawer version of Alcatraz, it didn't take long for the teacher I worked with to sense the lad in question still had his fidget spinner. Proud that their fidget-spinner radar was still in working order, the teacher proceeded to ask nicely for the child to walk to her desk and place the item onto the table. As he walked up, he looked very sheepish and nervous.

I initially thought my arms-folded, 6-ft-1, 18-stone figure of anger and disappointment (purely for effect) was causing the child to gulp as he slowly made his way to the front of the class. It wasn't. As he placed the toy on the desk, our annoyed teacher faces turned to pure shock when we realised that the fidget spinner was in fact ... BLADED! It was a massive relief we managed to acquire the weapon before he did some serious damage to himself or one of his classmates. Thoughts went through my head of me politely asking him to finish his yoghurt at lunchtime then being threatened with a modified ninja star! The only silver lining happened as I was taking down a class display and realised that the bladed fidget spinner was a cracking staple remover!

Going from hand-held crazes (and occasional violent weapons) that took the world by storm, to now more physical ones, we move on to the infamous **DAB.** The 'dab', and no it doesn't come with a dip, like the delicious classic sherbet confectionery of 'Barratt's Dip Dab'. (Yes, I know what you're thinking, I thought it was a Dib Dab too. Google it if you need to and you'll be even more confused when the Double Dip pops up!) While we're on the Dip Dab debate, they were so hard to continue to lick and dip, I would just eat my lolly and then drink my sherbet!

Adam, concentrate! You've nearly made it to the end of the chapter without mentioning food too many times.

Apologies, I digress. This kind of dab is merely a movement when a person drops their head into the bent crook in their arm while their other arm is out straight. Much like the way everyone now sneezes in schools since COVID! Dabbing was quick, it was popular and it was very annoying. As a member of school staff, children would be dabbing their way through the day, in the playground, on school trips, during tests. Shakira said it best: 'Whenever, Wherever', they would be dabbing. It was only a matter of time before dabbing was banned from the building.

While dabbing is not fully in the rearview mirror yet (along with whipping and indeed nay-naying), it has been superseded by something that was usually recommended by dentists to remove plaque and food build-up. Yes, it's that dance that every single child did at every single school disco or family party. It's **THE FLOSS!**

A repetitive dance move where your arms swing from the front to the back of your body. How can something so innocent be so painfully infuriating?! I think what annoyed me the most about the floss is that only a rare number of children could actually perform it correctly. I sound like an old, grumpy man and that's because I am, but also when you have a full class and even when some children were answering their name on the afternoon register, 'Good afternoon, Christopher,' instead of answering 'Good afternoon, Sir,' Christopher would stand up and floss while saying 'HERE!' I hit him (not literally) with the comeback of all comebacks: 'Instead of doing that silly floss, why don't you get some actual floss because you've got half the school pizza left in your teeth?!'

School wouldn't be the same without crazes. Whether dance moves, collectibles, horse-chestnut seeds or random dangerous weapons that the child clearly bought on holiday in Tenerife, they are some of the things that make school life so interesting. As a father myself now, I'll be in amusement park gift shops and glad I have children, purely so I can justify buying a slap-band, alien birth pod and another rainbow eraser to add to my collection!

Assemblies, or collective worship, are when the whole school gathers in the hall to listen to a visitor or a member of the SLT sharing insights into the values of the school, Bible bash (church schools), singing or just winging it.

Singing assemblies are the best!

Yes, I agree. Primary school life, no, actually, life peaks when you're in Year 6, sitting on the benches at the back looking down on the peasants before you as the whole school sings in perfect harmony to an absolute banger of a hymn or song.

Name your top ten assembly songs!

Ok, here we go. I have chosen these based on my youth at a Catholic school and my teaching career in a non-religious school.

10 'Here I am, Lord'

This hits deep. For me, I would have this higher. I know it isn't the most upbeat tune, but on a day when you've had wet play and you've worked your socks off to be team point champion that week and you are pipped to the post by Suzie, sitting in assembly, legs crossed with your head in your hands looking glum and then this tune comes on – it hits you on a different level.

9 'School rule song'

This is an absolute banger. If you haven't heard of this one just give it a listen on YouTube. It is one of those songs that starts slow but by the end is like a drum 'n' bass track. It also teaches the children some rules and expectations as they are belting out the lyrics.

8 'Life is a wonderful thing'

Again, a more recent track but a lovely positive one that makes you appreciate everything in life. This was always a hit on a Monday morning, although I think the music subject leader chose this one more for the teachers. They probably looked out at the staff looking tired, fed up and dreading another week ahead and so played this track to give them all a lift.

7 'Follow me, follow me, leave your homes and family'

If you still to this day don't know the lyrics of this by heart, can you even say you went to a church school back in the day? I mean, even as you read that line, you were singing it in your head to the tune of this straight-up anthem. It still gets a look-in at more adult events, such as weddings, and I've even heard it at a funeral too.

6 'Oil in my lamp'

To the king of kings, sing hosanna! Do you want some mash with this banger?

I particularly loved this track for the range on the 'king of kings' line. The high-low-high combo made you feel like you were Darius Danesh on *Popstars*.

That is one niche nostalgic reference.

5 'Lord of the Dance'
This was possibly the most memorable school hymn, purely for the fact it still gets banged out at most weddings we go to.

4 'Wake up, shake up'
No other song gets you pumped to attack a new day like 'Wake up, shake up'. A primary school anthem. I don't need to say any more.

3 'Cauliflower fluffy'
This is the staple of the harvest festival assembly. Don't even think of your harvest assembly being a success if this isn't the encore performance. Has the whole hall swaying, lighters in the air (or phone lights for health and safety), and never fails to hit the spot.

2 'Shine on me'
Just google this. Play it as you read this. There you are, it's summer term. You've just come in from a game of rounders on the field and now will finish the day with an assembly. You get to leave your jumpers in the class as the hall is warm due the mini heatwave we've had this week. At the end of assembly, the head announces we will finish with a song. Then the first few chords

of 'Shine on me' hit. You look left and give the nod, you look right to your BFF of that day and do a mini high-five. You know what's coming, so does everyone else. That is the beauty of singing assemblies. It's like you're at your own mini concert, just vibing. The fact you didn't finish your maths from this morning is nothing but a distant memory. The idea that you are only weeks away from leaving school and will never have this opportunity to savour the essence of a primary school singing assembly isn't even registering as you feel the chorus coming closer and closer. Then the moment hits, 'SHINE, JESUS, SHINE,' the whole hall erupts. This is the closest you'll get to a festival for the next decade. So savour it, take it in and let the good times roll.

1 'Spring chicken'
Certified banger. To finish off your Easter bonnet parade assembly there is no better anthem than this. The slow build-up to the chorus is yet to be replicated in any song I've ever heard. The hall would turn into a full-on mosh pit if children had free rein during this song.

The phrase 'packed like sardines' has never been more fitting than to describe an assembly, but for teachers it can be a welcome break from the classroom and can usually provide some sort of entertainment that will be discussed, re-enacted and laughed about in the staffroom. Or even better, when the SLT member leading the assembly says that staff don't need to stay. I used to think this was a very brave task to undertake, having to hold the fort down singlehandedly, but I have since learnt that it was the best option if you were completely winging the assembly. And let's face it, most heads and deputies are so busy with other things, the assembly will be the last thing on their minds.

Assemblies usually happen at the start or end of the day. A word of advice for any teachers looking at when would be best to schedule an assembly. Be wary of end of a school day assembly for the following reasons:

1. The stench. When it comes to smells, nothing will turn your stomach more than a room packed with 15 children per square metre. This is after a full day of lessons in classrooms that will still have the radiators on even though it's June, with morning and lunch breaks that consist of children running non-stop for an hour. To top it off, half the pupils will have school lunches smeared over faces and jumpers and the hall has little to no ventilation.

2. Attention. The likelihood of children's attention span making it past 9.30am is near on impossible, so by 2.30–3pm you're more likely to have the government paying attention to teachers than a room full of tired, fed-up kids listening to a story involving animals trying to convey a message about how to be nice to each other.

3. The content. Let's be fair, most teachers at half-two are already moving their focus to everything they will need to do after school, so the last part of the day is survival mode. This is the same for assemblies. I guarantee, 95 per cent of afternoon assemblies are winged, and rightly so – the kids aren't listening, so don't worry.

The worst part of assembly for most teachers is the process of getting to the hall. There will always be the teacher who will have structured their day to the second and so will have timed the process of tidying away, lining up, walking down the corridor and entering the hall. Others, like me, have a more inconsistent approach. I often think that my frantic approach is due to my ever-growing passion and immersion in the teaching that leaves my time management to be questioned. In all reality, it'll be because I have either not read the staffroom whiteboard, which clearly states in a faint whiteboard pen, 'Assembly 2.30pm', or I did see the staffroom noticeboard and completely forgot about it.

Either way, with only one minute before the assembly is scheduled to start, I have realised that we should be sitting in the hall by now. So I have to get the attention of the class. I just need them to clear their desks, put their books in their trays and line up outside.

This is where the clap is the tried and trusted method of gaining attention. I love technology and the ways in which it can enhance and transform so much in the classroom, but the clap is the one thing technology hasn't been able to improve. And by the clap, I mean physically clapping my hands to a quick rhythm to which the children instantly stop what they are doing and repeat the musical pattern back to me, not the other type, you dirty-minded so and so. For a while in my school the clap was discouraged for a different method, which I believe was known as '5' and played out like this. The teacher would hold their hand in the air. Not saying a word and using all the telepathic powers within this would make all the children stop what they were doing and hold their hands up until everyone in the class looks like they want to answer a question no one has asked.

The class line of '1 ... 2 ... 3 ... EYES ON ME' has been a mainstay in many classrooms, but with the ever-growing presence of social media and the need to hunt likes and followers, teachers have looked at remixing this to be more quirky, self-indulgent and downright cringey.

Here are a few examples I have seen or heard in primary classrooms:

- Scooby Dooby Doo ... Where Are You?
- Hocus pocus ... Time to focus! One usually introduced in the build-up to Halloween.
- Holy moly ... Guacamole! This has become more popular as avocados seem to infiltrate every aspect of our lives.
- To infinity ... And beyond!
- Macaroni and cheese ... Everybody freeze! (Funny how many of these are food-related.)
- Stop ... Collaborate and listen! (see also ... Hammer Time!)
- Are you focused? ... Yes, I am!

Ultimately, this voice call-back isn't the best as pupils can quite easily chant back while not giving you any attention. It ends up looking like I am an old-school garage MC trying to hype the crowd, who were expecting a Motown classic concert.

Here is how this rushed yet effective transition from class to hall goes in my head:

I clap, every member of the class instantly stops what they are doing and claps back, with 30 eyes staring, 60 ears listening.

'Ok, class, sensibly, table by table, please put your belongings in your trays and quietly line up outside ready to walk to the hall.'

Like a scene from *The Sound of Music*, each table, almost like it has been choreographed, puts books, stationery and worksheets away before sliding into the line like the hoedown of your finest line-dancing recital.

Without saying a word, the class then follows me down the corridor. We reach the hall, where pupils fill in the gap left by the other classes awaiting our arrival. The assembly begins and I remember what an incredible classroom practitioner I am.

In reality:

The clap happens, once, twice and three times, four ... 'BE
    QUIET!!!' is bellowed.

'Ok, class, we're late for assembly, I need everyone to put
everything away in their trays.'

Another mistake – in my haste, I have now sent off 30 children to put things away in their trays, which has resulted in a
pile-up of epic proportions. My hands reach my forehead as I
watch my class turn into the worst example of a cheerleading
squad attempting to create a pyramid as they desperately try to
reach their trays. I step in, commanding traffic with my hi-vis
jacket on. My failed attempts at co-ordinating my class can only
be salvaged by the line as I bellow, 'Just quickly line up outside,
and make sure you're not next to someone you will be silly with.'

'Quietly, line up in one line, just one. Why have we got more
than one line?'

Finally, the class is almost in one straight line. Now I have to
survey the dynamics of this line. Despite my previous statement
of not being next to someone you will be silly with, every child
has managed to stand next to a child that they most definitely
will be silly with. I couldn't have solved this mind-boggling
line-up brainteaser myself but somehow they've managed it and
now I need to unpick it. Frantic and impatient, I swap children
into an order that will hopefully mean my class doesn't cause a
scene in the hall. Moments later, we are ready to walk. Once
more I stress the importance of silence as we walk, until I have
to accept that it is impossible for my pupils to walk without
moving their mouths. I stop them, telling them that it shouldn't
be hard to walk without moving their mouths, even demonstrat-
ing how easy it is by doing it myself. I then start the backwards
walk where I walk towards the hall but facing my class so I can

shush, point and remind pupils to not talk as we shuffle along, hoping to make it in time.

Eventually we reach the hall, we enter, each year group is sitting in ascending order with Year 6 at the back. Have my colleagues remembered to leave a space for my class? No. I now have to work out where we should be and then ask the next year group to shuffle back but make sure they keep in their lines. No one offers to help, and my colleagues look on knowing that if I was more organised this wouldn't have been a problem. I often wonder whether they have a separate staff meeting to discuss how to stitch me up. My class sits down and I inevitably play a game of human chess, strategically rearranging them to make sure no one is sitting next to another child that would lead to a scene resembling UFC 211 because, despite our discussions about staying away from those who distract you, they have managed to find each other as we walk down the hall.

I then search for a chair to sit on, but as I am late I resign myself to the wooden bench. The bench that when I was nine years old seemed the ultimate achievement of primary school life. I would often sit in assembly on the wooden floor like a peasant, peering back at the Year 6s, dreaming of the day when I would be able to sit on the golden benches observing my kingdom as king of the school. Now, as a fully grown adult, I look like the naughty teacher hoping my knees can take the pressure when I have to stand up again.

I am just happy we got there on time; it could have been worse – I could have been that late the head has sent a runner! This is the child whose hand is raised the highest and once chosen, stands up in assembly, chest out, taking in all of the plaudits and looks of disappointment from those not worthy of being chosen. They then set off on their mission to walk down the corridor to inform said teacher that there's an assembly. The quickest turnaround and the class appear in the hall, with the teacher, red-faced, apologising profusely before parting the children like Moses and the Red Sea to create space for their class to sit.

The main challenge once the assembly starts is trying to stay awake. You wouldn't believe how quickly the afternoon lull can hit you like a freight train, so your focus now is to stay awake as every blink seems to get longer and longer. That is unless you are the teacher who takes the very important role of being the shusher. You eagerly spy the sea of children sitting on the wooden floor, waiting, hoping for one of them to twitch, move, speak, laugh, giggle or breathe so you can pull them out of the line and make them sit by you like Leia in Jabba's palace (without the costume, obviously.)

Every teacher has another teacher they telepathically talk with during assemblies. When things happen – and oh, do they happen – you need that colleague, someone you can give the eyes to; the 'did you just see that!' eyes or the 'did that child really just say that' eyes.

Every teacher has a role to play when it comes to the singing assembly. Here's a rundown of characters you will see:

1 The one who thinks they're performing their own concert.

Yes, this teacher, usually the music subject leader, the one leading the assembly, is front and centre and making the most of their moment in the limelight. They are pulling out all of the stops, making over-exaggerated claps, grabbing the air, maybe even starting sitting down, only to stand when the chorus hits like they're in Westlife. All of these are acceptable unless they go that one step further and wear a wireless microphone around their ears like Britney Spears. These are the same people who would take a straw on a night out and wear it behind the ears to replicate said microphone.

2 The one who has no idea of the words.

Yes, despite being at the school for years and having sat through the same assembly with the same songs hundreds of times, they have never once looked at the lyrics on the overhead projector, probably as they forgot to bring their glasses to the assembly, so they bumble through the songs, randomly guessing the words and barely grasping the tune.

3 The one who buzzes from doing the actions.

Yes, even for the songs that have no actions, they make it up. They are all arms and legs. These are the sort of teachers that tend to actually sit on the floor with the children, too. You'd see these teachers on a night out nailing the Macarena, Saturday Night and Cha Cha Slide.

4 The out of tune one.

That's me, I can't lie. Fair play to those teachers who know it as well but still go for it. They get involved, drowning out everyone else with their dulcet tones. It takes a brave teacher to join in. As in any singing assembly, you will either see a couple of children giggling hysterically or covering their ears from the horror of being sat next to the teacher.

5 The mime artist

This was what I became after feeling utterly embarrassed when pupils would giggle hysterically and look at me like I was rubbing cutlery on a plate. I became a master at the art of mime; I would know all the lyrics, all the moves, and to watch me from afar you could easily mistake me for the music subject leader. It is an art form tried by many and mastered by few.

6 The CBA one

There will always be a teacher who simply cannot be arsed with the assembly. They do not engage at all, they see no point in this waste of time when there are objectives in the curriculum to master. You can normally see these teachers carrying out the following duties: rolling their eyes, huffing and puffing, and checking the time every 30 seconds.

7 The behaviour monitor

One member of staff will take it upon themselves to monitor the behaviour of the children as the singing takes place. They may well struggle to hit any sort of note themselves but they make themselves useful by looking daggers at any children who are messing around or not singing. The best is always when they spot a culprit; they make the eyes and then point. The child has been caught red-handed. Their head drops as they know what's coming: the walk of shame. They have to stand up in front of everyone and walk down the row to sit down right next to the teacher in question.

No assembly would be an assembly without the school office secretary popping in to grab someone who needs to be picked up for an appointment. If the teacher is well organised (never me) they will have thought ahead and have said child sat at the side for an easy exit. Otherwise a game of Where's Wally ensues with the staff and everyone tries to get involved. 'Who needs to go?' they will mouth from the other side of the hall, and then a competition to locate the child happens.

The main event for most primary schools is the celebration/ good work assemblies, where pupils receive awards for doing great work in class. For example, many schools will award children with pen licences; that's right, a licence so the child can use a pen instead of a pencil. Children go mad for it, unless like me your handwriting is and always has been abysmal. If only I got my pen licence, I would have probably grown up to be able to write my own book. Oh wait …

My assemblies when I was at school were always a drag, involving some sort of message about doing the right thing and looking out for each other; basically someone droning on until my bum went numb! It was absolute doldrums usually until the dreaded figure of Mr Tyrell made his appearance to deliver his end of assembly announcements. If your name was read out at the end of assembly, it meant you had to stay behind and you were definitely in for a world of trouble.

One time, when I was in Year 3, I found my name was on Mr Tyrell's list of doom (admittedly, not for the first time), when I heard:

'Adam Parkinson, you need to stay behind!'

My stomach felt like I'd taken a Mike Tyson gut-punch. What had I done?

I mean, usually I would have known if a Tyrell roasting was on the cards, especially if I'd had a bad week up to that point. In my mind I'd had a pretty decent week so far.

I'll always remember the feeling: the classes lining up and leaving, yet I was standing there on my own, imagining all the eyes burning into the back of my head. I heard the older children tutting, adding to the pressure cooker. The hall was empty and Tyrell slowly walked towards me. He went straight for me:

'What the hell do you think you are doing graffitiing in the back of your book?!'

Confusion overwhelmed me, yet my eyes filled with tears, lips quivering. I was a mess, crying and trying to protest my innocence with Tyrell full flow. His rant seemed to last forever ... probably because he had impressive air flow due to his marathon running (he only came 3,156th, though). Continuing to launch at me, with saliva flying everywhere, it was pretty obvious he'd had muesli for breakfast.

I was full on screaming/crying at this point, wiping tears and crushed hazelnuts from my cheeks until another teacher arrived and whispered in Tyrell's ear.

'Erm... Mr Tyrell...That isn't the Parkinson child that graffitied his book...'

Tyrell immediately stopped the rollicking and looked at his colleague with a raised eyebrow.

'You've got Adam, but it was Ryan Parkinson you needed.'

Tyrell looked at me as I stood there (a quivering wreck), gave a half-arsed apology and then told me to pop back to class before I missed the spelling test. Nice one, Tyrell, I've got to change my underpants after that!

My saving grace was knowing that my goody-two-shoes brother in Year 5 was about to feel the wrath of Captain Alpen! Ryan was in for a tongue lashing from the Tyrell machine. Let's see how he likes them apples! I couldn't wait to see him after he'd had his turn. The bell rang at 3 o'clock and as we're making our way out, I excitedly ran over to Ryan ... but his face seemed fresh. Clearly no tears had graced his cheeks; in fact, he looked annoyingly relaxed.

'Ryan, did Tyrell speak to you about the graffiti?' He looked at me and smiled. 'Yeah, just told me not to do it again,' Ryan replied in a very nonchalant fashion. The spawny get!

Tyrell had clearly used up his one and only humdinger with me, and he had no energy left for the true culprit.

That one was a classic. I remember your face when you got home.

One of my favourite assemblies has to be the case of the missing identity.

Ah, this one is quality!

Every so often, a child or family decides to move schools. Sometimes the family are relocating due to the parents' job, and sometimes because the parents are not happy with the current school. If you were leaving because your mum fell out with the Year 5 teacher because she was overheard calling her a 'sulky b*tch' at pick-up, then don't expect a particularly jolly farewell. If you were switching to the other local school down the road then you got nothing more than a 'cheerio and good riddance'!

If you were moving away somewhere you got quite a nice send-off; possibly a card signed by the class or a little gift, plus the bit in the assembly where everyone wished you well as you went off to pastures new. The teacher leading the assembly would often declare that the school will stay in touch via email, but that seldom happens. If you were moving abroad then it was an even bigger deal. In my Year 5 class at the time were two Jacks: Jack G and Jack W. Halfway through the year Jack W's family decided to move to Australia. Jack's family were hoping to keep the news on the downlow to make the move as easy as possible. It must be hard for a family to uproot and move overseas, so I completely appreciated their logic.

When the day came for him to leave, we had planned to do our usual farewell at the end of the assembly. As the head was finishing the assembly, he started his mini-speech wishing Jack W well in his future endeavours 'Down Under':

'Now, just before we finish, I would like JACK G to come to the front.'

Uh-oh!

As requested, Jack G, a shy and easily embarrassed wallflower of a child, walked to the front, head down, with his face turning as red as his hair.

'Well, Jack, today is going to be your last day with us at school.'

Jack G looked concerned.

'And while we are sad you are leaving us, we've got a little gift for you to remember us by when you move to AUSTRALIA!'

Jack G was already a pale child, but now he was turning white! The look of utter bewilderment and worry on Jack's face is something that will stay with me for the rest of my days. It was clear to see Jack had no idea he was moving to Australia. Imagine being nine years old, shy and quiet, then out of nowhere, you're summoned to the front of assembly and in front of 250 of your fellow pupils, handed a pen as a parting gift and told that you were moving to literally the other side of the world.

All the staff were sweating, looking at each other and trying desperately to catch the headteacher's attention to let him know he had the wrong Jack. I tried to interrupt the proceedings but before he knew it, the whole school was belting out a chorus of 'For He's a Jolly Good Fellow'. Jack G didn't know what was happening, and I could only imagine what was going through his head. He was too shy to question it; it looked like he had accepted his fate, and despite the utterly bewildering circumstances of how he found out he looked ready to accept his fate and enjoy his new life in Oz.

He recovered from the experience (thankfully) and I obviously had to speak to his mum about the entire debacle.

Oh man, that kid must be scarred for life. Why does that stuff always seem to happen to the nice kids? The sensible ones that wouldn't say boo to a goose?! I'd have loved it if that had happened to one of the naughty b*ggers, the cheeky swines that used to mess around in assembly.

That would've been you, Adam. Be honest, did you ever behave particularly well during assembly as a child?

Bro, I don't even behave well now I'm one of the grown-ups! Especially when I'm winding my mates up.

I remember a brilliant one from my first teaching assistant job in a two-form entry school where the assemblies can drag and be a little bit repetitive … in fact, that's an understatement, they were drier than a cream cracker that had been left in the sun. In these situations, it's up to the staff to create their own fun. This is exactly what my old work colleagues and I did, but there was one man who wanted to mix up assemblies more than the rest, and that man was … COCKNEY JOHN.

When assemblies got boring he would sit by the side and start making noises during a quiet moment when a teacher was awarding Emily the 'Star of the Week' because, let's be honest, the teacher was running out of well-behaved children to reward this term. John would let out a subtle 'MEOW' to his Year 6 class and look away. This would carry on until a child put their hand up and reported the poor behaviour to their sensible adult at the side of the hall (?).

'Excuse me, Sir, but someone keeps making cat noises!'

John would reply, 'Don't worry, bruv, just focus on the wonderful assembly. Emily's getting Star of the Week, or somefing.'

Not only did CJ make cat noises, he also would wind up some of the children that looked as bored as he felt. At an opportune moment, he'd whisper their name.

One week it was Sammy. Now Sammy, who was always up for a laugh, was sitting legs crossed and arms folded, watching intently to the assembly until …

'Sammy,' whispered the cheeky cockney.

Sammy would look round and CJ would turn away. This would routinely carry on, purely for John's entertainment. One assembly, Sammy was sick of his Year 6 teacher's tomfoolery so he raised his hand during the presentation from a science guest speaker and declared, 'I think a ghost is trying to talk to me!' Cockney John could barely contain himself, but he had achieved his mission of making assemblies more enjoyable (for himself at least).

Not to be outdone by our Londoner pal, a couple of staff members and I thought we would turn the tables on him. We thought it would be funny to pick on John at the end of an assembly and, completely unbeknownst to him, the staff member at the front would tell the congregation that another staff member would like to share a prayer with them.

Miss Smith delivered her assembly and right at the end she said, 'To finish our assembly, a member of staff has prepared a prayer to share with you all, so please welcome ... COCKNEY JOHN' (not his actual teacher name, obviously).

John, who was near enough asleep at the time, had the shock of his life and with a bit of peer pressure from one of his colleagues (ME!) he made his way to the front. I whispered 'meow' to him as he was walking past and through gritted teeth he grumbled, 'I am gonna kill you, bruv!' I was so happy. There's nothing like a death threat in front of the children to brighten your morning. So John stood there at the front looking like a rabbit caught in headlights. He started his ad-libbed masterpiece of a prayer:

'So, like, right then, err... 'ands togevvah, eyes closed ...'

(As the children put their hands together and closed their eyes, I got my imaginary popcorn ready – this was going to be EPIC!)

'I'd like to fank God, for the school ...'

'I'd like to fank God for the teachers ...'

(This was even better than I'd hoped for!)

'I'd also like to fank God for the ... pencils, and the erasers, and the pens ... and the RULERS!'

He was definitely starting to panic, but he finished with the immortal line of:

'... and you know ... everyone stay safe at the weekend!'

I can confirm that not only was there confusion on the children's faces, probably wondering why Cockney John had just thanked the Heavenly Father for a whole pencil case, the staff were in bits.

Amen to that, Cockney John!

School Performances

There are two types of teachers – those who absolutely hate doing a school performance and those who love it. I fall into the latter category. As you will have read in my journey into teaching I was really into drama and performing in my youth, so a chance to put on my own performance was a dream come true. My first few productions – and I have purposely chosen the word 'productions', as that was exactly what they were – linked to Easter. I'm not going to say I took the productions seriously, but if you were to check my internet browsing history at the time, you would have found searches such as:

Can a school production win an Olivier Award?
How to get a play turned into a film.
What is Andrew Lloyd Webber's net worth?

You could say the film *Nativity!* was loosely based on my enthusiasm for school performances. In fact, I take that back. As much as I love the film *Nativity!,* and we annually watch it and have a laugh at the absurdity and bonkers plot line, which I agree is what is appealing about the film, I can't help but think, as a teacher, that this is up there as the most ludicrous representation of a primary school.

The way our school works is that Year 1 and Year 3 do a Harvest Festival performance, EYFS, Year 2 and Year 4 do separate Christmas performances, Year 5 do an Easter show and Year 6 do an end of year performance.

So as a Year 5 teacher, for my first few years of teaching I had to do the Easter performance. The first year, I actually bought the script for a show called *Good News*. My head teacher always wanted us to cover the traditional Easter story as he felt it was important to teach the children the reason behind celebrating the holiday. He did encourage us to be creative in our retelling of the story. *Good News* was a play that retold the Easter story through news reports. It was my first time dabbling with a bit of greenscreen, which has become a lot easier to do nowadays. The play went really well and I loved every minute of it, but I knew the year after I needed to emulate that first show.

My second production was a self-written triumph – *CSI Jerusalem*. Yes, just like the series you watch on the TV, the Easter story was retold through a CSI investigation that included examining the evidence and interviewing witnesses. It was a roaring success. The children loved this approach: becoming detectives, learning about the job and the different aspects of a police investigation. Again, it provided plenty of different cross-curricular links, with projects looking into the history of the police, providing different science investigations, writing persuasive reviews and trailers, and designing posters.

I felt I peaked the year after when I decided to write a new script retelling the Easter story through Michael Jackson songs.

After the untimely death of Michael Jackson, my stepson became obsessed with all of his songs. It seemed to inspire a whole new generation, so I harnessed this enthusiasm to help retell the Easter story in a whole new enjoyable and creative way. I sat down and re-wrote the lyrics for a number of MJ classics to fit in with the story. The children absolutely loved performing, they recreated some of his famous dance moves, sang all the songs with enthusiasm and never grew bored of singing. I am not going to lie, I was so proud of my handiwork rewriting the songs to fit the Easter story. Here is just a glance at the genius behind the songs:

Take 'Rock With You' and rename it 'Worship You' for when Jesus arrived in Jerusalem on Palm Sunday:

I wanna worship you (all night)
Worship into the (sunlight)
I wanna worship you (all night)
We're gonna sing for the new king

'Billie Jean' was reworked to be Peter's song when he denied Jesus and the cockerel crowed:

Jesus Christ Is Not My Brother
He's just a guy Who Claims That I Am The One
But The Kid Is Not God's Son
He Says I Am The One, But The Kid Is Not God's Son

'Thriller' became 'The Resurrection Song':

'Cause it's Jesus, Jesus Christ
He died upon that cross and you can't believe your sight
You know it's Jesus, Jesus Christ
He died on that cross but now he's living living tonight

As you can imagine, it went down a storm with parents and our school community. We actually had the BBC come in to film a feature on it for *North West Tonight*, but the head teacher wasn't sure about associating the Easter story with Michael Jackson. Plus, I wasn't actually sure on the whole copyright side. There was absolutely no association between MJ and Jesus, by the way; we had strictly just adapted the songs. Apart from Jesus moonwalking on the cross, that was it!

After such a positive response to the children using more appealing music, I took a similar approach the next year. As the Easter break came before the Easter weekend, we couldn't really do an Easter show three weeks before. Therefore we decided to try to introduce Shakespeare to Year 5 by performing a modern version of *A Midsummer Night's Dream* using songs by The Beatles. The added focus of The Beatles fitted in great with the KS2 history unit of looking at the life of a famous person – John Lennon. Having both The Beatles and Shakespeare as a focus provided so many learning opportunities, and the children really loved researching and making projects about these famous figures of the past.

As I changed to Year 4 the following year, we did a traditional *Christmas Carol* for the Christmas show. We focused on Charles Dickens, and learnt about him and his life and other work. But again, I rewrote some of the children's favourite Christmas carols and songs to fit in with the story. It seemed to have the children completely enchanted with the show and made such a big difference.

I can't stand teachers who say doing a school show leads to a loss in learning time; in my opinion, if that's the case you're not doing it right. The staple of every school is the Christmas nativity play.

To draw the curtain back on a school performance, it might appear during the actual performance that there had been no rehearsing, coordination, input or organisation. In reality, within being back a week in September, teachers will already be googling scripts, putting ideas together and considering parts. The thing to remember is that throughout their school career, children will have the chance to perform to the level they are comfortable with or just outside their comfort zone. A huge fulfilling moment as a teacher is pushing a child outside their comfort zone to perform and then seeing them absolutely smash it! Some children, however, just aren't made for the stage and so will never be forced into performing. If a primary school really does care about providing a broad and balanced curriculum, there will be a vast range of opportunities for children to shine – some are able to perform on stage, others on a football pitch, others academically. You do come across the odd pupil who is like a diamond in the rough, who seems to be incredible at everything. I have only genuinely experienced three, possibly four, children in my career who seemed to excel at absolutely everything they put their hand to. I was always so jealous of how talented they seemed to be at everything.

So for any parents wondering what it is like to put on a nativity play, here is a little insight …

The biggest piece of advice I could give any teacher who is about to start their first ever Christmas show is to understand no matter how much you practise, it will never be perfect. Even on the performance night, despite weeks of intricate planning and preparation, there will always be something that stops it being perfect. As long as you accept this and understand that this is the charm of a school nativity, it will keep you sane.

In the immediate build-up to the performance itself, teachers will go through a near mental breakdown from being unable to get the songs out of their heads. Initially, on first hearing the songs, you think, these are great, some absolute bangers.

Famous last words. There is a challenge in the *SAS: Who Dares Wins* TV programme where the recruits are blindfolded and exposed to the same dissonant sounds in an attempt to push them to breaking point and they voluntarily withdraw. This is a piece of piss compared with a couple of weeks of hearing the same songs on repeat, which are the last thing you think about before bed and the first thing you hear in the morning. Oh, and don't forget waking up in the middle of the night with the music going round and round in your head. Despite never being able to escape the songs, you still need to encourage the children to sing, not shout, as enthusiastically as possible.

There will always be one child who has been cast as a main part with plenty of lines but who point-blank refuses to learn them. You give them at least a month's notice and they just make no effort at all. You start by gently reminding them that they need to learn their lines before seriously contemplating giving away their part to someone you can definitely depend on. You have multiple discussions with fellow staff members to justify your imminent decision. You lose sleep over whether it is the right thing to do, then within a day the child miraculously manages to remember everything word for word.

Teachers will master the art of mime in the build-up and performance of the school play. They almost create their own sign language, creating hand gestures to signify 'smile!', 'not yet!' and 'get on the bloody stage now!'.

Depending on the size of the school, new characters may also need to be added to give everyone a part. Nativity plays featuring aliens, parrots, Simon Cowell and octopuses have all appeared on the podcast. One of my favourite stories we've shared on the podcast was this beauty:

Reception class nativity, and mum says to her class they need LOTS of animals so they can choose what they want to be. One boy says, 'I want to be a leopard' and my mum tries to convince him to be something more traditional with a 'Are you sure you wouldn't like to be a sheep, Billy? Or a goat ... or a donkey even?' But no ... Little Billy is adamant that he wants to be a leopard. Now there weren't any leopard-ish outfits in the dressing-up box, but mum's a dab hand with a sewing machine so she decided to make little Billy a really good costume! Anyway, the day of the dress rehearsal comes around and mum gets out Billy's costume, proudly showing him his spots and ears and tail but he bursts into tears and says, 'I don't want to be a leopard, I want to be a Leopard!' It took her and her TA a while to work out that little Billy didn't want to be an animal at all ... He just couldn't make a 'shhhhhhhh' sound. He actually wanted to be a SHEPHERD!

If only there were a video camera to film some of the things teachers say when rehearsing the Christmas play:

'How many times do I have to tell you, face the front! Your parents won't want to take a day off work to stare at the back of your head.'

'I don't think I've ever seen a donkey pick his own nose and wipe it on Mary's dress! Can we stop that, please!'

'Why don't you know these lines? Do you think Spielberg has to deal with this?'

'Do you know what, I may as well do it myself.'

'It is not Frankenstein! It is Frankincense!'

It is funny how teachers completely contradict themselves as well, mainly due to the pupils doing the exact opposite of what you ask them to do. Some of the contradictions I've said in the past are:

'You need to be aware of who comes on before and after you.' Followed by, 'Will you just worry about yourself!'

'If there is a problem, just come and speak to me.' The next moment, 'Do you know what, I can't be doing with all this fussing. Can we please just get through this?'

'You need to be as quick as you can getting changed, and then back round to the stage!' Followed by, 'Don't you dare run down the corridor!'

'I need to see lots and lots of expression when performing your lines.' In the next scene, 'Please can we not be so dramatic and overact?'

'Can you sit still, just sit still.' But, 'When you're on stage you can't be standing there like a scarecrow, you need to move.'

'When you say that, can you deliver that line with real attitude? I want you to really get into character!' Followed by, 'Don't you dare answer me back.'

'Hurry up, we've not got all day.' The next minute, 'Please don't rush when you say your lines, you need to slow down.'

There will also be a contagious bug that sweeps through your class mere days before the performance is due to happen. You can bet your bottom dollar that the main cast members – Mary, Joseph and the three wise men – will get it and you're praying for a speedy recovery. There have been a number of occasions when staff or older pupils have had to step in at the last minute as key cast members have ended up missing the big show due to illness. You have to respect the staff who go the full hog and even don an authentic costume to not ruin the illusion of the performance.

Some children will take ill during the performance itself. If Paddy Power were giving odds, it'd be evens that some sort of accident will happen, the most common being a child having an accident on stage or a member of the cast projectile-vomiting over other class members. The other thing to be aware of is that no matter how much you prepare, if you're brave enough to use any sort of technology, it will definitely not work on the night. PowerPoints will freeze, CDs won't load, sound cables snap, lighting fails – it is always a recipe for disaster. People consider me to be one of the leading teachers with technology in the country, but I end up just turning the computer off and then back on, and if that doesn't work I will stand at the front and start singing before the children decide to join in.

All that build-up, hard work, sleepless nights, dedication, endless rehearsals, comes down to the day itself, and teachers will never admit this but they love seeing the types of parents that rock up to each school performance. Here are some of the characters you will see at each school nativity:

Let's start with the bragger, the parent who as soon as they got a sniff that their child had one of the main parts, couldn't shut up about it. Every morning at the school gates, they are letting on to every parent who walks past, 'Have you heard? Oh, you didn't see my Facebook post? Instagram live? My YouTube vlog? No? Yeah, Jodie is going to be Mary. It has nothing to do with the fact she's been in drama school since the day she was conceived. I've already emailed the BBC to see if they want to cover the story.'

You also have parents who are so eager to get a decent seat, they camp outside the school. The show might be at 2.30 in the afternoon, and they're dropping the kids off at 9am and then queueing to come in. The show might be happening on Thursday but they're setting up tents, with flasks of coffee and sandwiches, to make sure they are first in line so they can be front row. It's hilarious to see their face when they realise the front row is always reserved for the esteemed guests, usually the headteacher, chair of governors or the local priest or vicar.

There is always a parent who gets there early and tries to reserve half the hall for her mates or family members. These are the same parents who, despite being told clearly that due to health and safety restrictions we can only allocate three tickets per family, go on to invite anyone they have ever met and even go to the lengths of forging fake tickets (true story).

The type of parents that wind me up are the distractors. As teachers we've spent hours telling the children not to wave to their parents; meanwhile the fully grown adults are throwing and flailing their arms in a desperate attempt to get their child to notice them, as if they've not just spent all morning with them or will be picking them up to take home five minutes later. Just chill your beans, trust me, they can see you. Just sit back and enjoy watching this masterpiece.

There is nothing worse than the parent who spends the whole performance stuck on their phone, scrolling through Facebook while their child is performing their lines. You just want to scream at them, 'PUT THE F****NG PHONE DOWN, BE PRESENT IN THE MOMENT, YOU ABSOLUTE ****!'

With GDPR being a huge responsibility for schools, safeguarding and other concerns, it makes a teacher's day when they've explained numerous times there is to be no recording for the safety of some of the children and there will always be that one parent who blatantly starts recording on their phone and then shares it with other parents.

There will be one of two parents who end up completely ruining and distracting the children on stage. It will either be the parent who comes straight from the office, walks in late, forgets to turn their phone off and so receives a call halfway through the show, or the parent who brings the toddler who resembles the Tasmanian devil and spends the whole show causing absolute chaos.

The overly emotional parent is always a treat; we've had bets on which mum is likely to cry first. You can also work out which parents' break-up hasn't been amicable, the ones who arrive separately, sit at opposite ends of the hall and spend most of the show looking daggers at each other before completely changing their demeanour as they smile at their child on stage.

There will always be a parent who has been helping their child learn all their lines and songs; they just end up acting and singing the whole play themselves. Or the parent who dares their child to try to steal the show, maybe hoping it will make a bit of beer money if it ends up on *You've Been Framed*, but there's no way a shepherd would bring a lamb to baby Jesus only to pick up the baby, pull off its head and then drop-kick it into the audience. Or I like to think he was dared, as this is the least worrying reason for this happening.

There is also always a parent who was a little bitter their child didn't get the desired part and can't help but put the play down at every opportunity, 'Yes, the children did well, but it's never going to win an award. I'm not being funny, but Mary's perform-ance was just so underwhelming, I mean, when she found she was pregnant, there was no emotion, I just was not convinced at all she was shocked, I was just left empty. If the teachers had made the right decision and put my darling in as Mary, it would have been a lot better.'

Finally, there is the parent that is also a teacher and who, unless they work at the same school, never gets a chance to see their own children perform.

Despite all the challenges, the ups and downs, the sleepless nights, the fact that some of the children forget their cues, mistime their entrances, forget their lines, make them up or just improvise, like when Mary and Joseph knock at the innkeeper's door asking if there's any room at the inn to be greeted by the innkeeper who confidently declares, 'No, f**k off!' there is a special feeling, a sense of pride and fulfilment that makes the whole process worthwhile. The children have learnt so much, stepped outside their comfort zone, overcome barriers and grown in confidence. You've created special memories for parents, and it is always a great way to end the most challenging term of the year.

PE. Two letters that when put together will produce such a range of emotions – delight for those that love it and pure dread for those that don't. Almost as divisive as maths, but definitely a Marmite subject. Unsurprisingly, Lee and I both loved it!

Primary school is different now. Some things are not as common as they used to be, things like 'smoking' candy sticks thinking you were all that at the school disco, bringing in toys at the end of the year and waiting to beat the one 'arrogant' child at their own game. But what I am talking about is the event that used to signal the end of the year, the event everyone wanted to be part of, the event that really made you feel like you'd made it in primary school. This was the 'staff vs kids rounders game'. This event may still take place in certain schools, but with risk assessments and the fear of injury to staff or children, mainly due to staff taking it way too seriously, schools are not willing to do it. Back in the day, this was *the* event I waited for. I always remember being a spectator from Year 3 right through to my selection in Year 6. I was a passionate member of the crowd, trying to get into the teachers' heads. My school chair would dig into the hallowed turf as I jumped enthusiastically throughout the game, cheering the pupils on.

Mr Ellis was the man in charge of all sport and PE at my school; he wasn't much of a fitness fanatic, more of a high-cholesterol fanatic – put it this way, he would get short of breath when he picked a pen lid up from the classroom floor. The one thing he had in buckets (no, not the Colonel's hot wings) was passion.

Ellis would start organising the staff vs kids rounders game once SATs were done and dusted. To be fair to him, in the games that I watched he had a fairly decent record. He wasn't the fastest, but all the doughnuts he scoffed in the staffroom seemed to give him power that most of us could only dream of. The year we played, Ellis knew he was in for a game. Tyrell always went 50 per cent. I truly believe if he had tried, he could have won the game in his sleep, but he would be trying to keep the children in it, keep the crowd engaged until the end. Remember, my primary school was a two-form entry, meaning in the crowd of our Year 6 game there was an atmosphere like no other, with 150+ children cheering (mostly for the children). Our game began, and I'd never heard noise like it. The occasion clearly got to some of our players. The whole game the staff remained cool, calm and collected, including Ellis, but it was a hot summer's day, so he looked anything but cool. Fast-forward to the unbelievable scenes towards the end of the game.

The score was close, with only a few hits remaining. The children had set the staff a solid six rounders for victory. Like a Hollywood movie, the staff had achieved 5 1/2 rounders going into the last batter. You guessed it ... Ellis stepped up, in his glasses (with strap for athletic comfort), to take his hit. I remember clear as day, it's like time stood still, the ball is bowled and Ellis watches it the whole way, his arm pulls back, bingo wings flying in all different directions, but as his arm swung around all that junk food solidified to make a monster contact with the ball.

As it flew over my teammates' head, the game looked over. Ellis set off – risk assessments weren't as big back in the day, so he was running around quite close to the animated crowd. As he was sprinting, glasses wobbling in the breeze, he turned past second base, and unbelievably his foot caught on the second base. In a last-ditch attempt to keep his footing, he sprinted with all his might, but unfortunately for Ellis, gravity was about to take its course. Down he went, but that isn't the best bit, as the crowd were completely losing it with the drama of this insane game. Ellis's blue Adidas tracksuit bottoms were pulled down with the force of the fall (bet he was glad the mothers of the rubbish football players weren't there), and unbelievably, in front of a crowd of Year 3s, Ellis tried to get up and continue to chase his rounder while mooning the majority of the school.

In the time it took Ellis to pull his pants up and make his way round third, the ball was back at fourth. Tap on the top of the base and Ellis was walking – it was a head in hands moment for the staff, but for him it was a pants in hand moment as he was still trying to keep them up (the elastic waistband must have snapped, just like his dreams of being the staff rounders hero).

Sports Day
This is a day that is highlighted on the school calendar far in advance.

It is the day when the PE subject leader steps up to the mark and finally gets their time to shine, organising sports day like it is a military operation. Unless you have a PE subject leader who is the opposite end of the scale and is so laid back they are just going to go with the flow, leaving the other staff to fret about the running of the event that they end up organising.

Although this date is given to parents in most monthly newsletters from the start of the school year, on the actual day, even though letters have been given out, reminders of kits for the children, texts being sent the day before, you can bank on at least one parent claiming 'they didn't have a clue' sports day was today.

The issue with putting sports day in the diary so early is you're trying to predict the summer weather in Britain, which is like trying to predict lottery numbers. It's impossible. No chance that every sports day runs smoothly on the day it's first pencilled in. By hook or by crook, the day will go ahead, parents will be in attendance, the children excited ... Well, most of them – maybe not the child who has scranned a huge packed lunch and looks more likely to throw up their bag of Wotsits than run the race on the 60-metre track.

Yes, sports day always happens on the reserve day. Even on that reserve day, it is either on the brink of lashing it down or is the HOTTEST DAY known to man!

The different variety of races is the absolute stalwart of any primary school sports day.

Until health and safety gets in the way, and you have to fill in more risk assessment forms than there are words in this book! 'Sorry, no sack race this year, far too dangerous! Three-legged race, are you kidding me? Skipping race, as if! Can you imagine the amount of accidents? We've not got enough wet paper towels in school, it is a no-go.'

But the bigger question is, apart from the obstacle race and the straight sprint, what preparation for life, health and fitness are the other races really contributing to? When you're making breakfast in years to come, will you have to balance an egg on a spoon and walk/run for 40 metres? When running to catch a bus, would it be quicker to hop in a sack and jump to your bus stop? When you're out with a friend, would it be best to walk across the dancefloor holding your friend like a wheelbarrow? Ok, that one actually happens. But let's delve deeper into the races ...

Egg and Spoon Race This is arguably the most controversial race; if it's done fairly it's like an OAP race, as they're constantly dropping their teeth and trying to get them while accidentally kicking them forward. Then you have the serial winners, who will do whatever it takes to win – they're literally sprinting with all their might to get to the finish line, and you think, how is that possible?! Then you realise they are clearly clamping the egg onto their spoon with their thick, chubby thumb. Now, as a teacher this is one of the situations that is up there with the worst. A child has clearly cheated, crossed the finishing line, sprinted to their parents like they've scored the winner in a cup final. Parents are embracing them with such pride, and now they make their way to the podium for the medal ceremony (by podium I mean the spare classroom desk that's been deemed surplus to requirements due to a major wobble). Parents have cameras ready to take pictures of their victorious (rule-bending) champion while you have to once again quickly remind them of safeguarding procedures – so put your bloody camera away! Why would you want proof of this act of treason in the egg and spoon race? Anyway, the time has come, and through gritted teeth you hand over the gold medal to the victor, a little part of you dies, until you think of the fact that no one else really cares. The parents of the cheat are buzzing, the second- and third-place medallists are amazed they medalled at all, and when it comes down to it, the medal is made from some of the cheapest plastic to ever grace the earth. So, hey ho, cheaters never prosper, but maybe they do, as a six-year-old egg and spoon champion will agree.

Wheelbarrow Race This is the race you always want to do with your mate, but it's also the race you want to do with someone of similar build and size. The track is usually cut short, because 60 metres there and 60 metres back when you've swapped over is far too long to be carrying the legs of another human being! This race is a clear show of teamwork and comradery. If it works correctly, you look like you have an electric lawn mower drifting down your lane with ease. If the technique is wrong, it can cause serious injuries to the arms and you could end up in a compromising position from the get-go, giving some parents new ideas. Teachers normally enjoy this race, due to the fact that the child that usually wins every race may struggle with the partner that is chosen for them. At the end of the day, everyone deserves the chance to win a gold.

Sack Race This cracker of a race should be known as 'the absolute banter' race. I've had more cry laughs watching the sack race than any other thing in my life (sad life, I know). This is a race where the winners are usually the children who surprise you; they watch the others fall and calmly jump in full control, and it's a thing of beauty. My favourites are the children who set off like a bullet out of a gun, but unfortunately the gun is clearly faulty. They are putting in unbelievable effort and their face is becoming redder and redder, but they have hardly moved further than a metre. The parents usually get into this race as they enjoy seeing their children in tough situations and witnessing them solve the puzzle in front of them, crawling and dragging their sorry bodies through the dirt to roll over the finish line, white T-shirt from their PE kit completely ruined. But everyone had a great time.

Obstacle Race This is the toughest race for any school staff, reason being, it involves benches (the dodgy, creaky ones in the hall, which sink into the grass even if it's dry), hula hoops (unfortunately due to Early Years taking some of them for fundamental moving assessments you have all different sizes), parachute (laid across all the lanes, for the army crawl underneath) and quoits (you may be reading this wondering what they are, but you will all know the pointless rubber rings that you have to balance on your head. If you have a ponytail or a bun, it will simply balance and you have a huge advantage). The issue is reloading every lane after every race; it can be soul-destroying collecting all the quoits in and one is missing, until you realise someone from the previous race has still got it on their head as they're back with their class, or another child has rolled it to see how far it will go.

Why is there always a big bite taken out of a couple of the quoits?

Sprint Race This is *the* race, this is when arguments are settled in the playground – and I'm not just talking about the children. Competitive parents dropping off and picking up their children wait for this race as it's a huge opportunity for a 'one up' on other parents – ones you like, or, even better, ones you don't! This is their race. They don't care if their child wins the 'novelty races', it's all about their child focusing on the win, not just so they will be collecting one of the finest medals a primary school can buy but so the parents can claim on social media that their child is the fastest in the year. If you win the sprint on sports day, it counts for a full year, too; it doesn't matter if you pile on the puppy fat. This is the closest many will get to an Olympics. A muddy field with lanes looking like they have been chalked by a drunk person on an unicycle. Hills and dips could be a friend or foe. If you get the uneven lane, you feel like you're Rocky Balboa going up the steps, which definitely doesn't help, but if you get the old mudslide down, as long as you can keep your feet then a record-breaking time could be in sight!

One year, I was working in my first school on sports day and it was announced that there would be a staff race after the children's sprint. I was carrying a slight ankle problem at the time. Now, I'm not going to lie, I didn't like a TA from another year group (let's call him Mr Costa) and he lined up straight away alongside another male member of staff. Mr Costa turned round as the children began to chant my name ... 'MR P! MR P!'

I couldn't let the children down. This was my moment, 20 years after my last sports day sprint, and I was ready to grace the hallowed turf again. I decided to slowly take my coat off and line up. I had full confidence that my glass ankle would not break and I could claim this win, not just for me, but so my parents could proudly announce that their 30-year-old teaching assistant son is still the fastest in primary school. The whistle went and I set off as quick as a flash. I made my way round the track, and as I approached the last corner, I had an unassailable lead ... or so I thought. I hit a mudslide down, going quicker than I ever thought possible. I had the legs of the Road Runner, but unfortunately the upper body of Porky Pig, and then it happened. With a crash, bang and wallop, I went down in front of all the children in KS2. As I crawled and scratched my way back onto my feet, Mr Costa and the other participant passed me on the finishing line, leaving me in a lonely third position. To make matters worse, even though I knew everyone witnessing that disaster knew if it wasn't for my fall heard around the world, I would have easily won. Mr Costa approached me and said, 'Don't worry, Mr P, I used to run cross country.'

I still think about this tragedy at least two to three times a week.

Parents' Race After all the effort you go through with organising a sports day, helping the children thoroughly enjoy a full, safe day of highly competitive events, this race is definitely the reward.

It all feels like it builds up to this moment. This is the repayment for all that hard work. I guarantee at least one of the parents' races will provide you with the medicine (and by that I obviously mean laughter) to make up for the rest of your highly stressful job.

Let's start with the mums' race. Now, if you're a mum you know all about the fascinating array of females that you're stuck with for your child's primary education. There's the 'mumsy mum' who is the first to share lovely ideas to the class WhatsApp group. The older mum who you definitely confused with nana when you first met her. The gobby mum (you know the one) who thinks whatever she says is fine because she starts every sentence with 'I'm not being funny but ...'. The gym bunny mummy who's never out of Lycra. The suited and booted mummy who is slightly intimidating. The exhausted mummy who has far too many kids and the hungover mummy who makes every other parent slightly jealous with her carefree antics.

After some begging and pleading from the children, the mums reluctantly make their way to the start line. Everyone is putting their money on the gym bunny as the firm favourite. Gobby mum chips in with her classic, 'I'm not being funny, but I've not even got the right shoes on!' The mums take their positions and blow kisses to their little cherubs; unfortunately mumsy mum is trying too hard to get her little one's attention so she misses the start whistle! Older mummy starts well but age quickly catches up with her as she's overtaken by the other mums and finds herself being the one who is sympathetically slow-clapped as she brings up the rear. Hungover mummy is going well until her Wetherspoon's full English begins to repeat on her. Suited and booted mummy was doing well until her stiletto heels sank too far into the turf. Gym bunny was always looking good but her early morning Pilates class dampened her progress as she began to look leggy in the final stretch. Exhausted mummy is so used to sprinting around town with her double buggy that she's out in front and charges through the finishing line. Hurray for the mummies! They all laugh and gossip their way back to their seats in preparation for the next event – the dads' race!

Now the main difference between the mums' and dads' race is that the dads need absolutely no encouragement. Half of them are already changed out of their work shoes and squeezing into their spikes. Home-workout dad is doing dips on a tiny plastic chair. Business dad is tucking his tie into his shirt. Builder dad is having a final sip of his brew – no preparation needed as he's running in his steel-toe-capped boots and hi-vis vest. Hippy dad is airing out his flares with a bit of meditation on the grass. Tall dad is still struggling to get up off the wooden spectator bench. Beer-belly dad is sipping on his 'energy drink', which has a slight resemblance (the exact colour and pattern) to a can of Stella.

The rules are clearly stated as competitive juices are flowing. The children are pumped, the mums are watching through their fingers and the head teacher is quickly counting the 'No blame, no claim' forms as no risk assessment would allow such an event to happen!

At the same time as the start whistle, two simultaneous pops go off … beer-belly dad and tall dad have only gone and done their hamstrings! Business dad is running well until cheeky builder dad 'jokingly' pulls him back. Phones, wallets and keys are sinking into the mud as builder dad is disqualified, leaving home-workout and hippy dad to battle it out. Home-workout dad is distracted by the pretty teacher he's been eyeing up since September and causes a lane violation, letting hippy dad claim the victory and his first ever sports day win.

There's one guarantee – sports days are never dull, especially with the parents' races!

If you are a parent reading this book, you are obviously amazing!

Definitely!

But dealing with parents can be the hardest part of the job. You can have a brilliant day where the children all work hard, make amazing progress and everyone gets along nicely with one another ... and then your phone rings at 3.31pm on a rainy Tuesday because Mrs Klein wants a chat about why little Calvin has a tiny bit of paint on his new jumper. That's when you know your day could be about to go downhill.

The key is to bribe the admin staff in the school office with chocolate to tell them you are in a very important meeting and can't be disturbed!

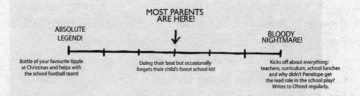

ABSOLUTE
LEGEND!

MOST PARENTS
ARE HERE!

BLOODY
NIGHTMARE!

Bottle of your favourite tipple
at Christmas and helps with
the school football team!

Doing their best but occasionally
forgets their child's forest school kit!

Kicks off about everything:
teachers, curriculum, school lunches
and why didn't Penelope get
the lead role in the school play?
Writes to Ofsted regularly.

On a scale of 'Absolute Legend!' to 'Bloody Nightmare!' (see above), most parents are somewhere in the middle, just trying to keep their kids safe and pay the bills. Don't get me wrong, there are plenty of teachers that deserve a lot of the stick they get because they don't engage positively, but for the most part teachers are trying their best to please as many people as they can.

Whether loved, hated, or something in the middle, parents are a huge part of a school community. They can make or break a job as a teacher. There has definitely been a shift over the past few decades where plenty of teachers will admit that they are not given the same respect from parents as they once were. There was a time when parents would believe everything a teacher said over a child who has no real understanding of the world and will happily lie if they sense it will get them out of trouble. The shift has been stark over the years, and the lack of support for teachers and school staff from the government and the constant bashing of teachers in the press certainly haven't helped. The rise of social media is also helping parents use these platforms to slag teachers off with no real evidence other than what their child had told them. That's the same child the parent will moan and complain about on their own social media timelines.

We're all brainwashed by various media to feel inadequate and unhappy. This constant feeling of inadequacy created by the models, millionaires and 'successful' people who clog up our social media feeds leads to the unrealistic pressure of portraying a perfect life online. This makes us portray everything in our lives as perfect – our jobs, our family and our children.

Alongside this constant feeling of inadequacy, we also seem to be manipulated to blame someone else for why we feel like this. Self-reflection is non-existent in the busy world we now live in. I usually discuss this on my CPD training when talking about technology. Technology can be such an amazing tool, but it can also be very detrimental to the mental health of young people and adults. The impact of technology all comes down to how we choose to use it. Our children are given access to so much technology at such a young age with this money-rich, time-poor approach to it. So many parents buy devices for their children at a young age because it is convenient and it keeps them quiet. There is no time spent educating children on using it safely, setting the necessary restrictions and boundaries. Once some of these children have issues – whether that is addiction or mental health – it is usually blamed on the platforms or the devices.

So, technology takes the blame for most of the issues we face, and if we don't blame technology, who else takes the blame? That's right, teachers. There seems to be a straight correlation between the government's austerity measures over the past decade and the number of hats that teachers and school staff now need to wear. Not only has this increased teachers' workload to a new high, it has also devalued our profession to an all-time low. I want to make it clear that I feel the majority of parents still value teachers and are supportive of the role we take. Honestly, 99 per cent of the parents I have experienced in my career have been amazing.

I have received numerous letters and messages and had discussions with parents in which they have thanked me and appreciated the job I do. However, I have also had the odd negative response. It seems to be human nature that no matter how many positive messages you get, that negative one will eat away at you. I've had this with conferences I've done and a lot of my online content. It is hard to not let that negativity affect you. There has probably never been a time where schools have to deal with as many fussy parents. I often wish we could be more blunt when parents phone up to complain, and I'd love to leave an answer-machine message that goes like this ...

'Hello, you have reached NO BS Primary School. This is an automated answer machine to connect you to the right member of staff. Please listen to all the options before making a selection ...'

If your child is absent even though they have been boasting over the past few weeks about their upcoming trip to Disney World, please press 1.

If you want to complain about a teacher because you believe everything that comes out of your six-year-old's mouth, even though we both know they're sometimes full of s**t, go and let them take a number two.

To ask why you didn't get the notice about the fundraiser despite us sending home a letter, the termly newsletter, the email, text message, the post on the school website, Twitter, Facebook post and Seesaw message, please press 3.

To slag off a hard-working member of staff on social media despite the fact they are working harder than any generation of teacher before them, please put your phone down and go and do something more productive.

To blame the school for things outside of our control, such as the government budget cuts to both schools and social work, curriculum tests, a lack of support and intervention for children with specific learning needs, please vote differently.

If you think that as teachers we should be taking on your responsibilities as a parent to teach your child manners, respect and the ability to use the toilet properly, please look in the mirror and have a word with yourself.

If, like us, you think your child is the reincarnation of Damien, press ... 6 ... 6 ... 6!

To request another teacher for the third time this week, GOOD LUCK! There's a huge recruitment crisis. Actually, if you do know anyone interested in a short-term contract maternity cover role, seriously, let us know.

To ask how to answer your child's homework because none of it makes sense and you were never taught any of it at school, and if the mention of SPAG reminds you to get some more Dolmio, phone Michael Gove and have a go!

To report an incident that has happened involving your child while they've been using social media, press 13, which, funnily enough, is the age they should be when they are ACTUALLY allowed to use it.

If, like most parents, you realise that we're here to help, we are not against you and just want the very best for your child, please just hang up and give us your support and respect. Keep doing the amazing job you're doing as a parent and we'll concentrate on what we do well, which is teaching.

One thing teaching has taught me is that you are quickly made aware of how weird some people can be. When you start to experience the different types of parents you come across as a teacher, other than the ones that are sound, some help you to quickly understand why half the UK regularly and intentionally vote against their own self-interests, or more importantly, why *Mrs Brown's Boys* remains such a popular staple of TV viewing!

There is no better place to experience the diversity of the British public than at parents' evening. These crazily tiring nights happen a couple of times a year. You have to cram in 5–10-minute meetings with the parents of every single child in your class (if they all turn up), which is a tough ask after a full day of teaching. However, the fact that most children know that you will be speaking to their parents face to face after school makes them behave impeccably for that day and that day only. Make the most of it! If you do have a child who is willing to act up on the day of parents' evening, then it is likely that nothing will work.

It is rare you will ever come across a teacher who has the intestinal fortitude to be completely honest when talking directly to parents face to face. We sugar-coat it as we know no one wants the direct truth that their offspring isn't as perfect as they think. I like to think I am realistic about my own children – I know what they are like, I know they have their faults and I am ok with being told the truth. My wife, on the other hand ...

So, for any parent reading this, I will quickly run through some of the phrases that teachers will use at parents' evening that might be interpreted as one thing but actually mean something else. This also works for end of year written reports, another exercise that is a complete and utter waste of time.

If we are truly drawing back the curtain on what it is like to work in education, here's a huge secret about end of year reports: teachers only write one set of reports, when they were an NQT and they didn't know any better. With your first class, they were with you through that first-year journey, and you both grew and learnt so much together. You therefore slaved for hours writing 30 personalised reports for each and every member of your first class. Fast-forward a year, and a year of more responsibility, pressure and workload, to the time when the staff meeting takes place and you are reminded to start writing your end of year reports. You think to yourself, I haven't got time to write 30 reports from scratch. So what you do is you load up the reports from the previous year and think, 'Ok, Zach in my class – who was most like Zach last year? Billy, Billy was similar to Zach.' And so you load up Billy's report from the previous year and use the best Microsoft Office shortcut known to man ... Find and Replace. If you're a teacher reading this and you don't do this little teacher hack, you're missing a trick!

So here is your guide to what teachers say compared with what they actually mean at parents' evening. We're not trying to insult your intelligence, but if we said what we were really thinking, there's every possibility we'd be sacked!

Parents, if you hear or read these phrases, you now have this handy guide to help you to translate them. <u>Teachers, apologies, you'll need to come up with some new ones!</u>

'Hi Mr and Mrs Jones, it is so nice to finally meet you ...'
(I have been bricking it, I am so nervous. I really wish I didn't have to do this, I would much prefer to just send a note home.)

'She is a very popular member of the class.'
(What a chatterbox. Honestly, I can't shut her up. No matter where I sit her, she just chats away and never gets anything done.)

'They are so enthusiastic.'
(Too keen. I love children to be interested but it is getting to a point where he is almost unbearable.)

'They can be quite shy.'
(I have yet to hear them speak a word. Even when I say 'Good Morning' during the register they look at me with such fear.)

'They are definitely a more sensitive member of the class.'
(Never stops crying. Honestly, how do you put up with it? I've run out of paper towels drying up their tears.)

'They are always so helpful.'
(If they ask me if they can do a job one more time, I will lose the will to live. They need to realise if I need them to do a job, I will ask them.)

'They are so organised.'
(I treat your child like my own PA.)

'They are so intelligent; they have their hand up all the time.'
(Flipping know-it-all! I am not going to lie; they need to rein it in a little otherwise they'll be called all sorts in secondary school.)

'They sometimes need reminders of what to do.'
(They need to start bloody listening so I don't have to repeat myself.)

'They have a great sense of humour.'
(I buzz off their Grade-A banter.)

'He is a lively character.'
(He finds it impossible to sit still. He can be a right little sh*t at times.)

'They can sometimes get a little bit confused about the task we're doing.'
(They literally get everything wrong, all the time! Bless them for trying, though.)

'They need to make sure if they're stuck, they should ask for me for extra help.'
(It is only once I've taken their book home to mark that I've realised they've done f*** all and if the head teacher spotted this, I'd be getting my arse handed to me.)

'They are starting to mature.'
(Today is the first day they have listened and done what I asked. I reckon it might be the fact that they realised I was going to be speaking to you tonight.)

'They love to help around the classroom.'
(Interfering busybody!)

'Their general knowledge is fantastic. Really impressive.'
(Their intelligence intimidates me. I think they're probably cleverer than I am.)

'They've made some progress this year.'
(We have managed to get them to stop licking other people's shoes. Small steps, I know.)

'When he applies himself, he is capable of some good work.'
(He never applies himself.)

'A huge target this term is handwriting.'
(I can't read a bloody word.)

'They really need to try to speed up finishing some of the work I set in class. They are capable but don't always reflect this in their work.'
(Lazy little b*stard.)

Now let's talk about the types of parents, based upon my experiences at parents' evening over the years. Again, I would like to emphasise that the majority of parents I have come across fully support us and want to work with us to ensure the best outcomes for their child/ren. Having some of the traits of these personalities is perfectly normal; it's the extreme versions of the characters who can sometimes cause teachers a headache. But if you are a parent reading this, the question is, which one are you?

The competitive one Usually this parent is recognisable within the first sentence they utter after sitting down at parents' evening. 'So, are they top of the class?' 'Top three? Top five? Top ten? They need to be top set. We've already picked out the grammar school!'
   'Your child is in reception.'

'Yeah, but I keep hearing about this "greater depth" phrase. Is my princess greater depth? She's in the top group at her ballet class, and the things she's doing in her horse racing!'

'Yes, but is she happy?' I often want to say.

Now I am a huge sports fan and think competition is a good thing. Raising children to want to compete sets them up in life, as ultimately life is a competition. However, balance when it comes to academic life is important. Parents who have been so focused on making sure their child is top of the class often fail to notice that while their child is working at 'greater depth', they can sometimes struggle to make friends or are so tired from doing so many after-school clubs they are on the brink of a breakdown and they are only seven. Having an active interest in how your child is progressing is crucial, but obsessing about where they are in comparison to others in the class is not. We develop at different stages; think about when you put a load of corn in a pan. Do all the seeds pop at the same time? No, but eventually you end up with a bowl of popcorn.

Nice. Is that a metaphor?

Children today have so many more challenges and pressures to face compared with when we were their age. I'd hate to be a kid nowadays, if I am being honest. I mean, can you remember at any point when you were at school feeling an ounce of stress or pressure about anything? Did you even know the word 'anxiety' when you were ten? Whereas now we have more Year 6 children being diagnosed with stress-related conditions because of a series of tests they need to sit in the last year of primary school that ultimately don't mean anything to them? The fact they are given all this technology at such a young age with this money-rich/time-poor approach where they become addicted and crave validation through things like a 'like' button. We need to have some perspective of this and be mindful.

The one with the toddler I swear there are parents at every school that go through a 10–15-year period where you only ever see them with a baby in their arms or a toddler stumbling around their ankles. They seem to be on a constant conveyor belt of spawning children, and not long before you hear about a new addition the next pregnancy is announced. These parents are quite the experience at parents' evening as they more often than not bring the toddler with them and present themselves as having some sort of split personality ...

'Hi, I am so sorry, I couldn't get anyone to look after the little one but please, how's she getting on?'

'No worries, well ...'

'GET BACK HERE NOW, I TOLD YOU TO SIT DOWN! Sorry, you were saying?'

'Yeah, she's actually ...'

'DON'T YOU DARE! COME BACK! WHERE ARE YOU GOING? I'm sorry, I'll be back in a second.'

The initial 5–10-minute appointment now turns into a 20-minute Benny Hill sketch where you and the mother are trying to chase and catch the toddler running riot in the hall.

The joker There is always one parent who was clearly the class clown when they were at school and their sole focus during parents' evening is making sure their child is emulating them.

'OiOY! How you doing, mate? So, how is he getting on? Is he keeping you entertained? Yeah, non-stop laughs? Top-quality banter! Yeah, don't worry about his targets. I just want to know if he entertains everyone like his old man.'

This tends to be the same parent you find playing tig with the kids in the playground before the school bell rings for the start of the day. This is the same parent who had to be put in his place on sports day.

The angry one It is likely you will encounter at least one parent who waits until parents' evening to unleash their frustrations and catch you off guard. It is funny as usually parents who have written letters of complaint, creating an impression that meeting them will be a nightmare, tend to turn up and won't say boo to a goose, are just pleasant to your face but will be straight online after to slag you off more. Or worse, they write daily notes of complaint but then when it comes to parents' evening, they don't show up.

I am not going to say that frustrations from some parents aren't justified. I am not going to say teachers never get it wrong. I completely understand how hard it is if you know your child has specific learning needs, and the process of getting a diagnosis is incredibly difficult, time-consuming and tedious. But again, I wish some parents understood that teachers are on their side. We do everything in our power to help, yet when the system is set up to fail, teachers take the brunt of the frustrations. The most infuriating angry parents are the ones who just point-blank refuse to allow anyone to speak about their child in a negative way.

'WHAT DO YOU MEAN THEY HAVE ANGRY OUTBURSTS!?! THAT DOESN'T SOUND LIKE MY CHILD. IF THEY ARE LASHING OUT AT OTHERS IT WILL BE BECAUSE THE OTHER CHILDREN ARE NOT PLAYING NICELY. I DON'T KNOW WHY THEY WOULD BE ANGRY.' With their face gradually getting redder, their fists clenching and teeth grinding, they'll say, 'I DON'T HAVE A CLUE WHERE THEY'D BE GETTING IT FROM!'

It amazes me how willing fully grown adults are to believe a six-year-old child over a fully grown (in most cases, sorry, Adam), professionally trained adult. To give you a taste of what this looks like in context, a parent once furiously complained that the spellings we had given out contained a swear word, going completely over the teacher straight to the head. When the head confronted the teacher to explain the complaint from the parent and find out why the teacher had purposefully and intentionally set the word 'arsehole' as a spelling to be tested that week, the teacher quickly replied with the fact that the word was in fact 'aerosol'. Yes, the child had copied it down incorrectly and rather than assume this, the parent believed that the teacher would give that word for the children to use. Unless that teacher had clearly had a few interactions with that parent previously ...

'Ok, class, question four, the word is "arsehole". "Arsehole". Kyle's mum is a complete and utter arsehole.'

The active one This is the parent you only ever see in Lycra. Dropping the kids off, gym top and leggings; picking them up, different gym top and leggings. Parents' evening, gym top and leggings; school fair, gym top and leggings. You need to be very careful with this parent, as if they get a sniff that you're willing to indulge them you're not getting out alive. Just like those children who go on and on and on and on and on and on when you let them talk during Show and Tell, these parents are itching to let you know what latest diet, CrossFit class or marathon they've run. My tip is to solely focus on the child and not deviate, as you will regret it.

The overly protective one These have to be up there as my most frustrating type of parent. Parachute parents who want to wrap their children in cotton wool, in my opinion, set them up to fail. Children are incredibly resilient. They need to learn to fail, they need to go through struggles and face adversity to learn, but some parents want to do everything – and I MEAN everything – for their child and then they expect you to do it too. Speak to teachers and they will all have some stories of the bizarre and utterly ridiculous requests from parents to keep their precious little pumpkins 'safe'. Genuine concerns will always be taken seriously and dealt with accordingly, but it is frustrating when you go out of your way to go above and beyond to improve the level of communication between school and parents by using online platforms to provide updates, pictures and examples of learning that are shared with parents, and then have parents complain over the most trivial of things. Once I allowed children to have some extra break time for working hard and sent a picture of the children enjoying the outside area to parents, then received a comment from a parent saying, 'I sent a note about James having a sniffle and I can't believe you have allowed him into the playground without his jumper on. Please can I have a word with you to discuss this further.' Jesus wept! Get a life!

The PTA one Parent–Teacher Associations are a crucial part of supporting a successful school. The role they play in fundraising, bringing the school community together and helping families get the most out of their school life is vital. But let's be honest, it takes a certain type of parent to adopt an active role in the PTA. There is only one word to describe these people and that is ... busy. They need to be really, but sometimes I can only deal with these people in small doses. Especially when their five minutes at parents' evening is instead used to discuss the Christmas Fair over their child's progress. I hope you realise the risk I am taking by speaking about these parents, as the power they can wield at the school gates can be intimidating, to say the least. Does the head teacher have the most power in a school? Or are they simply the pawn that the head of the PTA influences, like Dominic Cummings and Bojo?

The conspiracy theorist parent A new addition in 2020, the parents who really really need to get off Facebook and spend more time learning about primary and secondary sources. The letters doing the rounds at schools about testing, vaccines and so forth have been a new situation schools have had to deal with. You have to respect the diplomatic response from schools when in reality teachers would love to turn round and scream, 'STOP BEING SO F*****G STUPID! Coronavirus is real! Bill Gates, the lizard, isn't making this up and spreading it through 5G masts to infect us all so we take a vaccine that is laced with a microchip! You haven't done any actual research, you've watched a couple of YouTube videos, you plank.'

The 'obsessed with their phone' parent This has to be the worst one. Whether they are a wannabe Instagram influencer and so vlog the whole parents' evening or just unable to engage as they are constantly glancing, interacting and texting on their phone. I honestly think the issues young people face with technology and the negative impact it is having on children's speech is more to do with the lack of interaction from parents who are addicted to their phones. There is nothing more frustrating than seeing a parent pick up their child and not look up from their phone to greet their child. What message are you sending to that child when you are constantly prioritising that device over your child? Don't get me wrong, I often find myself distracted by my phone, but I am trying to be more mindful and when speaking to my children I will try to put the phone away.

Interestingly, I am always amazed at how many complaints I've had or seen that come from parents who themselves work in education. It astounds me how quick teachers can be in bringing each other down. Nothing has changed my view on education more than when I became a parent myself. It certainly gives you a different perspective. It changes your viewpoint on a number of things. How I am as a teacher vs what I am like as a parent is stark. Here are a few examples:

Homework
As a teacher:

Ok, class, here is this week's homework. You need to make sure you get it done over the weekend. There is no excuse, you need to do it and do it well. If it's not done, you will have to stay in at break to finish it.

As a parent:

What do you mean you've got homework this weekend? But we've got so much on! We're never going to be able to get it done. We've got football tomorrow, followed by swimming, and we're then going to see Grandma. Then *Strictly* is on, so I'm not missing that! Ok, we'll just do it now. If we get it done now, we've got the whole week to chill and relax. No, we need to do it now! GET BACK HERE! Listen, you're not having a biscuit until you've done this homework. Oh, can you hear that? I think it's the ice-cream man, but guess who won't be getting one! YOU!

I then sit next to my child, staring intensely while licking my 99 with a Flake.

As a teacher:

Right then, class, is everyone ok with the homework? I've gone through and explained exactly what you need to do but if anyone is unsure, please just ask and I will go through it again. No questions? Ok, go and put your homework in your bags.

As a parent:

How can you not know what you're doing? Your teacher isn't just going to give you homework and not explain how to do it. You should know what you're doing. Ok, let me have a look. I don't know why you're doing this, it's not even on the curriculum.

As a teacher:
According to our homework policy, homework is very, very, very important and something you need to do.

As a parent:
I am not being funny but, seriously, what you're doing here is a complete and utter waste of time! It is pointless!

As a teacher:
And when you are doing homework, children, remember it is *your* homework. I want to see that you're doing it so I can get a clear idea of how you're progressing with this work. Only when you're stuck can you ask your parents for some guidance.

As a parent:
Get back here and finish this homework. You're not doing anything else until it is finished. Fine. Go to your room! I'll just bloody do it!

There has been some research to suggest that homework at primary has very little impact on learning. I have to admit, I was a stickler for it before becoming a parent, whereas now I feel time at home can be used more productively. Obviously schools differ in their opinions about this, but one universal thing every single teacher will want every single parent to do is read with their child. EVERY. SINGLE. NIGHT!

Listening to your child read and reading a book to your child are the only non-negotiables I would have for parents. You can never underestimate the power of reading. Research has shown the single biggest indicator of how successful children will be later on in life is whether they read for pleasure. Modelling this as teachers and parents is a crucial way to help children with their ability to read. Putting 20 minutes aside each night just before bed to cuddle up and get lost in an amazing story that children will remember for the rest of their lives is such a gift and something I love doing. It is the highlight of my day.

Notes from Parents
As a teacher:

Oh brilliant, another nagging note from a parent. When will they learn I am just trying my best and want to help as much as I possibly can.

As a parent:

You what? You were kept in at break because your homework wasn't up to scratch. Hang on, I did that homework! Give me your reading record, your teacher is going to get a piece of my mind!

Letters Home
As a teacher:

I am so sorry, you can't take part in this bread-tasting lesson as we've not had written permission from your parents. I did send home that letter over a week ago. I have told you, you need to be more responsible and give that letter to your parents.

As a parent:

There was no letter! What is the teacher talking about? How can I sign a letter that hasn't been given to me! Where did you say you put it? On the kitchen side? I think I would have seen a letter if you'd have left it here on the side ... oh, you mean this letter. Why can't they just text me?

Reading
As a teacher:
It is important, so important, to make sure you read every night with your parents. Your parents NEED to be reading with you every single night without fail.

As a parent:
Yes, darling, I will read with you in a minute. I just need to finish this marking. I know it is pointless and my class won't be able to read it but if I don't do it, Daddy is going to be called into the head's office and be told off at the next book scrutiny!

As a teacher:
Ok, take your time, just sound it out. Well done, really good try! Keep going, you are doing so well.

As a parent:
Ok, let's go, sound it out, no, sound it out, don't just guess! SOUND IT OUT! It really isn't that hard! I can't do this unless you're going to try! I don't know how your teacher does it!

People have often asked me for parenting advice and honestly I don't feel qualified at all – just read the above. However, I do have a few life rules I try to instil in my children to hopefully help them grow into happy and well-rounded adults.

1) **Life's not fair.** It is a simple but incredibly effective point. Sometimes bad things will happen to you, and some people have more bad things happen to them than others – there is no balance. There will be some things in life you can't control, but you can control the way YOU react to them.

2) **You get nothing in life for free.** If you want to be successful in life you have to work hard. Expecting things to be handed to you will not only lead to little success but also to you having no drive or sense of the value of things. Hard work will outweigh talent every time.

3) **Not everyone is going to like you and there is nothing you can do about it.** No matter how nice you are as a person there will always be some people that don't like you. Don't waste your time on these people. Focus on people who like you for you. There will be some people who aren't your cup of tea. You should always treat people with respect in a way you would like to be treated.

4) **Comparison is the thief of joy.** This is one my children will understand when they are old enough to be online. As much as I love social media it can be a pretty toxic place. The only person you should compare yourself to is you, and if you are in a better place than you were six months ago you are on the right track.

5) **If you have a problem about something, the only way to solve it is to speak to someone**. That someone doesn't have to be your parents but the longer you keep a problem to yourself, the worse it will get.

Wow! Wise words, but why so serious?
Alternatively, you could follow my very simple life lessons:

1) **Recline.** When you're sitting down, try to recline. You may as well be as relaxed as possible when taking a well-earned seat, but try to pull that lever as silently as possible ... The kids (and my wife) can hear that sound from within a 5-mile radius!

2) **Don't iron.** If you're not leaving the house, don't bother ironing your clothes. Who cares? No one is going to judge your creased

threads in your own place and if you have unexpected guests, just blame the kids for having to recently get changed!

3) **Buy grated cheese instead of a block of cheese.** I was 31 years of age when I first used a cheese grater and my hand still hasn't recovered. It's just easier and a time saver to buy grated.

4) **Buy a dishmatic.** Arguably one of my all-time favourite creations. If you don't know what it is, it's a sponge on the end of a stick that you fill with washing-up liquid. It makes washing up fun ... seriously.

5) **Go large.** Last, but certainly not least, whenever you are ordering from a fast-food outlet and they ask if you'd like to go large, always, and I mean always, say yes – it's a bigger drink and more chips for like 30p, it's a no-brainer. Two words, guys, you're welcome. Especially when your partner claims that they're not hungry but still manages to eat 25 chips and a bite of your burger!

School trips – the most exciting day in the academic calendar. It doesn't matter if you are going to a science museum, Roman villa or a medieval castle, the kids will be bouncing off the walls by the end of the day.

Ah, I love school trips, especially when you arrive back with the same number of kids you set off with!

Have you ever not?

Erm, next question ...

I definitely found trips more fun as a child. As a grown-up, they are such hard work.

Do you remember it, though? Learning you were going on a trip, then dancing home with a permission letter. Your sole responsibility was to pass it to your parent or guardian in time for them to sign the reply slip and enclose the wonga.

Yeah, and on the day of the trip, some drongo usually still had their letter at the bottom of their school bag under some football stickers and a mouldy banana. The subsequent phone call to their parents on the morning of the excursion meant that even before it was 9.15am, the teacher organising the trip was stressed out.

If you were really lucky, you'd get to wear your own clothes, but when we were younger there wasn't a hi-vis vest in sight.

There was always some dope who forgot to bring a packed lunch. Packed lunches on trips were the best. I always tactically put myself near the kids I knew would bring the goods. A spare Wagon Wheel or a handful of Haribo Starmix would give you the perfect buzz for a day out with your mates. Dream stuff!

Did you ever actually learn anything on trips? Or did you just behave so that you could buy a rainbow eraser in the gift shop?

I've still got about 28 of those bad boys in a drawer somewhere at Mum's. The worst part of the day for me was when your teacher would announce, 'You had better be paying attention, we're going to be learning about this tomorrow!'

I bet your writing the following day was epic.

Only if I was allowed to write about eating four Milky Bar yoghurts and having a top laugh with my mates. I usually learnt nothing, bro!

The thing is, when you're a kid, a trip is something you look forward to all year, especially if it's one you've heard about before from older kids in the school. Whether it's Cadbury World or the local sewage works, it's a day out of the classroom with your mates where the most important thing is deciding which pal you are going to be sitting with on the coach. In complete contrast, fast forward to being the teacher in charge of the trip and you quickly find that:

SCHOOL TRIP = INSTANT MIGRAINE!

As a kid, you don't realise what actually goes into arranging a school trip. You may question on the day of the trip why a teacher's breath has a stronger hint of coffee than usual but the reason becomes far more obvious as you grow up. First, you have to choose your destination, then after that it's a whirlwind of logistics and red tape: getting permission from the head, permission letters from parents, checking enough parents have paid, booking the coach, ordering packed lunches, collecting medical forms, medicine and filling out a chuffing RISK ASSESSMENT!

Not to mention trying to sway which staff members are coming along for the ride (no one wants a mood-hoover in an already painfully dull museum).

As trip organiser, you arrive at school early, semi-eagerly awaiting all the children to arrive (secretly hoping that the child you know is going to ruin the day has car trouble and misses the coach ... but that NEVER happens).

I wondered why my teachers looked disappointed when I showed up on trip day!

The box of packed lunches is waiting, the support staff that are accompanying you on the trip are waiting — there's always one who is just buzzing because they still view school trips as if they were a child, and because they didn't organise a bloody thing (plus they get to miss a full day of actual work).

Speaking of missing work, if you don't have enough school staff joining you then sometimes there are a few parents on the coach as well. It's always important to rope in your go-to parents in advance. You know the ones, your dependable stalwarts that are veterans of school trips past.

The ones that are usually CRB/DBS cleared to work with children as they help run the local Brownies. These guys are like gold dust.

The ones you don't want are the molly-coddling morons that make the trip way more stressful than it needs to be, undermining the staff at every point, putting them on edge and reprimanding children that have done nothing wrong while letting their own offspring behave like a brat.

Funnily enough, those parents don't get invited back.

At the start of the day there's the pre-trip briefing with the class. The sensible chat begins, including which groups the children are in and which grown-up they have been allocated. This is usually met with cheers and groans (more groans if the mood-hoover got the nod). Then the most important question gets asked if it hasn't already – 'Who gets travel sick?' Your eyes are scanning the room as one, two, three or even four rascals out in the crowd put their hands up. You'll know exactly who they are; they are the already slightly sickly ones with the potential to turn green. This means it's time to get the plastic bags and buckets at the ready. Potential vomit-artists are placed at the front of the coach, just behind the adults in the first few seats.

There is always a feeling of relief when the coach doors close, and you know they're all on and accounted for. You throw a 'stage one completed' look, wink and give a thumbs-up to a fellow staff member.

Yeah, but you come crashing back down to reality when after approximately three minutes of driving, one of the front-seat sick-merchants has gone so pale they are almost translucent. I once had a girl named Alice. As we were travelling on a school residential trip she sat in the front seat, and early into the journey said she felt like she was going to be …

Did she finish that sentence?

… Nope! The seat was plastered with beige lava; it looked like it was rice for last night's tea. The worst thing was there was a bucket and bag on the seat next to Alice but she went rogue and decorated the interior of the bus. I had to act quickly to stop the flow and make sure we didn't have travel sickness dominoes going on. One whiff of the spew and the kids would have been following suit.

Not the way you want to start a day trip.

Day trip? This was a school residential! Fortunately, we isolated the spew-meister and gave her mints to suck on to stop her losing her breakfast for a second time!

Once you finally pull up to the destination, you have one last pep talk that usually sounds something like this:

'Right, guys, we're here to have fun, but in the right manner. We are here to learn and we are representing the school. If anyone isn't doing that in the right way, the head teacher is one call away and they will pick you straight up.'

If you don't threaten getting picked up by the head, are you even on a school trip?

Grouping the pupils sensibly on a trip is essential. If you are a member of staff and you do not organise the groups meticulously, you're asking for trouble. You make sure the kids that are going to be a problem are definitely not in the same group.

That probably explains why I was often in a different group to some of my pals!

I should imagine that was a top priority, mate! Although you definitely make sure your chosen group has a few kids that you can have great banter with so the day isn't truly dull. You get to see another side to the kids out of school and, in turn, they get to see a different side to their teachers.

School trips are brilliant to make memories but can also be a test of patience like nothing else. Try overseeing 30 kids taking turns in a gift shop smaller than your front room.

Children nowadays will be allowed to bring up to a fiver in order to purchase some random, overpriced twaddle bearing the logo of the place you are visiting. One kid will have brought a crisp £20 note and will buy bouncy balls, a slinky plus a plastic catapult that almost takes out a classmate's eye. You'll have to have a chat with their parents, who will no doubt feign ignorance at the stated £5 limit on the letter.

There's never this problem when your school trip is to a farm!

Why's that?

No gift shop!

Good point. You had a school trip to a farm, didn't you?

Yes indeed, with a teaching assistant called Mary, and it was a rather mooo-ving experience.

There's a cow in this story, isn't there ...?

Yeah, there's a cow.
　　Now old-school Mary, was as ... erm ... 'old school' as they come, but funny as hell (not always on purpose). A real team player ... but only on her terms.

Sounds like one not to be messed with ...

Strap in, though, it's about to get weird.
　　On a trip to a farm with the Year 2 class, I witnessed a sight that will never leave my memory. Mary would do anything to look after the children she works with – and I mean **literally anything**.
　　The trip was going as planned; the children were enjoying a nice day at the farm – bumpy tractor rides, feeding the lambs and there was even a nice play area, meaning we could have a lovely drink in

peace as we watched them. The trip was going swimmingly until we went to watch the cows getting milked towards the end of the day. The milking demonstration area wasn't the biggest space; children and staff were crammed near the barriers next to some of the cows. During the demonstration, Mary was standing next to a boy by the fence when a cow (as cows do) leaned over and let out a 'MOOO' right into the boy's ear. This startled him, and he was clearly in shock and started to get really upset. Quick to respond, and to my surprise, Mary yelled 'BACK OFF!' and with unexpected strength, open-palm-shoved the cow's head away from the boy.

After she gave the cow a hand-off Jonah Lomu would have been proud of, it surprisingly all calmed down ... that was until the cow swung its head over the barrier and licked the petrified child's arm. I mean, what would you do in that situation?

Panic!

Exactly! Not Mary, though. With no regard for the thoughts of the farm workers in close proximity, Mary clenched her fist and full-blown PUNCHED the cow straight in its chops and bellowed,

'I DID WARN YOU, YOU SILLY COW!'

The cow let out a huge 'MOOOO' and backed away from the barrier.

What the fudge?

Oh, yeah! Lennox Lewis would've loved the right hook she delivered. I can honestly say I laugh about this tale roughly once a week and it was nearly a decade ago! Luckily for Mary no further action was taken, as the farm staff were rolling in the hay laughing their arses off. Moral of this story: you don't want to have a 'beef' with old-school Mary!

Disclaimer: No cows were harmed in the making of this story ... apart from the one with the extra black eye!

Dinner
Times

Break duty. At no point during my four-year university course did anyone even mention the fact that once or a twice a week you would have to stand in the freezing cold watching and trying to keep the peace among hundreds of children. Depending on the size of your school and staff you will probably have one break duty a week, possibly two if you have afternoon breaks. Midday assistants or old-school dinner ladies hold the fort during lunchtime unless, of course, due to the budget cuts from our caring government, midday assistant duty has now been passed on to teachers and support staff. I would like to state that teaching is incredibly draining – mentally and physically: having to impart knowledge in a way that can be understood by a class of 30+ with a huge range of ability, considering questions to pitch at the right level for a particular child then instantly differentiating another question to further challenge a different child, trying to keep on top of behaviour and low-level disruption to ensure pupils can focus on their learning, while also considering how you are going to manage marking the work children do after the after-school club and then getting home to sort your own children out with their homework, tea, extra-curricular clubs. The point I am trying to make is that teaching an effective lesson to a class of children is hard work. Therefore, teachers need a break. Having 10 minutes to get organised for the next lesson, grab a brew, run off some worksheets from the photocopier makes a huge difference to the rest of the day. This is why most teachers will say doing break duty is up there as the worst part of their job.

Every teacher will know that on the day when it is their break duty, it isn't going to be the best day. It's hectic, it throws you off your rhythm, it is only made worse if you make the fatal mistake of forgetting your coat. The only way in which this can be drastically made worse is by the two words that send shivers down every school staff's neck, the two words that mean the rest of the day is a complete write-off and that turn a normal day of learning into one of simple survival. I am talking, of course, about ... WET PLAY.

But WET and PLAY aren't the only two words to send a shiver down any teacher's spine. In fact here are plenty more of what we like to call ...

HOMEMADE CAKES If that comes from the mouth of the most snot-ridden, mucus-filled child in your class, you will obviously thank them and then keep the cakes as a greeting when Ofsted come to visit.

WET LACES On a sunny day with no puddle in sight, you know there's only one reason why those shoelaces are wet.

FIRE DRILL There goes my lesson in one fell swoop.

BROWN MARKS Use your imagination.

QUICK WORD When this is uttered by a member of the leadership team, you will know that a) it won't be quick, and b) you've done something wrong.

BOOK SCRUTINY This is explained later in the problem with the education chapter.

GOVERNMENT INITIATIVES More often than not, these are cooked up by people who have never worked a day in the classroom, which ultimately results in a greater workload for those at the chalkface.

PARENTS' EVENING Yes, believe it or not, this is a scary experience for most teachers.

HEAD LICE Just the mere mention of them will make any teacher become paranoid about catching them.

THE CALL This means Ofsted are on their way and you are about to enter the most stressful few days of your career.

BROKEN PHOTOCOPIER Although frustrating, the fact it happens so regularly means you get used to it.

LESSON OBSERVATION More on that later.

THAT PARENT Yes, the parent who makes your life a living hell. If you're a parent reading this thinking, I don't think there's anyone like that in my child's class, it's probably YOU!

PARENT COMPLAINT Of these, 9 out of 10 will be completely irrelevant, but they will still take up a lot of your time.

CAN YOU ...? You wish you could say no, but you can't.

YOU BUSY? Obviously I am, I'm a teacher! And even if I weren't, you're about to make me busy!

WRITTEN REPORTS As discussed earlier, a pointless exercise that wastes so much of your life.

But in classrooms all over the world, WET PLAY – or INDOOR RECESS for our friends on the other side of the pond – will definitely ruin your day. I can never get my head around the teachers who are quick to decide on wet play; just a dark cloud on the horizon and they're calling for classes to stay inside? Granted, you don't want to get wet on duty, but that's a small price to pay compared with a long afternoon after your class has been penned into the classroom for nearly four hours straight! If it is spitting, we're out; light rain, get outside, make sure you have your coats on and get some fresh air.

Talking about random things you only find in primary schools, every class will have a wet play box. This is usually kept in the teacher's cupboard and will be a collection of broken toys, board games with half the pieces missing and random McDonald's toys added from Happy Meals over the years. The scrap-paper drawer is raided by some of the class and parents will know it's been wet play when the children come home with a collection of random drawings, using usually yellow pens as they are the only ones teachers are happy for the children to use so they don't waste the good ones. Teachers can't set their classroom up for the next lesson and children don't have the opportunity to burn off energy and instead release it during the next lesson.

Not much has changed since I was a child when it comes to what you see in a playground. Technology might improve, curriculums will be different, but the same characters will be found in the playgrounds of every primary school up and down the country. The only real difference is the fact that apparently children can no longer differentiate between a fellow pupil and a teacher. I understand that beauty products are helping plenty of adults look younger, but the fact teachers need to make it clear they are the adults by wearing a hi-vis jacket if they're on break duty is taking the health and safety risk assessment culture we now live in to another level. I've never had a child mistake a 30+ year old for a 6 foot 4 …

… 6 foot 4? Are you having a laugh? You're 6 foot 2 at best.

Alright, 6 foot 2 then. As I was saying, I have never had a child mistake me for a nine-year-old. Anyway, back to the different types of characters you find in a playground.

First we need to start with the most important child in the whole playground, the teacher's PA. Not that anyone employs a PA, we're talking about the child who steps into the role and reminds the teacher of everything they need to do. I wouldn't survive without these children. I'll be in class, in full flow, dropping knowledge bombs, and before I know it the bell has gone. You completely forget until the PA steps up to remind you that it is your break duty, so you whizz down the corridor to make sure you're on time to carry out your other important role. Only when you get to the playground do you realise, you haven't got your coat or whistle. Who is there to save the day? Yes, you guessed it, the PA, who will nip back to the class to get all the equipment you need to fulfil your duties perfectly. They are a lifesaver.

There will always be a group of children who eat, sleep and dream for playground football. It is the highlight of their school day, and they live for those 20 minutes during lunch. The marked-out pitch in the school playground is like Wembley. Both Adam and I were part of this group when we were back in school. It was the place where you could replicate the skills you'd admired watching *Match of the Day* over the weekend. If you're a die-hard playground-football enthusiast, the game will start with a walkout from your classroom, doing the sign of the cross as you enter the pitch, a rendition of the Champions League theme tune, thanking the thousands of imaginary fans that have come to watch and the toss-up to decide who will kick off. You can recognise these children as they will be limbering up in class from around quarter to 12 to get themselves ready for the big game. If you gave them the choice, they'd quite happily change into full kit before playing the game, even if it meant reducing the actual game time by half.

The only person who annoys me when it comes to playground football is the child who brings the ball. They've been to Decathlon at the weekend, picked up a fresh sponge ball and they are now in complete control of everything – teams, rules and ultimately the results. If things aren't going the way they want, they can at any point call the game there and then and walk off with the ball to start another game. We have had a couple of power-hungry children who would threaten the whole game if they didn't get their own way. We have even bought our own set of sponge balls to try to stop these dictators of the pitch, but they didn't last long as within a week they all had a huge chunk bitten out of them.

There will always be a child who, as soon as break time comes, puts their coat on – and by putting it on I mean just their hood – and they transform into a superhero. These children have never been seen with their arms in their coats, it's just a hood on their heads; their coat is now a cape and they fly around the playground looking for anyone in distress to help. Is it a bird? Is it a plane? No, it's Kian in Year 3. There is no sadder sight than when that child gets a new coat and it doesn't have a hood. It is like kryptonite; they lose all their powers and spend the rest of their playground days traipsing round the playground like Mr Incredible when he has to just live a normal life.

Effective break duty will not just rely on a teacher having their wits about them. It is a team effort, as any teacher worth their salt will have spies dotted around the playground, ready to report on any incident that might go down. Some teachers might call these children tell-tales, other children will call them snitches, but they are crucial when you're dealing with children who have a completely different view on what has just happened on the playground. A child might have just chosen to start their own WWE Royal Rumble where they decide to 'open a can of whup-ass' on everyone, and when you question this child who thinks he's The Rock or 'Stone Cold' Steve Austin and the playground is Wrestlemania they refuse to accept responsibility and instead protest that 'I didn't punch him, he walked into my fist.' You then turn into a lawyer from *Law and Order*: 'Well, let me call my first witness ...' One of your spies then appears: 'Do you swear to tell the truth, the whole truth and nothing but the truth?'

'I do your honour!'

'Ok, did you see him punch him?'

'Yeah, he walked up to them, flipped the bird and then tried to rock bottom them!'

Rock bottom! Another of my go-to playground wrestling moves!

I turn to the offender: 'Right, you, on the wall!'

Every school has the WALL. It was a familiar location for Adam back in the day, and is a place of reflection for those who don't make the right choices. It often looks like the scene from *The Usual Suspects* where they all line up and are questioned, all two metres apart, practising social distancing way before 2020. At the end of break, teachers will come to collect their class, hoping, praying that the wall is clear.

There will always be a couple of wheeler-dealer children, the Del Boy wannabes, the ones who are able to bring illegal objects into the playground. And before you wonder what kind of school does he work in, I'm not talking about drugs. I'm talking about some of the objects we've covered in the Classroom Crazes chapter. They have been discussed in assembly, with the head stating they are not to be brought into school, but somehow they still find their way into the corners of the playground.

Some children use the playground as their own arena stage, spending each and every break time choreographing, practising and performing the latest dance, TikTok trend or music video. I just love how seriously they take it. It usually coincides with some sort of talent show or school performance. These children will spend the following 364 days practising for the next audition. There may well be a leader of each group, the diva that will accept nothing but the best from everyone. They take absolutely no messing and are relentless in their pursuit of talent-show gold. Anyone who doesn't perfect the moves is cut, and it quickly turns into a *Britain's Got Talent/X Factor/Cheerleading* talent show. As a teacher you take the Dermot role of consoling those children who didn't make it through to the next round.

You will also have a group of children who turn the playground into their own reality TV show. Forget *TOWIE*, *Geordie Shore*, *Real Housewives of Wherever*, the real drama is in the St John's playground! Gossip is taken to new heights as decisions about who's going out with who, dumpings and new couplings-ups are a daily occurrence. The fallings-out are non-stop and always the most draining to sort out for teachers, as it's all 'He said', 'She said'. Funnily enough, a child came to me recently to tell a tale on his friend who wasn't playing nicely, and when I said, 'I'm sick of this "He said", "She said",' he replied with, '"She said"? There's no "She said"!'

Finally, there will always be at least one child who from the moment they step foot in the playground will latch on to your side and remain there for the full duration of break. No matter how much you encourage them to go and play, run around, burn some energy, they are quite content to play the role of your shadow. You then spend the whole break time trying not to fall over the child.

Dinner times in a primary school, the second-best part of most children's day (second to the end of the day).

As a child, this is the time when you can sit with your friends to have either your school dinner or your packed lunch. I used to find that the rest of my day and lunchtime behaviour would depend on what school dinner it was. Back in the day, if I saw Turkey Twizzlers and potato smiles, I knew the day was going to be a classic. On the flip side, if I saw quiche and veg, I knew it was more than likely I would have to stand on the wall at dinner due to pure 'hangriness'.

Anyway, once you had wolfed your lunch down you got to play some classic playground games, but sadly you don't see the games that made our lunchtimes so exciting as a child any more.

Games that are rare now are kiss chase (basically, you chased the person you wanted to kiss), which was a perfect way to declare your love to a potential suitor in Year 5/6, but usually by the time you caught them, you were red as a tomato, sweating all over and those weird white spit bits had gathered around your mouth – not how any of us imagine our first kiss going. Remember conkers, marbles, pogs and wrestling? All these games have fallen out of favour and mostly been banned. Playtime now is much more structured than it used to be, with more options and organisation, and plenty of staff rotated to provide the safest and most enjoyable lunchtime for the children. It's not like it used to be when there would be one dinner lady (two at a push) looking after about 70 children, and if you found the right space, it was free rein. Nowadays, all bases are covered, and as someone who works every dinner time, I love trying to provide fun and laughs throughout the break for my children as I feel it benefits their work in the afternoon.

For me as a child and as a semi-grown up, the highlight of any lunchtime has to be playground football. At 6 foot something and weighing in at 18 stone (16 stone hopefully by the time this is published), there aren't many primary age children who can match up to the colossus of breaktime football ... yours truly! Joking aside, when I do join in, I play at a walking pace and try my best to encourage good sportsmanship and positive play. Well, I do when a member of SLT walks past! As soon as they are in the distance, I'm sticking a bicycle kick in the top bin!

The con of me acting as dependable referee was definitely over on the day I was due to be giving a presentation to the governors after school. Unlike with most things, I had actually remembered the meeting, so I came to school dressed in a smart shirt, shoes and suit trousers. All was going well until I was faced with a moral dilemma; the school football captain was missing their lunchtime game due to making the wrong choices earlier in the day. They were a player short. How could I turn down the opportunity to be a breaktime hero? Oh, how I wish I had turned it down!

The two teams were going tit-for-tat in the latter stages of the game when I spotted a hole in the opposition's defensive line, mostly because I had sent the best defender to 'THE WALL' for using foul language. I signalled to the goalkeeper to hit me with a long ball. As it was played, I realised it was going further than I had anticipated. Showing my commitment, I stretched my leg out in an attempt to bring down the long pass ... and that's when it happened. 'That's torn it!' I thought to myself, but it wasn't the familiar feeling of a tearing a hamstring, oh no, 'twas the embarrassing sound of my trousers tearing! This wasn't just a slightly inconspicuous hole but one that started at the base of my zip and followed my entire bum crack round to my belt line!

Unfortunately for me, the closest area of refuge was my head-teacher's office. I gathered what was left of my trousers and tiptoed off the pitch. This was when staff knew that I had taken 'reffing' to the extreme. Fortunately, my head teacher has a great sense of humour; she found it hilarious. What the hell was I to do, though? The spare clothes box that usually has a few replacement items for kids that wee themselves or fall in a puddle was hardly going to have replacement attire for a giant buffoon that should've known better! Luckily, I remembered that I had a bag of clothes in the boot of my car that I was supposed to take to the local recycling bank. Jackpot (sort of)! I walked like John Wayne through the school car park, and in amongst the clothes I was delighted to discover some beige slim-fitting chinos that were a few inches light on the waist. I managed to stretch my shirt enough to cover the fact that I couldn't do the button up. Result! At least there were trousers to cover my blushes. I was very grateful that I was too lazy to take that bag to the clothes bank, and thank goodness the head teacher found it so humorous.

Despite my wardrobe malfunction, the governor meeting went without a hitch until the end, when the head governor said:

'Maybe next time don't join in the football game and rip your trousers.'

The news had clearly travelled fast and the people in the meeting were finding it very amusing.

As a child, the staffroom where teachers congregated at lunch-time and break was a complete mystery. Only a very lucky few were ever able to see inside this enigma. I remember once being sent to the staffroom to ask for something, then nervously knocking on the door. The door opened ever so slightly, just enough for a head to appear with a look of utter disdain issuing a tutting, 'Yes?' As I tried to explain that a teacher was needed in the dining room, my eyes desperately tried to peer in and see the wonders of the infamous staffroom, the place where teachers went every day to escape. Granted, the smoke that wafted out of the room as the door was opened only further added to the mystique. As the bell rang to announce the end of lunch, the teachers would appear like contestants on *Stars in Their Eyes*. That tradition of keeping the staffroom a place of complete mystery is still maintained today.

When I eventually got to enter a staffroom as an adult the disappointment on my face must have been a picture. This special room that teachers escaped to was nothing like what I pictured. I imagined pool tables, slot machines, a bar maybe. Weirdly, there are some schools that don't have a staffroom, or they have one but staff don't go in it, or if they do it is frowned upon. For anyone who has never seen a staffroom, whether you work in education or not, let me break down pretty much every such room in a UK primary school:

There will be a cupboard of random mugs and cups in all different shapes and sizes, to provide the caffeine shots needed for teachers to make it through the daily grind, with plenty of 'World's Best Teacher' mugs that were given to teachers as a Christmas or end of year thank-you gift. As an NQT, these felt more important than your actual teaching degree – I don't know if there are actual teaching trophies, but getting one of these was when you knew you'd made a difference.

You'll always find a couple of mugs with some witty teaching banter on it, something along the lines of 'Keep calm and pretend it was on the lesson plan', 'I am a teacher, what is your superpower?' or 'I put the tea in TEA-cher'.

There will also always be personalised mugs with a teacher's actual name on it. Under no circumstance can these be used by anyone other than that teacher themself. If a visitor makes the mistake of using it, they will be blacklisted and never allowed to step foot in the school again.

The only thing more random than the collection of mugs is the collection of cutlery in the drawer. There will be some odd plastic cutlery left over from the staff party three years ago. However, you will never – and I mean never – be able to find a teaspoon, as these are as rare as a Pritt Stick in July. The only plates are ones from the dining hall where a teacher has got themselves a school lunch, brought it to the staffroom and never returned the plate.

The noticeboard is a staple in every staffroom, a wall with a whiteboard bordered by policies, development plans, probably the latest Ofsted guidance and a poster with who your union rep is. I find it funny that the union rep usually pictured on these posters hasn't been seen in school for years. Signed off with stress or worked at the school over a decade ago and now no longer works in education at all. There may be another display next to the main one that an eager member of staff has created and which consists of motivational quotes alongside a staff shout-out section where colleagues can nominate and put up a Post-it note giving someone else a big shout-out for doing something. Great idea to start with, but fast-forward a year and everyone is so busy they have no time to write and put up a Post-it note, so the few that were stuck up within the first week of the display being put up remain there for years and years. The main noticeboard, which can only be used by SLT, will consist of details of the upcoming week and of the next staff meeting. There may also be some sort of list, sometimes a staff night out, secret Santa or Christmas do list that staff can add themselves to. There is another list that teachers do not want their name on, and that is the tea money list of shame – make sure you get that tea money in on time.

Around the staffroom will be stationery of every kind – pens, pencils, markers – you name it, you'll find one in the staffroom. However, they never work. Next to that will be the pile of magazines; every month you get delivered the latest edition, which is read by all of one member of staff when you're on PPA and just want to procrastinate. As soon as another staff member walks in you quickly put the magazine down as you don't want to be seen as the ultimate teacher geek. No one actually knows the member of staff who subscribed to it, and so for the rest of eternity you'll receive your monthly dose of education-related news and articles.

There is one plant that lives somewhere in the corner, slowly soaking up all the negative energy of the staff moaning about their struggles in class, and so it can barely stand straight. That plant really represents the energy levels of the staff throughout the week.

There will be a table with chairs for staff to sit at while they eat their lunch. You will also find these weird blue chairs that are ridiculously low and have no arms, but there are enough to create a square with a coffee table in the middle. This is where the staffroom clique will sit. Everyone has their place, and very rarely do people move or swap places; you find your spot in the staffroom and that will be yours for the rest of your time there.

There will usually be some sort of card or collection on the coffee table too. Everyone needs to chip in for a new baby, wedding gift, retirement or special birthday. Why is there always that one teacher who spends their whole lunch reading through everyone else's comments? I never know what to put; I try to think of something really witty but usually just end up wishing the person good luck and signing my name.

Let's not forget the cakes and sweets that are always on tap in the staffroom. Except, of course, when one staff member takes the last Celebration but doesn't bin the tin, and so you walk in, pick up the box hoping for a quick choc fix and are greeted by the empty box and heartbreak. My advice would be to also check where the cake has come from. There's nothing worse than a staff member watching an episode of the *Great British Bake Off* and getting giddy, then trying to make some cakes that upon eating give everyone food poisoning and the school has to close for a day. Or, worse, accepting homemade cakes from a pupil. And we're talking here the child who has more snot than sense. Always ask the question, 'Who baked these again? Jenny in Year 5? The one usually seen with her fingers up her nose seemingly tickling her brain? Yeah, I think I will pass, thank you!'

Talking of eating in the staffroom, let's now look at the types of teachers and their lunch. Every staff member will fall into one of these categories:

1 The Leftover King

This is a teacher who seems to always just have the leftovers from tea last night. Whatever it was – pasta, lasagne, spag Bol – was dumped into a Tupperware box and put in the fridge ready to be transferred to the staffroom fridge. They then hog the microwave as they warm it up. What is it with microwaves in schools being the worst microwaves known to planet Earth? I mean, the highest setting seems to be lukewarm and you need 55 minutes of your lunch to heat your dinner. Depending on what they had last night, these teachers can engulf the room with the aroma of korma. Just pray they don't warm up fish.

2 The Spiller

This is the member of staff that no matter what they eat they manage to get it all over them. They are fully grown adults yet can't go one lunchtime without spilling or dropping food either on themselves or all over the table. Don't sit next to these people when they bring soup in and be careful around them with yoghurts. They love wearing white clothes, too.

3 School Dinner Binger

There will be a member of staff who can't get enough of school dinners – school pizza, Turkey Twizzlers, cheese whirls. First port of call each day for them is walking straight to the dining hall and putting down their order for the day. I can't lie, I love a good school dinner.

4 No-lunch Renegade

The staff member who looks at themselves and thinks I've not got time to stop and take two minutes to scoff down some scran. Think about what I can do in those two minutes: I could dash to the photocopier, mark two books, write up my lesson evaluation or check my PowerPoint for the afternoon. This, by the way, doesn't make anyone a better teacher, trust me – take five minutes, refuel your body. You'll need it.

5 The Takeaway Queen

Day in, day out, these teachers are eating their daily recommended calorie intake in one sitting by doing a chippy run, picking up a Maccy D or devouring a bargain bucket within the hour. There's not a McDonald's in a 10-mile radius of the school, but somehow they'll be there with their large Big Mac meal and milkshake. What infuriates me about these teachers is they are always the skinniest of the staff. I put on a stone just looking at their dinner – I am so jealous of these teachers. I've joined them on the odd day for a Subway and I have to then run for two weeks straight to burn it off.

6 The New Day, New Diet

Every single Monday, they are ready to start their new diet. They have spent all of Sunday prepping kale alongside a rich protein dish for each day of the week. They are telling everyone about this new diet and how it will definitely be the one that will help them achieve the results they've been craving since they started working at the school seven years ago. When booksellers come in to show the latest titles, this teacher will always buy the new Joe Wicks or Jamie Oliver book as inspiration for the new diet that will inevitably start on Monday. And just like every week previously, the two days of carb-free, protein-rich, kale-laden meals that guarantee you'll lose a stone before the day is over are quickly forgotten about, because on Wednesday they are with the takeaway queen having a cheeky Nando's for lunch.

7 Random Concoction Maker
These teachers baffle me. They seem to make the most random concoction of food and find it delicious. 'What are you having there? Chocolate-covered Snack a Jacks with liver pate? Lovely, please excuse me while I go and throw up.'

8 Plain Jane
Day in, day out; week in, week out; month in, month out these teachers have the same meal every single day without fail. Always the most dull and boring choice, too, a ham sandwich with ready salted crisps. I have no problem with these teachers but please add a bit of variety to your life. Variety is the spice of life, but they order korma when you go for a curry. Not my kind of people.

9 The Unsolicited Critique Merchant
The wannabe Gordon Ramsay spends the whole of break making comments on everyone else's lunch, how they can make it better, what to add next time. Their lunch is always vanilla as anything but they think they are judges on *Masterchef.* If I want your opinion, I'll ask for it, thanks ... now leave me to my Angel Delight.

10 The Bring Your Whole Kitchen Diner
Lastly, there is always a member of staff who seems to bring their whole kitchen into the staffroom. They may even have their own pantry as they can never decide what to have, so they keep the staffroom stocked with an array of foods like they've just won a round on supermarket sweep. You need to keep these

staff members on side as if for any reason you forget your lunch, they will always be able to knock something up for you.

Then it comes to the lunch hour itself. Every staff member has a role to play. If the lunch hour is a typical 12–1pm, no one will dare enter the staffroom until at least 20 past. It seems to be an unspoken rule. There will no doubt be staff who can't believe some teachers have the time to have a break, so you need to take the first 20 minutes to look busy. More often than not you will be busy: keeping back those children who haven't made the right choices; making sure children have actually written something more than just the date in their book; setting up for the afternoon. But there has been the odd occasion where I have sent all the class out for lunch on time, sorted my afternoon lessons (photocopied worksheets, got the necessary equipment, downloaded the PowerPoint from Twinkl), we've self-marked in maths and the English was a comprehension that we've gone through together. I could have easily waltzed to the staffroom and taken a full 50 minutes. But what would the mood-hoovers think? How would they possibly be able to keep the knowledge that a staff member has taken more than 30 minutes for their lunch without so innocently dropping it into the next conversation with leadership while also explaining how they've not taken their break in seven whole years of teaching?

Before we go into the ins and outs of a typical lunchtime in the staffroom, we do need to acknowledge the members of staff who are always too busy to have a break and see the staffroom as a sign of weakness and temptation. Why would they spend 10 minutes chatting to a colleague when they could be getting next week's photocopying done?

As staff start dripping in and sorting out their lunches there will always be one teacher who takes the role of being the official timekeeper. The huge Ikea clock that is displayed is monitored and scrutinised by this member of staff all the way through lunchtime. There will be two reactions as the time is read out by this teacher, either one of utter surprise and excitement:

'I can't believe we've got another 20 minutes of lunch left!'

Or one of utter despair at how little time is left:

'How can it be ten to already? Where has the time gone?'

Then there is a staff member who is sitting there every lunchtime eating their lunch and who never says a word, just lurking and absorbing everything that happens. They are often invited to share their views but usually reply with a one-word answer.

Somewhere else a teacher, the lazy one, is sprawling all over the chairs, treating the staffroom as if it's their bedroom and they're a teenager at the height of their puberty journey. Mugs are left, spoons are rarely even put in the sink let alone washed or stuck in the dishwasher. They take the idea of a break to the extreme, using any surface they can find upon which to recline ...

Yes, but it is so important to recline. One of my first life lessons on the podcast was exactly that whenever you can, recline. The ability to do it in a range of locations is crucial.

What about the brewer, the member of staff that is always making a brew and has everyone's order down to a tee, your very own Starbucks barista? Sometimes you wonder what their other responsibilities are around school, because making the break-time brew is never missed by these people.

The ghost of the staffroom is always a treat to experience – this is the member of staff that is there one second and gone the next. They show their face just to feel part of the team or not to make them be labelled as a mood-hoover, but as soon as they have entered the room, they're back out on their way to their classroom. On the other side of the room is the teacher who believes that if they bring all their marking into the staffroom, they will be able to get it done in 20 minutes while also having their lunch, getting involved in some juicy gossip and counting that daily staffroom poll based on the random questions someone will throw out. And with the right mix of staff these questions can be pearlers, let me tell you, as we talk about all sorts – making the perfect class of characters you've taught, doing impressions of the children, 'shag/marry/avoid' featuring celebrities, parents and colleagues, and 'would you rather?' questions being discussed for days on end. It is a safe haven where teachers can feel human for 20 minutes each day and I find that has the biggest impact on keeping teachers sane in a profession of madness. So that teacher who continues to bring a set of books with them in the hope that one day they will be able to actually mark something, always ends up getting involved in the random discussions – and rightly so. The human connection of talking with a friend for just five minutes about something other than school will have a more positive impact on the teacher and their class than getting ahead on marking will ever have. If a group of teachers can spend a few minutes halfway through the day laughing and giggling with each other, the release of endorphins will rejuvenate the staff for a more enthusiastic and successful afternoon. A huge shout-out has to be given to those staff members who can bring a smile to their colleagues' faces without knowing how truly powerful it is.

My favourite part of being a member of school staff is if I ever forget my dinner or just plain and simply fancy a hot lunch from the school canteen, I can cut the queue and get no blowback. As a staff member you need lunchtime just as much as the children do, because not only have you more than likely missed breakfast, or you have shoved a breakfast bar in your gob in the sprint to the photocopier at 8am, you also need the 30-minute recharge, and there is no better place than a staffroom filled with people wanting to unwind only for a short time. Every staffroom is much of a muchness: table and chair, a couple of couches, a fridge/freezer and a microwave (two if you're lucky). Now the staffroom is usually a jolly old place, but if an argument were ever to occur, it would definitely be linked to the fridge/freezer.

People have their 'unofficial' own zones, and if you shove your dinner in their zone or edge their dinner further back, there could be hell to pay. At my old school we had a TA named Debs who was in charge of keeping the peace with the fridge and freezer; alongside this, it was to keep it clean and empty enough to store things. One lunchtime I entered the staffroom and Debs was on all fours with a knife, scraping out the freezer. There was complete silence, and I could hear the huffing and puffing coming from her. I knew I probably shouldn't interfere but I asked, 'Is everything ok?' in a concerned tone. She replied quickly and angrily, 'NO! It's not! Someone left a can in the freezer and it's exploded everywhere!' I'd never seen Debs so angry, she was usually such a jolly soul, but the freezer was her baby. I announced in the staffroom, 'Now come on, guys, it's out of order. If you left a can in the freezer go and help Debs because it shouldn't be her doing it as it's not even her can,' shaking my head in disappointment. I looked at Debs and she gave me a smile of approval as if to say thanks for looking out. The bad thing about it all is the night before, I had placed a can of Dr Pepper Zero in the freezer before my after-school club, to get it nice and frosty for home time, but I did not go back to the staffroom to collect my can. Debs, if you're reading this, I'm sorry, I was scared of you, plus you were chipping the Dr Pepper out with the best knife in the staffroom!

If you have a staffroom where everyone is on point and talking about everything and nothing for half an hour, it's one of the best places to be. You know you're in the right staffroom when either of these things happen: you check the clock and celebrate the fact you have a few minutes left because you thought it was later, or there is a collective sigh when the bell goes for the end of lunchtime.

The true classics of any primary school lunchtime in the staffroom is when a lunchtime supervisor knocks and enters, and everyone waits with bated breath to see which child needs assistance or which teacher needs to go out and sort an incident. My very mature and instinctive response to this was always 'Oooooooohhhhhhh' while patting my knees and stamping my feet, and a communal 'Whayyyyyyyyyy!' from the rest of the elated staffroom when their lunchtime was still theirs and not being eaten up by spending it with the children.

The most important member of the staffroom is not the head, deputy or any member of the SLT. It is of course the member of staff who is the social secretary. Usually nominated into the role by themselves, they have the most important role of organising the infamous Christmas do. Planning starts on day one of spring term – yes, that's right, the first day back in January – when the social secretary, hot off the heels of another successful Christmas party, starts to put the wheels into motion to try to better it next year.

They will already know where the staff do will be, but just to give everyone the chance to have their voice heard, they will ask for suggestions. Anything that gets suggested is quickly dismissed: 'That'll be too expensive,' 'You've got to think about every member of staff and not just the young ones,' 'We need to try to keep it local so it's accessible to everyone.'

When the social secretary makes the decision, then comes the hard part ... collecting everyone's deposits and payments. What a nightmare! They try every tactic, give people plenty of time, but there will always be a couple of staff who never pay on time. The passive-aggressive approach with a list on the noticeboard, 'the following people still need to pay the deposit for the party ...' doesn't work. Daily reminders ... nope. To be fair, the school secretary needs to up their game; they need to understand that no one carries cash anymore. My solution? Invest in a card reader.

It is weeks before the event and things are heating up. The venue has emailed through the set menu and the social secretary has printed it off and placed it in the staffroom. Why is there always one staff member that takes a whole lunchtime to study the menu as if they're going to be tested on it in the afternoon!

'Duck à l'orange? Does that have orange in it?'

'No, Yvonne, it's pineapple! Of course, it's duck in an orange sauce.'

'What is this? Calz-o Calz-ooon?'

'Calzone, love, it's a folded pizza.'

An hour later and they're now moaning that there's nothing for them to eat.

We're now in the week of the do. If you've planned the night out towards the end of term, the week will be filled with colouring in, a Christmas DVD and plenty of singing. But you do need to be tactical with your planning. There's nothing worse than waking up the night after with a killer hangover and the prospect of a marking marathon ahead. Here is my tip: plan activities that need little to no marking, artwork the children can take home, a Christmas-inspired story that is subsequently stored in your green filing cabinet (aka the green recycling bin) or do some ICT – no marking there.

Ah, so that is the reason you specialised in that! Explains a lot.

You need the full weekend to prepare. This is your opportunity to show everyone you can actually scrub up ok. The chance for everyone to see you in a different light. Your hair can be done nicely without glitter all over it. You can put makeup on without it running throughout the day through a mix of crying, children coughing directly into your face and forgetting your coat when you're on break duty. Get your nails done instead of them having paint, chalk and board marker all over them. Wear clothes that aren't tarnished with snail trails, snot, glue or, worse, urine (from the children, although I wouldn't put it past some teachers). You are going to go through a bigger transformation than Laney Boggs from the 90s teen romcom classic *She's All That.*

The night itself starts very tame. You all have your bets on who will end up being the most drunk. NQTs or new staff are always front runners, but you can't discount the staff who have come back from maternity leave recently, for whom it may well be their first night out in a year. If they have planned this correctly – and let's be fair, as a teacher they probably have – they'll have made sure their partner will be taking babysitting duties the next day, so that's a green light to go hard and go heavy!

If you've not had one staff party where you've ended up being the most drunk, you've not lived. We've all been there. It should be part of getting your QTS (Qualified Teacher Status).

You have to love a Christmas do for getting to see a different side of people. The most strict, most straightlaced colleagues are suddenly Fun Time Frankie, throwing shapes on the dance-floor like they're on *Strictly*. Get a drink down them and it's like they're auditioning for *Geordie Shore*. They are on it big time.

I am always jealous of the sensible Sallys who, despite the bullying, the jeers and constant pressure to come to town, make the adult decision to go home. They are so smug as they walk into school on the Monday, fresh as a daisy, while you've still got the shakes.

We live for the Christmas do as there will always be an incident that provides the staffroom gossip for the next 12 months. It almost becomes tradition.

Right, Lee, I am going to leave you to it, I can see how eager you are to unleash your views on the bad side of education. You've got rants in your pants. Me, on the other hand, I like to focus on the positives.

Be honest, you don't engage purely because you still, five years in, don't know half of the teacher lingo.

What do you mean?

You often say, you'll be sitting in a staff meeting and someone will mention an acronym – the SEF, for example (School Evaluation Form) – and you completely disengage from the meeting that's taking place while you try to work out what the acronym might mean or, more importantly, what you wish it meant.

Imagine if it stood for Sexy Elephant Farms!

Why, in the name of all that is holy, would it be called that? I think you have a thing for elephants; for a while you thought the DfE was a rap group called Da Funky Elephants!

I can show you my elephant trick if you want?

No thank you!

Readers, strap yourself in, as Mr P is going to unleash ...

What are you going to do?

I might put up a new display in the school corridor.

As if! I thought you were banned from touching or creating displays.

That is true, I am going to cook myself some Turkey Twizzlers! Try not to send all the readers to sleep ...

As stated in my opening chapter, if I were about to start my teaching journey today, I don't know if I would. I love my job, I do, but there are certain parts of it that I hate. If teaching were just about teaching the children, no one would leave the profession. Unfortunately, the UK still has some of the worst teacher recruitment rates and even worse retention rates. The actual teaching part makes up a fraction of the job in today's classroom. It is the aspect that so many people outside the profession never see that is the hardest. In this chapter, I want to explore these parts, look at why the job is the way it is, offer some solutions and just have a bit of a rant, as it helps me. Despite the humorous elements of the job we've discussed, I couldn't write a book about education without discussing some of its downfalls and problems. All of which can be solved to create a profession that trusts teachers as professionals.

To see the drastic way in which teaching has changed over the past decade is so sad when you realise that teaching can be the best job in the world when you get the environment right in a school. The problem with teaching at the minute (2021) is that not enough schools are getting the environment right. There are a few people to blame for this and each of the parties mentioned in this chapter needs to take some responsibility. I think the biggest illusion that has plagued our profession over the past few years has been ...

'The more you monitor and scrutinise teachers, the more you'll raise standards.'

This is ridiculous. Here's the fact: the more you monitor and scrutinise teachers, the worse the teaching is. All that leads to is teachers wasting so much time proving they are doing the job they should just be trusted to do. Does this mean that there should be no accountability? Of course not, but when this obsession with accountability contributes to stress levels in staff going through the roof, it needs addressing. So how have we got to this point? Who is to blame? Well, let's start from the bottom up.

Teachers

Yes, teachers. Now don't get me wrong, the majority of teachers are great, wonderful, incredibly hard-working individuals, but there are some that let the rest of us down. I have a few in my school, and you get them in every school. You know the teacher I am talking about; you may know them as the lemon-sucker, the mood-hoover, the negative nelly, the teacher who loves to moan about absolutely everything. EVERYTHING. They could win the lottery and they would still turn around and say, 'It is just too much!' They let the rest of us down because they refuse to move forward. They will say things like this to me:

'There are two things I hate about my job, Lee, two things.'

'Go on ...'

'Number one, I hate the way things are. I hate the pressure, the workload, the accountability, the ridiculous policies we are forced to follow. I just hate it!'

'And the second thing?'

'The second thing? I hate change.'

I have noticed that these teachers tend to be the ones who are also hot on 'growth mindset'. Here's another example of teachers being the ultimate hypocrites; any new idea or strategy that would either improve teachers or improve their workload, they are against, and if it involves any use of technology, then that is it. They may try it once and if it doesn't go the way it should, as most things never do, then that's that. I tried, it didn't work, so I'll go back to what I have always done. But then they stand up in an assembly and give it the big one: 'Right, children, growth mindset. It is all about trying new things but never giving up; FAIL stands for first attempt in learning; you've never failed until you've stopped trying.' Kids aren't stupid, they'll be sitting there thinking, 'That's rich coming from you. Remember the time you tried to use technology and when the wifi dropped out, you lost your head, threw the laptop at the window and all we've ever done since is sit while you show a PowerPoint and we do a worksheet in our books.'

I think growth mindset is great, but you don't need to spend thousands of pounds to encourage this idea in your school – just have staff that live the values and go on the same learning journey. Every day is a learning day; we never fail, we either win or we learn.

So these teachers end up holding the rest of us back. Why? Because SLTs would rather create a policy full of non-negotiables that both patronise and create a culture of mistrust. More on non-negotiables later, but ultimately, rather than creating a culture that moves everyone forward, SLTs create policies that are designed to the lowest common denominator, which means teachers are forced to work in a micromanaged way.

Next in the firing line ...

SLTs

Senior Leadership Teams are the management team within a school. They make or break a school. SLTs fall into two categories: leaders and bosses. I have nothing but respect for leaders; these are SLTs who support staff, go above and beyond to help staff reach their potential and don't put unnecessary pressure or workload on them. Then there are bosses ...

SLTs usually consist of a teacher with a TLR (teacher and learning responsibility), which effectively is the teacher getting a tiny increase in pay to take on huge responsibilities within the school. Middle managers, phase leaders, assistant head teachers, deputy head teachers, head teachers, executive head teachers. You can ask me to explain the difference between some of these roles, but to be fair, I don't really know with some. Over the past few years it seems you have to be everything other than an actual teacher. Some teachers love the labels and roles they have – the more the merrier.

Ultimately, these people are the deciding factor as to whether the school creates the right environment. Most of the SLTs I come across are absolutely brilliant, but there are some absolutely shit ones. I often get messages from SLTs who tell me all I ever seem to do is slag off leadership teams. I want to make something clear in this book: I don't have a problem with the majority of SLTs; in fact, I have the utmost respect and admiration for them. It's the toxic ones I cannot stand. The ones who quickly forget what it was like to be at the chalkface. I understand the pressures that are put on head teachers, but that pressure needs to be deflected from the staff, not passed on with more intent. 'Be an umbrella that deflects this rubbish away, not the drainpipe that pours it onto staff,' as Simon Smith, a head teacher in the North East, tweeted recently. So how do you spot a toxic SLT? Here are a few things to look out for:

Policies about things that have no real impact on learning.

Staff meetings about wellbeing that do nothing to improve wellbeing (more on that later).

Weekly book scrutinies.

Weekly staff meetings to introduce a new initiative that adds to workload without it replacing anything else.

Unannounced Learning Walks every other day.

More than one observation every half term, unless there is an identified issue.

Basically, any SLT that plays up to the belief that the more you monitor and scrutinise teachers, the more you will raise standards, is exactly the type of SLT that's causing the problems in education.

LEAs/MATs

Then we get the LEAs (Local Education Authorities). Although these are now dying a death in a lot of places, those that are still around are a bit of a mixed bag. This can also apply to MATs (Multi-academy Trusts) now. While there are some that are doing incredible things to support, help and guide schools, there are others that are simply dreadful, visiting schools and advising on things that are simply bad practice, expecting to see things done in a way that completely contradicts what Ofsted's guidelines are and then just adding more pressure, accountability and stress on schools. I was very dubious of academies, but I can see why some schools do it: more freedom on budgets, less accountability to people who are detached from the classroom. But then you hear about some of the dreadful and truly ludicrous expectations from certain MATs. Ultimately, I think with every school, academy or LA-maintained school, it comes down to leadership.

STA and DfE

Between the Standards and Testing Agency and the Department for Education, they couldn't organise a piss-up in a brewery. Their decision-making and approach to school assessment over my time as a teacher has been nothing short of a joke. When I started, SATs were a genuine test to see how the cohort were doing. It was expected that the average was level 4, with perhaps a few level 3 and a couple of level 5. Within a couple of years, it was minimum level 4. A couple of years later, minimum level 5 for ALL children. Then levels got scrapped with a 'let's see what schools can come up with' type of approach, before then introducing categories of working towards, expected and greater depth, which is purely levels without the levels.

Assessing children's writing was left to the teachers, which was welcomed by a lot of teachers until their livelihood became based purely on such results. This led to a massive narrowing of the curriculum, schools modelling and scaffolding writing so there could be no natural flair or creativity, and if that didn't work, cheat!

Year 2 and Year 6 teachers have to attend writing moderation meetings. Teachers from local schools would all meet to discuss, compare and share pupils' writing to ensure everyone was on the right track. It usually becomes whoever has the loudest voice has their way. When writing is so subjective it is hard to justify and get that consistency, but when your best writer is being denied greater depth because another teacher just 'doesn't have that feeling' about it, the whole process becomes very tedious. The inconsistency with moderators (teachers who would visit other schools to check their judgements) made a mockery of the whole process. If LEAs needed results to be higher, suddenly Jack who struggles to write a correct sentence is told he's expected standard, whereas if the results the previous year showed too many greater depth, the next JK Rowling was being deemed bang average. Again, I don't want to make out like I think all moderators are bad, they're not, but some are. Some have ulterior motives. For example: a school that had attended my training and had used some of my resources told me that they had the best writing the teacher had seen in 20 years, but when the moderator visited they received the worst results they'd had in years. Turns out, the moderator writes and sells her own resources, so the school down the road, who used all of these moderator's resources, got the best results in the local authority.

Maybe this whole process wouldn't have been as bad if it weren't for the next group, who have constantly moved the goalposts over my career, meaning that teachers always feel like they're chasing their tail ...

OFSTED

Where to start! First of all, I would like to start by saying I don't mind Ofsted as an idea. I think having a body that visits schools to check standards is necessary. But let's make this clear, that's all Ofsted do, check standards. However, if you look at the Ofsted website they have a logo that states: 'Ofsted, raising standards, improving lives'. THE BIGGEST LIE IN EDUCATION. Ofsted don't raise standards, they never have, they never will.

Although my interactions with Ofsted over the years have been pleasant, I have never had an inspector give me any advice that made me a better teacher. Here's the thing: I don't mind the fact that Ofsted don't do that and I am happy for them to check standards. Just don't lie about it. An example: one of my best mates is a secondary school art teacher in one of the most challenging schools in Manchester. He was recently observed by an inspector who said the lesson was dreadful. Imagine the worst lesson you've ever taught and multiply it by 100, and you'd be near how bad this lesson went. He had to go and meet the inspector for feedback, can you imagine? My friend was crapping it as he walked to meet the inspector and receive feedback, but he wanted to try to turn it into a positive experience. Sitting down, the inspector immediately said, 'Didn't go very well that, did it?'

To which my friend replied, 'No, but just out of interest, what would you have done differently?'

The inspector looked him square in the eyes and said, 'I don't know!'

Yet we hail these people like they're something special, because they 'raise standards'. Do me a favour!

What could Ofsted do to bring more trust to teachers? The best change we could make to our profession would be to scrap Ofsted labels. I hate them – they are unnecessary and complete bollocks. A fallacy, illusion. There is no such thing as an outstanding school, we are all human. Despite most teachers and schools knowing this, we are our own worst enemies. When you have ex-secondary school geography teachers inspecting EYFS settings it becomes a bit of a lottery. I am not saying schools aren't brilliant, most are, but there are also some schools that are dreadful. But I don't think labelling these schools as such helps. A huge problem for me with inspectors is that for a body that bangs on about consistency, they seem to be the biggest hypocrites. I have encountered some amazing inspectors, who recognise the pressures teachers are under and therefore seek out ways in which schools are dealing with this, through technology, for example. Others refuse to look at anything other than books. I had a teacher once tell me that their inspection was awful and they were given the Requires Improvement grade. This ultimately meant they would be taken over by a MAT — turned out the executive head of this MAT was the lead Ofsted inspector.

More often than not, the inspection process is a complete and utter lottery. The right roll of the dice will get you the right inspector on the right day, one who agrees with your vision, sees what you're doing and why, and may reward you with the Outstanding grade. What does every school do? Celebrates, boasts, turns it into a business and starts running courses for other schools so they can learn how to be outstanding. The staff turnover rate may be through the roof, with the workload and wellbeing of staff dreadful, but that doesn't matter now as we're outstanding. We can't afford TAs anymore but you can bet your bottom dollar we will be splashing a few hundred pounds on a huge banner to display outside our school telling everyone how outstanding we are.

Then you might have a school, half a mile down the road, who gets the wrong roll of the dice. The wrong inspector who wants stuff done in a certain way, and therefore completely disagrees with what you're doing and so labels you as Requires Improvement. And now the staff are fighting for their jobs.

I say to every teacher that getting a 'good' grade is the best option. But ultimately, if we were to get rid of the labels, things would be easier. No school is perfect, every school will have positive points and areas for improvement, so just inspect and report on that. At the end of the day we are all human, so I wish we would just aim for everyday excellence. Can we be our very best on that given day?

There will be times in your life when you can't be at the top of your game – there's an illness in the family, a relationship is hitting a rocky patch, you're feeling under the weather – but as long as you're there giving your very best, you will still be having such an incredible impact on these young people. Not impact as in you're getting them through a phonics test (check, phonics, check, sorry), but that for that child in your class you might be the only person in their life that makes them feel valued and worthwhile. For those six hours that they're with you each day, that might be the only time they feel safe and content. You're that person for someone, even if you don't realise it.

My biggest issue is with schools that revolve everything around Ofsted. I am linking this back to bosses and not leaders. You can choose to let Ofsted consume you, so that every decision you make as a school isn't out of the best interest of the learners, but what you think Ofsted want to see. You can waste some of your very tight budget sending staff on 'be Ofsted-ready' courses run by schools who fluked an outstanding and have a completely different context and demographic to your school. You can choose to waste more of your budget inviting external companies, who have no affiliation to Ofsted, to come into your school and do MOCKSTEDS, even though Ofsted tell you not to do this. That is all a choice.

The alternative to this is that you can choose to focus on providing the best possible education for each and every child in your care, making sure every decision is in the best interest of your pupils, then when you do get the call, you will argue that what you are doing is right. And it is these schools who seem to be getting better outcomes. I wish this would be recognised more in the society we live in but it's not, no thanks to the next group ...

The Government

I could write a whole book on the government and education, but I want this book to be a positive one. Yes, this chapter is recognising all the negative sides of education, but it is just one chapter in the whole book. No government has ever got it right with education. Why? Maybe the fact that we've never had an Education Secretary that has worked a day in the classroom. I think the biggest problem with this current government is the level of austerity that has left schools to pick up the pieces. I remember when I was at school, we would do fundraisers to raise money for different charities. Now schools and families are the charities. Schools are being encouraged to fundraise just to make ends meet. The cuts to police, social care and elements of the NHS have led to schools and teachers having to wear more hats than ever before.

All we ever seem to hear from the government is them banging on about recruitment: we are recruiting more teachers than ever before, we are ploughing more money into recruiting teachers, etc. There is not a recruitment crisis in education; there are millions of qualified teachers in the UK. In fact, there are more qualified teachers working outside of education than working in it. The issue in education is with retention. Twenty-two million pounds of taxpayers' money has been wasted in the past two years on bursaries for teachers who have already left the profession. One in three teachers leave the profession in the first three years. Why? One word ...

Workload.

Now, workload is a funny one. It's not, obviously, but the way our profession deals with workload is. We've had this workload crisis for five or so years. Every *TES* article mentions it, the DfE have had a workload reduction toolkit for the past three years, teachers are probably onto their tenth workload questionnaire. But every day I ask teachers the same question, 'Has your work-load got any better in the past year or so?' One in every 30 will usually put their hands up. I was doing some CPD in Wales recently and asked the same question, and three teachers put their hands up. I said, 'Great, what has changed?' All of them replied, 'We used to work in England and now we work in Wales.'

So why, despite everyone knowing we have this workload issue, is it, generally speaking, that most teachers are still strug-gling with their workload?

All fart and no poo with workload.

It is that simple. As a profession we are great at talking about stuff. We will have staff meetings where we talk about how crap our lives are. We won't do anything about it, but talking about it helps. At one school, where the head teacher (a boss, not a leader) decided to let the staff do an anonymous suggestions box about workload, when she didn't like the responses, she went to the governors to get some of the staff disciplined.

You may be greeted first thing by a member of SLT: 'Did you get my email last night?'

'No.'

'The email I sent last night, I sent it about half nine. It is that workload questionnaire, no, the other one, it should only take you a couple of hours, but I need it by the end of today.'

Directly linked to the workload problem is the wellbeing issue we have in education. This is such a huge problem, with the latest research showing that primary school teachers' suicide rate is nearly double the national average. This is some-thing I feel very passionate about and is one of the main driving forces behind what we are doing with this book, the podcast, my social media and CPD. I will receive messages pretty much every day now from teachers who are really struggling with their mental health, and it is so frustrating when so many of the causes can be prevented. I had one teacher recently who stood on a bridge ready to end it all; she had left a note at home, and it was only for a passerby talking her down that she didn't do it. It can be quite tough for me reading these sorts of messages, as I can't necessarily solve the problems, but I often think about that passerby and it fills me with hope. I wonder if that person knows the impact that act will have had. That teacher hopefully got help and recovered and may return to the classroom to help hundreds of children through the rest of her career. We never tend to stop and think about how our actions can lead to so many positive outcomes.

Here's the thing. I honestly believe we can Thanos snap the wellbeing problem (well, most of it) if we actually did something with workload. But because most (not all) schools are just paying lip service to the workload issue, wellbeing is now turning into this really frustrating, token-gesture approach that may have a short-term impact but in the grand scheme of things does nothing for wellbeing. So here is my list of top ten wellbeing fails I have seen or heard schools do. Now if you are guilty of these, I am not having a go (well ...). Your heart was probably in the right place as you are now part of the 'wellbeing team' and have to do something, as Ofsted will ask about wellbeing.

Top Ten Wellbeing Fails
10 This genuinely happened at my friend's school. The wellbeing ambassador organised for an ice cream van to come to the school on the last day of term for the staff. It didn't help my

friend as she is lactose intolerant. Funnily enough, the wellbeing ambassador has since been signed off with stress. This came at the end of a term where my friend had five different observations in ONE half term.

9 Ofsted's guidance on wellbeing: we care, they said, we want to help, they said. And they nearly had us, we nearly fell for it. When they announced the new inspection framework and how this wasn't data-driven or based purely on SATs, it was about the broad and balanced curriculum, even though they had created that system themselves, we nearly fell for it. Their line was that this approach should help schools with their workload and wellbeing, and we should be ready to back them. But then we had to remove our clown masks once deep dives were introduced, which have since increased workload exponentially in so many schools. They have completely ruined that phrase for me. Acronyms are another one. Some of the garbage I see being pushed in schools by people on Twitter who have nicked ideas from someone but repackaged it as an acronym, and teachers think it is the best thing since sliced bread. You can literally take any random group of words, and if the first letters spell out the name of an animal you'll make millions. Most of it is rubbish but makes a nice display. I might start introducing my own acronyms into education. Everyone keeps telling me I am an educational influencer, so I want to introduce the following:

ARSE Assessment Reflection Systematic Evaluation Time.

KNOB Kinaesthetic Numeracy Observation Books.

SHIT School Hall Interactive Time – another word for assemblies.

If you think the brilliant *Line of Duty* on BBC is difficult to understand with all the acronyms, it has nothing on education. You can easily be walking down the corridor and hear something like this:

'Just heard that the SLT have put the NQT on capability over the fact that the NQT did not evidence the LO in the PSHE book. So they don't know if the AFL for the RSE was being covered for the SEN. Now I don't know if it was the HT, AHT or DHT that made the call, but clearly the NQT needs a bit more CPD that they didn't get on their ITT to look at EHCs and EAL. The LSA needs to step up and keep on top of CPOMS, otherwise the MAT isn't going to approve the PIP, meaning that the NQT isn't going to get their PPA to then plan RE.'

Which roughly translates to:

'Just heard that the Senior Leadership Team have put the Newly Qualified Teacher on capability over the fact that they did not evidence the Learning Objective in the Physical Social and Health Education book. So they don't know if the Assessment for Learning for the Relationship and Sexual Education was being covered for the Special Educational Needs children. Now I don't know if it was the Head, Assistant Head or Deputy Head that made the call, but clearly the Newly Qualified Teacher needs a bit more Continuous Professional Development that they didn't get on their Initial Teacher Training to look at Education, Health and Care plans and English as an Additional Language. The Learning Support Assistant needs to step up and keep on top of CPOMS (safeguarding software for schools), otherwise the Multi-academy Trust isn't going to approve the Performance Improvement Plan, meaning that the new teacher isn't going to get their Planning, Preparation and Assessment time to then plan religious education.'

As you can see when you do understand it, it is nowhere near as enthralling as when AC-12 do it.

8 Asking parents to donate money to a teacher wellbeing fund.

This has genuinely happened, and it backfired, as you would expect. I think the way the current government has funded education over the past few years has been borderline criminal.

However, there are ways in which we can help ourselves. I have been sent numerous JustGiving pages from schools to try to raise money to keep support staff on roll. Despite the executive head driving a new Porsche, the budgets are so tight they can't afford to keep staff on roll. I have become reluctant to share these JustGiving pages until the school has passed a series of questions. Usually they fall at the first hurdle. What is your annual photocopying cost as a school? When schools come back with £25–30k a year, I'm out. Asking parents to provide books, stationery and supplies is one thing, asking them to give money to buy biscuits and treats for the staffroom, you are asking for trouble. You have to remember, most teachers earn more than the majority of the parents, and with the austerity measures leading to over four million children living in poverty in this country, to ask parents to give money for prizes for staff and discounts for spa breaks is sure to go down like a lead balloon.

7. Emails about wellbeing. I don't mind these; my issue is when they are sent. Imagine receiving a work-related email past 6 at night or one that talks about wellbeing. The worst are the ones sent on a Sunday! Give it a rest. Teachers need a break.

6 Colouring-in sheets. Yes, some schools have dedicated staff meetings to get teachers to sit there colouring in a mindfulness picture as this can be therapeutic and relaxing. Face palm! These are the same schools that expect teachers to spend three to four hours every night colouring in children's work in five different highlighters as this is a non-negotiable in their marking policy. I am not having a go at these activities, it just winds me up when they are forced on teachers without taking away anything else.

5 Having a staff meeting about wellbeing. Let's be honest, they are just patronising and most of the time are a waste of time. The number of teachers who will message me, saying:

Hi Mr P, I have just been asked to lead a staff meeting on wellbeing. Can you suggest any activities we can do?

My response is always the same: Cancel the staff meeting. Giving the teachers time out is better than any activity or staff meeting.

4 Group meditation. I was once messaged by a teacher at a school that decided to do staff group meditation every Friday morning at 8 for 20 minutes. This was compulsory. The teacher admitted that this led to her Fridays being disorganised and rushed. I couldn't help but think that the best way for me to relax would have been to stay in bed for an extra half an hour.

3 Filling a mug with chocolate. I am sure you will have seen this on social media. It is when a teacher gets a mug and fills it with sweets or chocolate, then leaves it on the desk of a colleague with a Post-it note saying: 'You've been mugged.' I think the intention behind this is a really nice token of appreciation. My issue is when schools play this off as wellbeing. It's not. It does nothing for my wellbeing if I am on a diet. Someone did it to the Other Mr P, and as a type 1 diabetic it was like a slap in the face.

2 Surveys. As mentioned earlier, schools that use workload or wellbeing questionnaires tend to personify the 'all fart and no poo' approach. Especially when nothing happens on the back of it. Just have an open conversation. The time it takes to make the questionnaire, fill it out and document the results isn't exactly going to reduce workload.

1 Yoga. Winner winner chicken dinner! I know a lot of people love yoga. We even do it in my school, but it is optional. That's the difference. The number of schools that are forced to do yoga so it helps with wellbeing is embarrassing. There was one school that forced the staff to do yoga after school on a Friday. If staff didn't attend they would receive an email from the head, berating them about their lack of support and how they cannot moan about their workload and wellbeing if they're not willing to join in with these initiatives. Needless to say, that

three-form-entry school had only one teacher in KS1 who stayed on this academic year. I can't think of anything worse than being in the hall doing the downward dog and farting in someone's face. It'd be better for me to be sitting on a couch with a bag of Doritos binging on a new true-crime Netflix documentary.

The only universal way to improve a teacher's wellbeing is to give them the two Ts: Time and Trust. Wellbeing is completely subjective; what works for me isn't necessarily going to work for you. What really helps my wellbeing is doing the podcast. Every episode, there will be a point where I lose it laughing my head off at Adam. I know that so many other teachers use the podcast to help their wellbeing, too. The fact we've been able to do live shows all over the UK and have hundreds of teachers give up their Saturday night to hear Adam and me share funny stories is incredible, but I know there are so many other teachers and school staff who would hate the podcast and couldn't think of anything worse than sitting through one of our shows. There are some people on this planet that love to spend their Sunday mornings dressed in Lycra biking up hills. Can you imagine?!

The only way to improve teacher's wellbeing is to give teachers time. STOP THE FAFF! Trust the teachers to do the job they are very capable of doing. I always say that I feel we are the best generation of teachers, yet we're the least trusted. Very few teachers get into this profession now for the holidays, as we work most of them. We don't come into it for the pay, as you can get paid more working for Aldi. We choose this job because we care and we want to make a positive impact on the pupils. We aren't always going to get things right, but if we can create an environment where teachers feel valued, trusted and appreciated, they will take care of the rest.

So here's an alternative list of things schools could do that would actually reduce workload and at the same time improve wellbeing by giving teachers time.

Scrap 'Book' Scrutinies

This is the big one. This is what I am seeing becoming the most toxic thing in education. I am not against the physical act of looking through books, but I am against the mindset this is creating in teachers where they now seem to feel they are being deemed a success or judged purely by the way their books look. It is the way schools approach book scrutinies, or 'book looks', as some schools call them. When they are happening weekly, when there's a list of non-negotiables to follow, when teachers are expected to include four pieces of writing a week, then it creates unnecessary workload. Teachers will waste so much time and money printing and photocopying evidence to go in a book to show what they have done, it is ridiculous!

It makes no sense in a world where technology is so easily accessible and pupils can evidence their learning online, that books should be the be all and end all. I remember around four years ago, when I was team teaching in Year 1. I got into school at around 7.45am, and the teacher must have been in for at least an hour already as she had just finished handwriting the learning objective in all the pupils' maths books. What bewildered me was the fact that children didn't end up doing anything in their maths books; they were making number sentences with Numicon. Great lesson, but you should have seen the teacher. I don't know how many cups of coffee that teacher had had that morning, but she was wired. She was whizzing round the classroom like Road Runner, her iPad in hand, snapping pictures of the children every time they made a number sentence. She spent her whole break sending the pictures from her iPad to her computer. She then jumped straight into phonics, followed by English and then lunch. We have an hour for lunch, but this teacher didn't; she spent most of the time printing the pictures, photocopying and trimming them down. The TA then spent the rest of the afternoon sticking the pictures into books. How does that use of time have any positive impact on children's learning? Not only is the TA not working with the children, but the time it takes the teacher to do that every week, every term, every year – just think what they could be doing instead? That was the point where we looked at using technology to evidence learning alongside books. Which is why we should BAN book scrutinies and instead look at learning reviews where SLT will take books and devices into account when looking at coverage and progress.

One more point on the problem with book scrutinies is that you narrow your curriculum massively. Take the English National Curriculum. Every year group's English Curriculum will start with the following objectives:

Spoken Language
(The objectives for Spoken Language are common across Key Stages 1 and 2)

En6/1a listen and respond appropriately to adults and their peers.
En6/1b ask relevant questions to extend their understanding and knowledge.
En6/1c use relevant strategies to build their vocabulary.
En6/1d articulate and justify answers, arguments and opinions.
En6/1e give well-structured descriptions, explanations and narratives for different purposes, including for expressing feelings.
En6/1f maintain attention and participate actively in collaborative conversations, staying on topic and initiating and responding to comments.
En6/1g use spoken language to develop understanding through speculating, hypothesising, imagining and exploring ideas.

En6/1h speak audibly and fluently with an increasing command of Standard English.

En6/1i participate in discussions, presentations, performances, roleplay/improvisations and debates.

En6/1j gain, maintain and monitor the interest of the listener(s).

En6/1k consider and evaluate different viewpoints, attending to and building on the contributions of others.

En6/1l select and use appropriate registers for effective communication.

None of these can be evidenced in a book. In fact, some schools don't even bother with this. Why would you if you're solely judged by what your books look like? Teachers are forced to see speaking and listening as the poor cousin to reading and writing, and so they don't give it anywhere near as much time, or value it as much. There is a reason those objectives are the first part of the English curriculum, as they are the most important. 'Effective reading and writing floats on a sea of oracy.' If a child can't talk through a piece of writing, they can't write it effectively.

There are also wider society issues with this. Most schools I work with admit that they are finding more children are starting school in EYFS with severe speech and language difficulties. Schools aren't even helping by prioritising the most important part of the curriculum. They are simply welcoming these children into class: 'Hi, what's your name? Oh you can't verbalise anything orally, that's a shame. Never mind, come and sit at your desk and get on with this worksheet.'

Another wider issue linked with this is to look at the biggest killer of men under the age of 50, which is suicide. We currently lose 12 men a day to suicide. What do we need more men to do? Talk. Yet we're not instilling the skill set into young boys by valuing that part of the curriculum to give them the ability to open up and share their feelings and emotions. The obsession with accountability in education has been contributing to this wider society issue.

Stop Evidencing Objectives

This is very closely linked to the first point. Whatever you call them, Learning Objectives (LO), Learning Challenges (LC), WALT, WILF, WELL, I CAN statements – whatever garbage acronyms you use to share the focus of the lesson, these weren't around when I first started teaching, you just put a title in the book and off we go. Now you need to make sure the children evidence this in the book before they actually start doing work. WHAT A WASTE OF TIME! About five years ago, someone did some research into this that found that if you get children to copy out learning challenges for every single piece of work they do, it can waste up to 32.5 hours a year. That's a week of school! For some of the pupils I work with, it is half of what they write in a whole session. It completely kills the momentum of a lesson and is one of the most distracting things. In so many lessons I have taught I can sense that my class have grasped the concept, and this excites me greatly as it rarely happens, and then I ask them to apply all the impressive knowledge I have bestowed upon them.

'But first, children, make sure you put today's learning challenge at the top of your page alongside the date, yes the long date.'

Ten minutes later ...

'Mr P, what are we doing again?'

The worst example of how clueless some schools are, are the ones that have recognised that it wastes children's time so they now expect teachers to do it. It's just another way to increase teacher workload as they now have to get into school at 6am to be first to the photocopier so they can print 30 sticky labels with the Learning Objective for that lesson. These are then physically stuck into each book. My word!! One teacher once said to me, 'I am ok for this, as guess what I got for Christmas? My own Dynamo sticky label printer for my classroom, so whenever I need to, I can just print them off in class and stick them in books.'

My only thought was, wow, I bet Christmas was a right hoot around your gaff.

Would it make any difference to children's learning if teachers didn't waste time sticking these in books? If you're answering no, stop doing it.

Get Rid of Marking Policies

I wouldn't wipe my arse with a marking policy.

I reckon that will be left on my tombstone. This has been the biggest bane of my life since I did my first placement as a teacher. I had to sit there for three hours doing all this written marking, and then realised the next day when the pupils either completely ignored it or couldn't read it what a complete and utter waste of time it was. The way marking has evolved in my short teaching career has been ridiculous. I am starting to see some schools moving forward, but, generally speaking, it is still a huge factor as far as workload goes. Every teacher knows that 99 per cent of marking teachers do isn't for the pupils, but instead for the book scrutiny (see above).

I ask teachers this question every single day and always get the same response:

What is the best form of feedback you can give your pupils?

Every teacher on this planet will answer with:

Oral/verbal feedback.

So if every teacher on the planet knows that oral/verbal feedback is the best form of feedback, why oh why would any school STILL have a marking policy? I put it down to the fact that school misinterprets the word 'consistency'.

'Consistency' is the real buzzword in education at the minute. It is in every Ofsted document and all DfE guidelines, and I want to make it clear it is important; it is always my banker when I play staff meeting bingo.

For those, who have never played staff meeting bingo before, all players before the staff meeting need to write down six words or phrases that they think the person leading the meeting will say. As the meeting starts, you tick off anything you have written down but you can only win if you shout BINGO! This usually is disguised in a cough to go unnoticed to those who aren't playing. Some people think this is distacting, but I have never listened so intently to a staff meeting. Some go-to phrases:

Ofsted window
Workload
Community cohesion
Assessment
Tracking
Data
Progress
Cultural capital
And, of course, consistency.

The problem with some schools is that they interpret the word 'consistency' as 'everyone needs to do the same thing', which leads to policies being designed full of non-negotiables that force every teacher to mark the exact same way, because if everyone marks the exact same way we'll get consistency. This means we completely miss the point of feedback.

Here's my definition of consistency: consistency has to come by the outcome not the process.

In any class, no matter what age, you will not be able to give the exact same form of feedback for every single child because of the differing levels of ability. However, if every child no matter what their ability is being challenged, supported and moved on with their learning, should it matter how you give the feedback? But what we've done over the past few years is obsess over how we mark, and in a lot of schools it's become how we can show we're marking the shit out of a book and feedback isn't even a focus.

It doesn't help that we still have a lot of teachers in this profession who associate time with being effective. They think the more time I spend doing a task, the better I must be at it. Again, this is complete and utter rubbish. I know some teachers enjoy working this way, they find it therapeutic, and I get that. So if teachers want to spend every day of the summer holiday making their classroom look like Hogwarts, that's fine. If they want to spend four or five hours a night marking with 10 different highlighters, that's fine. If they want to spend hours each night laminating a new display about single-use plastic, that's fine. But none of this means they're a better teacher. In some schools these teachers are put on a pedestal and used as an example for how all the other staff should be. 'Why are you lot not working as hard as this teacher who eats, drinks, sleeps, repeats teaching?' My answer is simple: 'Because I have a life outside of teaching. I have to be a dad, a husband, a brother, a friend. I need time to switch off and escape this world of teaching, so that when I come back to class I can work to the best of my effect.'

Some schools' lack of understanding about this is mindblowing. The worst is when these busy teachers become SLT and the faff they've created becomes policy, policy becomes non-negotiables, which means you're forced every night to spend hours writing all this waffle – what went well, even better if, two stars and a bastard wish.

One of the worst examples of faff when it comes to marking has to be the introduction of highlighters. I remember the staff meeting at a school I was seconded to when this was introduced. It started because a school down the road had just been inspected and got Outstanding. We therefore did what every school does, which is send staff to that school to see exactly why they were outstanding so we could replicate it, even though what we were already doing was better. The following staff meeting:

'Right, staff, we know exactly why that school is outstanding. They don't just tick anymore, ticking is so 2012! If they see something good, they highlight it pink and this is called tickling pink!' While gesturing your hands as if you're tickling something. 'So, staff, after three, 1 ..., 2 ...'

You are now sitting in a staff meeting, as a fully grown adult, questioning your life choices as you chant back, 'Tickling Pink.'

'If it's not so good, we highlight it green and call that Green for Growth! Mmmmm, alliteration!' (As they seem to have a mini orgasm.)

'So we have spent £500 of our budget on highlighters for you all, we've already made this a non-negotiable in the marking policy, now off you go, minions.'

I looked around, making eye contact in a way to say, look, we're not having this, let's rebel! Break into some sort of *Les Misérables* number. Instead, it looked like a scene from *The Walking Dead*, with most of the staff resembling zombies in their burnt-out state.

I questioned it: 'Just out of interest, have we trialled this yet to see if it's any more effective than what we are already doing? I already waste enough time doing all this marking, knowing a quick conversation would be more effective. You're telling me I need to now paint by numbers to mark a book. I don't think it will save me time.'

This was met with, 'Yes, but Ofsted like it so we're doing it.' That was the problem then and it is still a problem now in many schools. Schools do things because they think that's what Ofsted want to see, even though in all of the Ofsted documentation it basically says you can do what you want, we don't expect things to be done in a certain way as long as what you're doing works.

This is the problem with the workload and wellbeing issues discussed earlier. Ofsted are now making this a focus in their inspections, which I think is a bit of a lose-lose situation. If an inspector collars you and asks about your workload, what are you going to do? Tell the truth, explain it is a nightmare and even though you're 23 you're greyer than Phillip Schofield. What will happen? This will go against you, your school will be downgraded to Requires Improvement and what will happen to your workload? It will increase!

Or you can lie and make it out like your school has it nailed with workload, and then nothing changes.

Luckily, my school has moved on a lot since then and we don't make decisions for Ofsted. Instead, we make decisions in the best interest of our children.

I know a lot of schools are starting to move away from this, but they still show a complete lack of trust in teachers. Certain schools will say, 'Yes, we give verbal feedback, but we expect teachers to write in the book everything the teacher said to the pupil,' or 'We have to then use the verbal feedback stamp or write VF.' WHY??

The verbal feedback stamp, which has probably become the best-selling piece of teacher stationery over the past year, is the most POINTLESS thing in a school. It proves nothing. I could quite easily stamp a book and it doesn't show whether I have or haven't given feedback. Again, it is purely for show and has no impact on pupils' learning.

As I said earlier, consistency comes from the outcome, not the process. There are so many ways in which to give feedback. Teachers should be trusted to know their pupils and use their professional judgement to give the best form of feedback for the task. The proof is then in the pudding for how pupils improve in the next piece of work. It isn't rocket science.

Don't Grade Lesson Observations

How do you define lesson observations? Recently, the comedian Guz Khan, who was a teacher before becoming a comedian, said on *Would I Lie to You?*. 'A lesson observation is essentially how teachers are judged on how good they are as teachers. It is not based on how you move these children on emotionally, spiritually, how you build them as human beings. It is a 15-minute window in which a wasteman who can't teach themselves, comes in and judges you.'

I've had a fair few observations in my time, some great and some not so great. It doesn't matter how long you have been teaching, these observations will consume you. You lose sleep, you think about it all day and night. If you're brave enough, you just do what you had planned to do but many teachers will cherry pick a solid lesson they may have already taught just to tick the box. It depends on what the observation is for; most schools use it just to check up on everything, the SLT just want to ensure you're following the policies, etc., which is fine. Others have their whole performance management based around these observations, which provide a very brief and limited insight into your teaching.

Things have changed now. Schools have clocked on to this and want the process to be more natural or to catch teachers out and put them in a constant state of worry and apprehension by doing unannounced learning walks. Whether it is an observation or learning walk, they are a very mixed bag. I think having someone watch you teach is an important part of our job, and we should be constantly looking to reflect and evaluate to improve, but a lot of the time this is NOT what lesson observations are. Mostly they are to justify why the SLTs are paid more. The best observations I have ever had have been from fellow colleagues where the pressure is off and it feels much more of a team effort.

Feedback from observations is also a very mixed bag, and this is a real reflection on the leader. I am lucky, in that my SLTs are very positive, honest and helpful. I did have one SLT early in my career who didn't grade my lesson outstanding because I didn't have tissues on my desk.

If you thought the tissue feedback was bad, there was a recent Twitter hashtag #nobservation that shared some awful and rather bizarre feedback teachers have received. Here are some of my favourites:

@DavidCummins86: My #nobservation told me my jumper was too similar to the school uniform and I need to stand out. I'm a 6-foot tall man in a girl's school.

@Misterbodd: My favourite #nobservation was a colleague teaching RE – the 5 pillars of Islam. The feedback was: 'could you have differentiated by only giving the lowers the 3 pillars of Islam?'

@Vickilkelly: #nobservation Y4 Maths lesson on fractions a couple of years ago. HT: Why didn't you use puppets?

@curliclare: #nobservation I got told my lesson would have been outstanding if I had removed a dead plant from the back of the classroom.

@HannahLucyM: 'I'm not sure what you can do about it but your voice is annoying.' #NOBservation

@curlycarol34: #nobservation 'I couldn't give you an outstanding as I couldn't see the board properly. The light was creating a glare.'

Me: 'Couldn't you have moved?' Silence.

@ruth_ashbee: 'Pupils should have come up with their own learning objectives' for a lesson on magnetic flux density. #nobservation

@mrsbarker_teach: A colleague was graded 4 because the (German) lesson was all in German and the observer couldn't speak German so 'didn't know if it was any good'. True story!

@miss_coster: Told my lesson was RI (Requires Improvement) once, when I asked for feedback on how to improve. The response was 'book your observation in earlier because we had already hit our quota of good teachers before we made it to you!' #nobservation

@lucy_crehan: I'll add my own: NQT year, and I'd written my lesson plan in five-minute chunks. My feedback was that I needed to plan what was going to happen in EVERY MINUTE of the lesson. #NOBservation

As you can see from these examples, lesson observation can be a ridiculous process that has little to no impact on learning. Used effectively, they can be great, but it is down to what they are done for, how often they are done and what is learnt after that determines the effectiveness of them.

Forget Wellbeing Staff Meetings

If the staff meeting can be done in an email it should be. End of.

Two Mr Ps' Final Thought

When we started writing this book in mid-2019, the world was very different to the one we are in now. Mostly this is due to the COVID-19 pandemic that we'll never be able to forget. It is a world where home-schooling became a reality for everyone with school-age children, regardless of economic background, ethnicity or geography.

Before the pandemic many Western countries were already very divided nations, with populism on the political agenda and everybody taking sides against the other because they were pro/anti-Trump in the US or pro/anti-Brexit in the UK. There was a huge rise in disinformation for political gain, a reliance on memes, GIFs and angry tweets for people to get what they consider as news, and the fact that Adam is starting to care about what the president or prime minister is saying shows how the world has changed.

Yeah, the fact that I said on our podcast that I watched a grown-up programme such as *The Andrew Marr Show* – it shocked a few people!

When I go into schools to deliver training, I talk a lot about social media and how people engage with it. If you look at Adam's Facebook timeline from 2009 ...

I'm a cool dude!

Doubt it! It's mostly pictures of him looking like a boy band reject with his vest top, dog-tags around his neck, bandana on his arm and strawberry-blond hair straightened to inexplicably look like Chris Tarrant.

Like I said, a cool dude!

What about quoting song lyrics on your status updates? Like, really cheesy ones?

Erm ...

Making this bad boy your profile picture ...

Ahem ... FAKE NEWS! Can we move on, Lee? (Wish my man-boobs looked like that nowadays!)

FAKE NEWS, a term (possibly) coined by the most famous, orange, Village People fan and former leader of the free world: Mr Donald J Trump!

Shall I do the impression?

Adam, it's a book!

Oh yeah! I'll save it for the audiobook.

But the answer to combatting 'FAKE NEWS' is **EDUCATION**. The more you know, the better the choices you can make. The more you know, the more you can empathise and understand people who are different to you. As Nelson Mandela said, 'Education is the most powerful weapon which you can use to change the world.'

As primary school staff we're not expecting to change the world, but if we've learnt anything from the last decade it's that we need people to champion the pursuit of knowledge in a positive way more than ever. For much of 2020 the world has had to educate the next generation from their homes. During this time, parents have seen that it is not easy teaching or helping their own little darlings with schoolwork. While the newfound appreciation for educators will never last, it is definitely a stepping stone for building a much bigger bridge between home, school and, hopefully, the wider world.

We need to teach children together to think for themselves and not be led by everything they read online. Watching people of our parents' age engaging on Facebook is a sight to behold. It's baffling how the people you trusted and relied upon to guide you through your childhood are so easily duped by online twaddle. They go from being oracles of information to sharing missing dog posts from other countries.

'Every generation, blames the one before ...'

That's semi-profound, Adam. Who wrote that?

Mike and the Mechanics – 'The Living Years' (1988).

Ffs! The point is, we all need to work together to help our children to thrive and not just survive in the world we are leaving them in the future.

In this book we hope we have demonstrated that teachers are human; we love what we do and we would love it more if we were trusted to do it. We're not perfect, but you'd be pushed to find a more passionate and dedicated workforce. Teaching isn't easy, and our system isn't perfect, but find the right school with the right environment and it is the best job in the world. The difference you can make, the many lives you can inspire and the impact that can have on the future of this planet is truly a special gift. So to everyone who continues to graft day in, day out in classrooms up and down the country, providing the best education for your pupils, we thank you. Keep going! You'll probably never fully appreciate the true impact you have on your pupils, your community and the world.

We need to heal the world; make it a better place. For you and for me and the entire human race.

Michael Jackson? Really? I should have had that as the final song in that Easter play all those years ago.

Exactly! We're just trying to heal the world, one wet paper towel at a time!

That's the plan! Take care of yourselves ... and each other!

Acknowledgements

Right, ok, so how is this going to work? Obviously we're not going to thank the same people, are we?

No, this is my time to gain some serious brownie points ...

Well, let's get the joint thanks out of the way. Then we can do our own personal ones.

Yes, sweet!

First, thank you to everyone at HarperCollins for their incredible hard work, helping us every step of the way with this project. Thank you to Kelly for the faith she's put in us, and to Holly and Helena for all their hard work too.

To Paul, our agent at Headway Talent, thank you for everything. You manage to keep your cool despite hundreds of WhatsApp messages every day. To Tim Sadler (@Sadlerdoodles), who has been so much more than just an illustrator, a soundboard, a helping hand and a great friend in this whole process.

To our parents, thank you for everything you've done for us. You have always believed in us and continue to be our biggest fans. To our brother Ryan, good luck winning son of the year this year after this is a bestseller! Of course we have to mention the legend Nana Maureen, who never fails to make us smile and now has the same effect on everyone who listens to the podcast.

A thought for our amazing grandads, who are sadly not here to enjoy this book (or use it as an ashtray). I'm sure you've played a part somehow.

Of course, to every person who has supported the podcast and my social media over the years, your support has helped us so much and we are incredibly grateful.

And to every teacher and school staff member, we hope this book has reflected the profession we all love so much. We know the system isn't perfect but the hardworking staff are the reason why so many children go on to reach their potential. Keep being amazing!

Don't forget the teachers we had at St Monica's and St Ambrose who had to deal with me for many many long painful years.

Yeah, good shout.

Ok, now on to my personal thanks.

I wouldn't be anywhere without my wife Claire. She is the most understanding, patient and supportive person, who encourages me to reach my potential in everything I do. To Callum, Harry, Charlie and Lily, I am truly the luckiest person in the world to have you call me Dad and I am constantly inspired to make you proud. To Claire's family, thank you for everything you do to help with the kids, allowing me to pursue this adventure. To my other family and friends, thank you for your love and support, you are all amazing.

To Alan and Julie Peat, I will always be eternally grateful for how you took me under your wing at the beginning of my journey and I wouldn't be here without it.

To all the staff and pupils (well, most of them☺) at Davyhulme Primary both past and present, thank you for all the special memories and support. You've made it the best school to work at over the past 13 years. But in particular, the Hooters (yes, we're that cool, we have our own little name); you aren't just colleagues but close friends and you've been a massive support with everything I have done.

Over to you, Adam …

Straight off the bat, I'd like to thank my darling wife Kim. She is truly one of a kind (you've probably guessed that, as it's doubtful anyone else would marry me). She has given me the belief that I could do more than I ever thought possible. She also blessed me with my two gorgeous children, Isla and Max, who I am immensely proud of, and I will continue to try and be the best Daddy I can be.

I was going to mention Kim's family, but I know I'm running out of ink, so I will say to Kim's Nan Kath, thanks for being my biggest fan (alongside the late great Grandad Wilf).

To my boys, thanks for keeping me grounded, for never listening to the podcast and for ripping apart all my achievements; you make me strive to make you eat your words, but I wouldn't have our friendships any other way. See you at the bar soon, fellas.

To everyone who I have worked with and am currently working with in my brilliant school, thank you for your constant support. Even though we're colleagues, many of you are friends I will have for life. On that note, my Moston crew from my first TA job, you know who you are; we made memories for life and continue to do so!

Finally, to the children who I have taught and worked with for the last ten years, I hope I made an impact on you in some way and gave you primary school memories you've never forgotten. Thank you for allowing me to teach and inspire as best I could. I hope whatever you are doing with your lives, you always remember that manners don't cost a thing, never have any regrets and always reach for the stars.